New Decorating with Architectural TRIMWORK

PLANNING • DESIGNING • INSTALLING

Jay Silber

CREATIVE HOMEOWNER®, Upper Saddle River, New Jersey

CREATIVE
HOMEOWNER®

A Division of Federal Marketing Corp.
Upper Saddle River, NJ

VP / Editorial Director: Timothy O. Bakke
Production Managers: Rose Sullivan, Kimberly H. Vivas

Senior Editor: Fran J. Donegan
Contributing Editors: William Brockway, Neil Soderstrom, Clem Hallquist
Assistant Editor: Dan Lane
Copy Editor: Ellie Sweeney
Editorial Assistants: Evan Lambert, Lauren Manoy
Photo Editor: Stanley Sudol
Technical Consultant: Roy Barnhart
Indexer: Schroeder Indexing Services

Senior Designer: David Geer
Designer: Robert Strauch
Illustrations: Robert LaPointe
Art Development: Glee Barre, Mark Sant'Angelo
Photo Assistants: Dan Lane, Frank Krumrie

Manufactured in the United States of America

Current Printing (last digit)
10 9 8 76 5 4 3 2

New Decorating with Architectural Trimwork
Library of Congress Catalog Card Number: 2003112511
ISBN-10: 1-58011-181-5
ISBN-13: 978-1-58011-181-2

CREATIVE HOMEOWNER®
A Division of Federal Marketing Corp.
24 Park Way, Upper Saddle River, NJ 07458
www.creativehomeowner.com

Photo Credits

All photography by Gary David Gold except where noted.
Directionals: T-top, M-middle, B-bottom, R-right, L-left, C-center

P. 1: Eric Roth, design: Sally Degan Design **p. 2:** Mark Lohman **p. 10:** Tony Giammarino **p. 11:** Mark Lohman **p. 12–13:** Mark Lohman **p. 15:** M. Barrett/H. Armstrong Roberts **p. 18:** Brian Vanden Brink **p. 26–27:** (C) Jessie Walker; (TR) Mark Samu, design: Sherrill Canet Design; (BR) Rob Melnychuk; (BL) Lisa Masson; (TR) Tony Giammarino **p. 28–29:** Mark Samu, design: Mojo-Stumer **p. 30:** Mark Lohman **p. 31:** Mark Samu, design: Bruce Nagle **p. 32:** Mark Samu, design: Sherrill Canet Design **p. 33:** Jessie Walker **p. 34–35:** (R) Mark Samu, design: Sherrill Canet Design; (BL) Mark Samu; (TL) Tony Giammarino, design: Jack Shady, Freeman Morgan Architects **p. 36:** Tony Giammarino, architect: William Prillaman **p. 37:** Mark Lohman **p. 38–39:** Tony Giammarino, architect: William Prillaman **p. 40:** (T) www.davidduncanlivingston.com; (B) Jessie Walker, design: Lorrie Brown **p. 41:** Jessie Walker **p. 42:** Mark Lohman **p. 43:** (TR) Jessie Walker; (BR) Tony Giammarino; (BL) www.davidduncanlivingston.com; (TL) Tony Giammarino **p. 44–45:** Mark Lohman **p. 51:** Don Wong/CH **p. 54:** (T) Mark Lohman; (C) Nancy Hill; (B) Mark Lohman **p. 55:** John Parsekian/CH **p. 56:** John Parsekian/CH **p. 57:** (T) Jessie Walker (B) Carolyn Bates, artist: Deborah Pratt **p. 58:** Don Wong/CH **p. 59:** (T) Mark Samu, artist: Luciana Samu; (B) John Parsekian/CH **p. 60:** Don Wong/CH **p. 64:** Nancy Hill **p. 65:** Everett Short **p. 66–67:** (TL) www.davidduncanlivingston.com; (B) courtesy of Brewster Wallcovers **p. 68–69:** (TR) Mark Samu, design: T. Michaels Contracting; (BR) Jessie Walker, architect: Stephen Knutson; (L) Jessie Walker, design: Carol Knott **p. 70–71:** John Parsekian/CH **p. 72:** (BR) John Parsekian/CH **p. 74:** John Parsekian/CH **p. 79:** John Parsekian/CH **p. 80–81:** (B) John Parsekian/CH **p. 83:** (BR) John Parsekian/CH **p. 84–85:** Lisa Masson **p. 86–95:** John Parsekian/CH **p. 96–97:** Lisa Masson, design: Tracy Hoppe Interiors **p. 102–103:** John Parsekian/CH **p. 105:** John Parsekian/CH **p. 106–107:** John Parsekian/CH **p. 108–109:** (R) www.davidduncanlivingston.com; (BL) Rob Melnychuk; (TL) www.davidduncanlivingston.com; (C) Rob Melnychuk **p. 120–121:** (TC) Lisa Masson; (R) www.davidduncanlivingston.com; (BC) Tony Giammarino, architect: Aquino & Associates; (L) www.davidduncanlivingston.com **p. 122–123:** Lisa Masson **p. 126–128:** John Parsekian/CH **p. 132–133:** (sequence) John Parsekian/CH **p. 137–140:** John Parsekian/CH **p. 142:** John Parsekian/CH **p. 146–147:** (TR) Lisa Masson; (BR) Tony Giammarino, architect: William Prillaman; (C) Jessie Walker, design: Carson Pirie Scott Designs; (BL) courtesy of Fypon; (TL) Bill Rothschild **p. 148–149:** John Parsekian/CH **p. 153:** John Parsekian/CH **p. 158:** www.davidduncanlivingston.com **p. 159:** Jessie Walker, design: Katie White **p.172–173:** John Parsekian/CH **p. 178–179:** (TR) Mark Lohman; (BR) Bill Rothschild; (BL) Mark Lohman; (TL) www.davidduncanlivingston.com **p. 192–193:** (T) John Parsekian/CH **p. 194:** John Parsekian/CH **p. 196–197:** (C) Tony Giammarino, architect: William Prillaman; (TR) Mark Samu, design: Delisle/Pascucci Design; (BR) www.davidduncanlivingston.com; (BL) Jessie Walker; (TL) Tony Giammarino **p. 198–199:** Eric Roth, design: Benjamin Nutter Architecture **p. 204–205:** John Parsekian/CH **p. 210:** (TL), (TR) Mark Lohman; (BR), (BL) www.davidduncanlivingston.com **p. 211:** Mark Samu **p. 224:** (TR) Jessie Walker; (BR) Eric Roth, design: Hallmark Home Builders; (BL) Mark Samu, design: Bruce Nagle; (TL) www.davidduncanlivingston.com **p. 225:** Lisa Masson

SAFETY

Although the methods in this book have been reviewed for safety, it is not possible to overstate the importance of using the safest methods you can. What follows are reminders—some do's and don'ts of work safety—to use along with your common sense.

- Always use caution, care, and good judgment when following the procedures described in this book.
- Always be sure that the electrical setup is safe, that no circuit is overloaded, and that all power tools and outlets are properly grounded. Do not use power tools in wet locations.
- Always read container labels on paints, solvents, and other products; provide ventilation; and observe all other warnings.
- Always read the manufacturer's instructions for using a tool, especially the warnings.
- Use hold-downs and push sticks whenever possible when working on a table saw. Avoid working short pieces if you can.
- Always remove the key from any drill chuck (portable or press) before starting the drill.
- Always pay deliberate attention to how a tool works so that you can avoid being injured.
- Always know the limitations of your tools. Do not try to force them to do what they were not designed to do.
- Always make sure that any adjustment is locked before proceeding. For example, always check the rip fence on a table saw or the bevel adjustment on a portable saw before starting to work.
- Always clamp small pieces to a bench or other work surface when using a power tool.
- Always wear the appropriate rubber gloves or work gloves when handling chemicals, moving or stacking lumber, working with concrete, or doing heavy construction.
- Always wear a disposable face mask when you create dust by sawing or sanding. Use a special filtering respirator when working with toxic substances and solvents.
- Always wear eye protection, especially when using power tools or striking metal on metal or concrete; a chip can fly off, for example, when chiseling concrete.
- Never work while wearing loose clothing, open cuffs, or jewelry; tie back long hair.

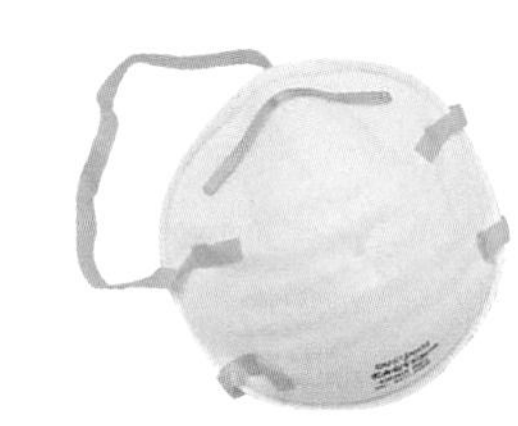

- Always be aware that there is seldom enough time for your body's reflexes to save you from injury from a power tool in a dangerous situation; everything happens too fast. Be alert!
- Always keep your hands away from the business ends of blades, cutters, and bits.
- Always hold a circular saw firmly, usually with both hands.
- Always use a drill with an auxiliary handle to control the torque when using large-size bits.
- Always check your local building codes when planning new construction. The codes are intended to protect public safety and should be observed to the letter.
- Never work with power tools when you are tired or when under the influence of alcohol or drugs.
- Never cut tiny pieces of wood or pipe using a power saw. When you need a small piece, saw it from a securely clamped longer piece.
- Never change a saw blade or a drill or router bit unless the power cord is unplugged. Do not depend on the switch being off. You might accidentally hit it.
- Never work in insufficient lighting.
- Never work with dull tools. Have them sharpened, or learn how to sharpen them yourself.
- Never use a power tool on a workpiece—large or small—that is not firmly supported.
- Never saw a workpiece that spans a large distance between horses without close support on each side of the cut; the piece can bend, closing on and jamming the blade, causing saw kickback.
- When sawing, never support a workpiece from underneath with your leg or other part of your body.
- Never carry sharp or pointed tools, such as utility knives, awls, or chisels, in your pocket. If you want to carry any of these tools, use a special-purpose tool belt that has leather pockets and holders.

Contents

Introduction

TRIMWORK CAN CHANGE THE CHARACTER OF YOUR HOME. *It not only covers rough edges and seams between different materials, but adds a distinctive touch that gives a home architectural detail and character. Even simple additions, such as replacing thin window casing with a more elaborate molding profile, can improve the look of a room dramatically. But in many modern homes the architectural detail and character of trim are absent. Passageways often are formed with drywall corners, and where trim is used, such as baseboard molding, it's often small and plain. This book will help you change that and transform spaces with plain-looking walls into elegant, handcrafted rooms. You'll learn to design and install everything from basic window and door casings to elegant wainscot walls and elaborately trimmed passageways.*

Decorating with Trimwork

Until fairly recently, designers and builders of homes often included trimwork in their designs. Even modest homes contained the molding and trim details that reflected the trends of the period and the tastes of the people who lived in the houses. Many of the housing styles that we think of as American architecture are identified, at least in part, by the trimwork that graces their walls, doors, windows, and mantels.

Having a grasp of the trim details used in the past is a good way to begin thinking about the designs that would work best in your home. Chapter 2, "Elements of Design," page 28, will guide you through the world of interior design, showing how elements in a room relate to one another in terms of size, scale, and proportion. These are important concepts when selecting molding for window and door casings or when designing a wainscoting system for your living room.

Pillars *aren't confined to entry halls. The one at right anchors a short wall on top of a vanity.*

Fireplace mantel trimwork, *below, is rarely one piece, but rather constructed of built-up moldings.*

Adding Distinction

One of the decisions you will need to make is in determining where you want to install new trimwork. Just about any room in the house will benefit from the addition of distinctive moldings and trim. Many homeowners begin with door and window casings and choose the more elaborate designs for more public rooms, such as living and dining rooms.

Chapter 6, "Casings for Windows & Doors," page 96, will help you choose and install molding that will not only enhance the door or window on which you work, but give a design boost to the entire room as well.

Details that Make a Difference

Window and door casings are only the beginning, however. One of the best ways to enhance the overall look of a room is to install distinctive cornice, chair rail, and baseboard molding. Each has a function and design value of its own, but when used together, they turn any blank wall into the focal point of the room. You will find the design and installation information you need in Chapter 7, "Crown Molding, Chair Rail & Baseboard," page 122.

Installing wall frames is another distinctive way to add texture to a wall surface. "Creating Wall Frames" begins on page 160 and is followed by "Staircase Wall Frames" on page 180. Chapter 10, "Wainscoting, Pillars & Pilasters," begins on page 198 and shows easy ways to include these elements in your home's design.

A well-trimmed room, *below, contains a variety of trimwork styles and techniques.*

designing women
OLD BEIJING IN PANORAMA
AZZ
Holland

CHAPTER 1

The Power of Trimwork

Molding and trimwork can transform a room from an empty box to a richly textured living space. In the past, homes contained a wealth of architectural trimwork that lent character, beauty, and substance to their interiors. But the trimwork used in most modern homes serves to hide joints between surfaces while providing little in terms of ornamentation or style. This book will show you how trimwork can transform your home. Trimwork—door and window casings, crown molding, wall treatments, picture rails, base trim, and the like—can have an almost magical effect on the look and character of your home. It can completely alter a room without changing its basic structure, giving your rooms the warmth, harmony, and sense of completeness trimwork alone can impart.

Trimwork, such as crown molding, *wall frames, and chair rails, was once standard fare in home design.*

Changes in Home Design

Until the mid-twentieth century, the use of decorative trimwork was standard in the construction of new homes. Most new houses incorporated trimwork that reflected the interior design style of the day. The early colonists brought with them a taste for dark, formal wood paneling of England during the seventeenth and early eighteenth centuries. By the mid-1700s, classical details such as pilasters, arches with keystones, and doorways with pediments—all elements of the English Georgian period—began to find expression in American homes. Heavily influenced by both archaeological and architectural discoveries of the time and by the English masters, America's own Federal style evolved during the early nineteenth century. Federal style also relied heavily on classical architecture and motifs, in particular those of ancient Greece. But it was heralded for its lightness and grace. Toward the end of the nineteenth century the Victorian style took root, and Victorian-era houses usually displayed ornate, intricate door and window casings, elaborate baseboards, and elegant crown moldings.

In the early twentieth century, architects, builders, and homeowners reacted against the perceived excesses of the Victorian Era, opting instead for the cleaner, simpler lines and square profiles of the Arts and Crafts movement. Influenced by the Arts and Crafts movement, homebuilders in the 1920s abandoned elaborate cornices and instead used small picture molding where walls and ceilings converged; doors and windows were cased out with flat boards usually about 4 inches wide. The subsequent Modern movement espoused that all ornamental features should be stripped away so that only a pure statement of function, process, and material remained. This took home design further away from the use of architectural trimwork.

But even if evolving tastes gradually rejected more ornate styles, trim remained a standard feature of new homes during the first half of the twentieth century; chair rails and crown moldings, though simplified, were still being installed, and carpenters didn't ask whether you wanted architectural trimwork in your new home—they just asked what style you wanted.

Vanishing Trimwork

The postwar building boom of the late 1940s and 1950s radically changed homebuilders' attitudes toward trim. When World War II veterans returned home and started families, demand for housing skyrocketed. Builders realized that if they reduced the amount of trim in a house to the bare minimum, they

While modern architecture *lends a sense of space to a home, it also sacrifices the warmth and intimacy of the traditional approach.*

CASING DEVOLUTION

The elaborate curves and bevels of Victorian-era casings gave way to square, flat profiles of the Arts and Crafts movement in the early twentieth century. During the building boom of the late 1940s and early 1950s, the plain clamshell casing emerged and continues to be widely used today.

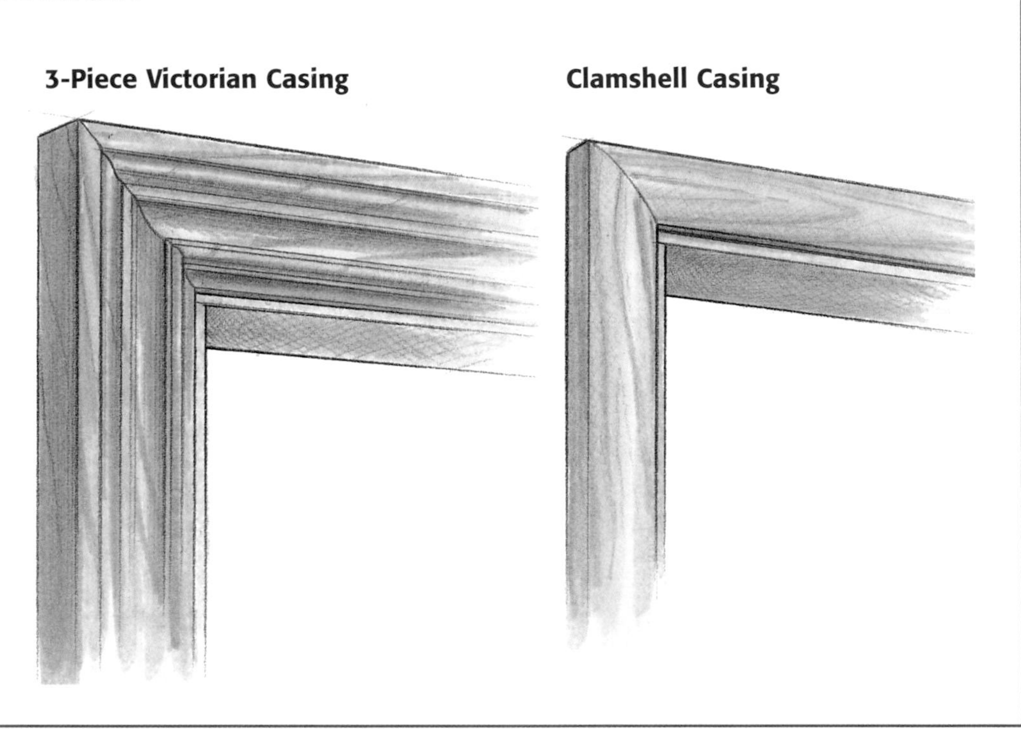

could build faster and cut costs. By using a simplified molding to cover the gaps around the window and door frames, and between the wall and the floor, builders saved on both materials and labor. This molding, called ranch or clamshell molding, was designed to have a streamlined profile that was consistent with the minimalist interiors of the new ranch and raised ranch houses. More recently, so-called Colonial trimwork has come into vogue for window and door casings as well as base trim. Colonial casings, like clamshell, are 2¼ to 3¼ inches wide but are milled with a more complex (though still simplified) profile. They are designed to look more at home in traditional settings.

Today most new houses are built with a minimal amount of simple trimwork of the clamshell or Colonial type, unless the homeowner and architect want to look to the past for inspiration and incorporate some of the beauty, warmth, and character imparted to an interior by the use of more ornate architectural designs.

Trimwork as a Design Tool

With the trend toward simplicity has come both a loss and a challenge. Most homes built today lack the ornamental details that provide a space with architectural character and identity. Rooms are often plain and featureless. Open floor plans commonly seen in contemporary houses create large, undefined areas and undifferentiated spaces.

This is where architectural trimwork comes into play. Installing decorative molding not only adds beauty and substance to a plain home but also is a superb—and often surprisingly simple—solution to the design challenges posed by many contemporary houses. In addition, the versatility of molding makes it adaptable to a variety of design treatments, from informal to ornate.

Consider some of the advantages of using architectural trimwork to enrich, enhance, enlarge, and define space.

Without trimwork, *as shown in the before photo, below, the front door of this house looks too small for an entry with a vaulted ceiling.*

TRIMWORK SOLVES THE EMPTY BOX SYNDROME

Rooms owe their architectural identity to their basic size and shape, the balanced placement of windows and doors, and the trimwork on the walls and ceilings. In most well-designed older houses, elaborate, built-up molding treatments lend character and beauty. Today most houses continue the minimalist trend discussed above. Decorating them usually involves "applied materials"—such things as window treatments, wallpaper, and paint—that homeowners can apply or remove fairly easily themselves.

The applied-materials approach goes a long way toward improving the appearance of some houses, but it has its limitations. This fact becomes especially clear when you're faced with the "Empty Box Syndrome"—walls and ceilings that are as featureless and nondescript as the inside of an empty box. You can dress up rooms with curtains, paint, and carpeting, but stark and sterile walls will remain the dominant feature of a room's background. If you are surrounded by plain white walls in your home, consider them a blank slate upon which you can create beautiful rooms with fresh architectural identities.

Without resorting to major reconstruction, such as moving walls and windows, the best way to enhance the character of a house architecturally is to install or upgrade the trim.

Trimwork Solves the Challenge of the Open Floor Plan

Modern architecture introduced the open floor plan to American home design, but with it came new decorating challenges. In this type of layout, rooms are not separated from each other by walls with cased-out passageways. Instead, they flow freely and openly from one area of the house to another. In addition, ceilings are often raised, creating what are known as vaulted or cathedral ceilings.

When people began to live in these houses, they realized that areas that are physically open to one another had to share the same or similar wall treatments. But if they did, where did one room begin and another end? What if the homeowner wanted to use a different color palette in the family room from the one in the kitchen? Did an open plan preclude using more than one wallpaper pattern in the public areas of the house? With no differentiation of space, the easiest decorating solution for these rooms is either to paint them the same color or to wallpaper them with the same wallpaper.

The alternative, using architectural trimwork, is much more creative, especially when you consider

The addition of stately columns *helps delineate space while preserving an open, airy feeling in this handsome room.*

A three-part, or tripartite, design *consisting of wainscoting, wall area, and crown molding creates a classic look in any home.*

incorporating the tripartite wall. It is a three-part horizontal treatment of wall surfaces consisting of wainscoting (panels or wall frames) and a chair rail on the lower portion of the wall, a cornice at the top of the wall, and the field between them. The tripartite wall evolved in response to the most common decorative treatment of wall surfaces during the mid-1800s, which was to cover them, top to bottom, with a single pattern of wallpaper or decorative paint.

The tripartite wall is an ideal decorative solution for the enormous walls created by cathedral ceilings. Installing raised-panel wainscoting or a wall-frame treatment at the bottom of the wall, plus cornice or panel molding just below where the ceiling begins to depart at an angle, transforms the entire character of the room. Not only that, the trimwork effectively changes the perception of the space. What may have felt cavernous before feels cozy now.

Another solution to meandering open-plan layouts is to build partition walls with cased-out passageways. Extra-wide passageways outfitted with pillars resting on podiums are also quite attractive and dramatic. Installing pilasters is an elegant design alternative to consider.

***Trimwork** can make a small space seem larger. This plain entryway, below, opened up dramatically once the chair rail and wall frames were installed, right.*

TRIMWORK MAKES ROOMS APPEAR LARGER

As you consider redecorating, you might be concerned that extensive trimwork will make small rooms feel even smaller. In fact, however, the opposite occurs. Through a phenomenon known as "geometric illusion," trimwork often makes a room appear larger and wider. Long horizontal lines, for example, can make you perceive that a room is longer and wider than it really is. Likewise, long vertical lines can make a low ceiling appear higher than it actually is.

Different molding types *include: (**A**) cornice; (**B**) door casing; (**C**) chair rail; (**D**) subrail; (**E**) wall frame; and (**F**) baseboard molding.*

Molding Types & Functions

With the proper tools, an understanding of some design basics, and knowledge of how trimwork is applied, most homeowners today can install and enjoy architectural trimwork. Between standard stock items and custom-milled possibilities, the choices available to you are nearly endless. Although the most popular types and their use are described here, you can also find cross sections of all of the common moldings displayed on a molding board at most lumber supply dealers.

Molding used to trim doors, windows, and other openings is called casing. (See Chapter 6, "Casings for Windows & Doors," page 96.) It is also commonly used for chair rails, cabinet trim, and other decorative purposes. Casing is perhaps the most typical molding used to conceal faults in a room's architecture and carpentry.

Cornices create a decorative transition between walls and ceilings and work especially well in rooms with high ceilings. (See Chapter 7, "Crown Molding, Chair Rail & Baseboard," page 122.) Crown molding, the most popular type of cornice, has a profile that projects out and down and gives a rich appearance. Cornices are also used in combination with other moldings to form decorative mantels and frames.

Chair rails, which protect walls in areas subject to damage by chair backs, have nosings that give way to curved and beveled surfaces that taper back to the wall. Picture rails, developed to hang framed pictures without damaging plaster walls, are similar in design.

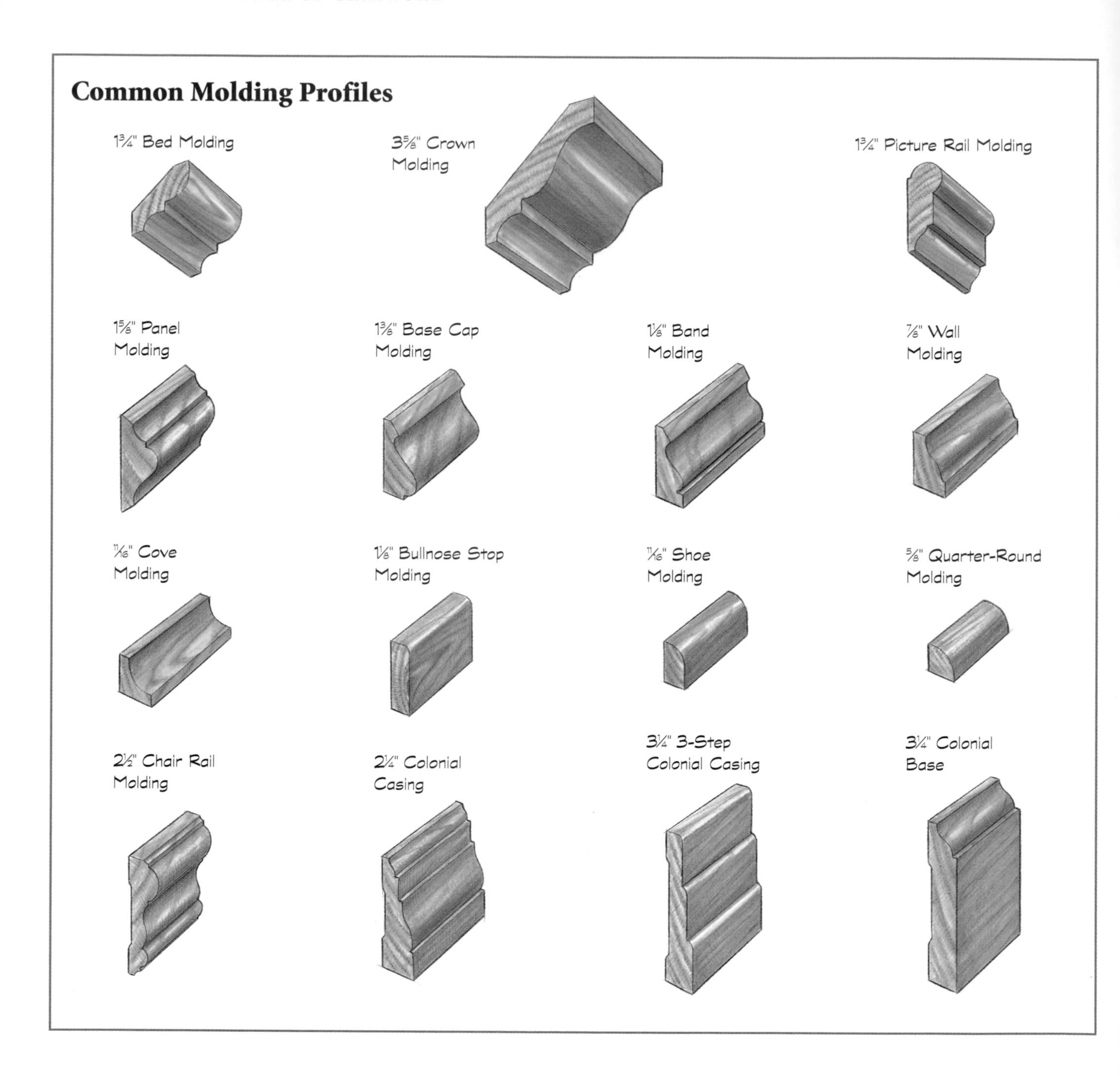

Baseboard protects the bottom of a wall from wear and tear and hides irregularities where the wall and floor meet. (See Chapter 7, page 152.) A shoe molding is installed along the bottom front edge to hide unevenness in the flooring and give the baseboard a finished look.

Wall frames look like a series of empty picture frames running along a wall. (See Chapter 8, "Creating Wall Frames," page 160 and Chapter 9, "Staircase Wall Frames," page 180.) Painted in the same color as the surrounding walls, they lend a sculptural quality to a surface. Painted to contrast with the surrounding wall, they can create a striking three-dimensional appearance of varying depths and densities.

Other moldings can be used in conjunction with those described above. (See Chapter 10, "Wainscoting, Pillars & Pilasters," page 198.) Wainscoting can impart a country look to kitchens and bathrooms or a more formal appearance to living or dining rooms. Pillars are useful as a way to define space in an open floor plan. Fluted pilasters are elegant architectural elements.

Most moldings are made of wood, though some are also vinyl-coated, metal, or plastic.

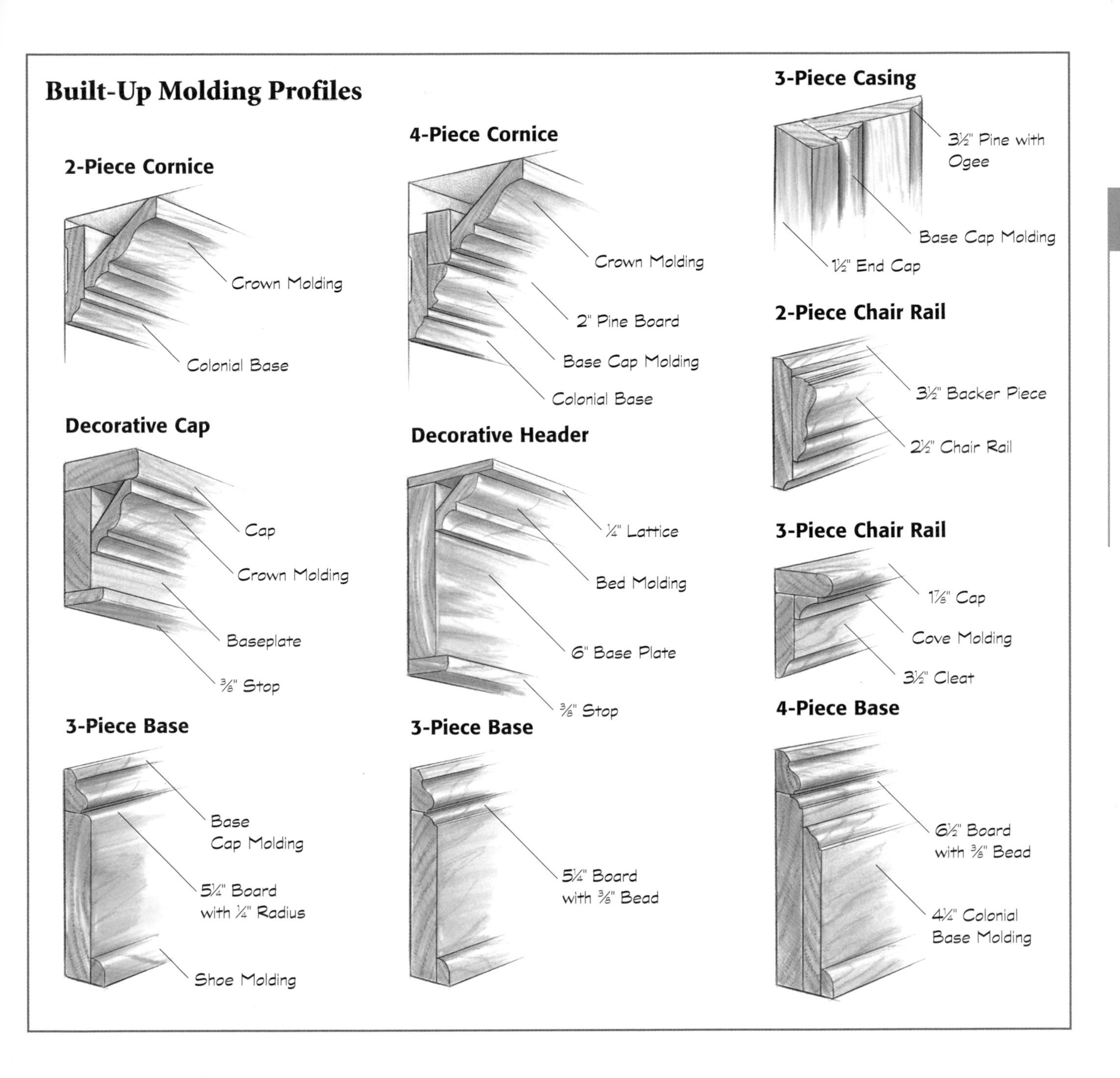

Stock versus Custom Milled

The moldings just described typically come from stock profiles available in lumberyards. If you install these profiles properly and give careful attention to the design elements of a room, they offer very satisfactory results. Yet the look you wish to achieve may not be attainable with stock profiles alone. Single-piece stock moldings may be too small or too thin, making them appear insubstantial in their surroundings. In such cases, your best choice may be to use built-up, or multipiece, moldings, made by combining various complementary profiles to produce what appears to be a single piece of molding. You can combine different pieces of stock molding, although this can be tricky because stock molding is not designed for this use. Or you can combine single-piece stock moldings with custom-milled profiles—an easier way to achieve attractive multipiece profiles.

Obtaining custom-milled profiles is less costly than most people believe, and the results can be markedly superior. Small woodworking shops can create built-up molding components at a reasonable price and will work with you in achieving your specific profiles design.

Gaining Confidence Using Trimwork

Redecorating with trimwork gives you a chance to create new warmth and beauty in the home you originally fell in love with. To do so with confidence, you'll want to make design choices appropriate to your space and decor. In some contemporary homes, for example, elaborate molding treatments could be out of place. But don't make the common mistake of underestimating the amount of trim that rooms can tastefully accommodate.

This book will guide you through the process of planning, designing, and installing both simple and more complicated trimwork. The next chapter summarizes design basics and trends that can help with your project planning. After that, the book covers the tools you'll need to install trim and the basic techniques for doing it yourself. Then it turns to the major categories of architectural trimwork, from cornices and baseboards to chair rails and pilasters, and shows you step by step how to install them. Throughout the book, photographs of trimwork provide ideas and inspiration you can draw on in developing your own plans.

A pillar standing on a podium *lends a touch of distinction to a simple open passageway and helps to delineate space.*

Transforming a Room

Basic Trimwork

A dining room in a typical house built today will be trimmed with ranch, or clamshell, molding around doors and windows and at the base of walls, creating a sterile, empty box of a room.

Enhanced Trimwork

Installing crown molding at the top of the walls, a chair rail around the perimeter of the room, a more substantial baseboard, a wall panel under the window, and wider window and door casings lends architectural character.

Complex Trimwork

Installing beams, a framed opening, wall-frame wainscoting, built-up base molding, and substantial door and window casings transforms the empty box into a room that looks more spacious, warm, elegant, and complete.

White painted moldings, *above left, can complement a very strong color scheme.*

An elaborate cornice, *left, works well in this traditional-style living room.*

Fluted pilasters, *above, seem to anchor a large passageway between two rooms.*

Decorative columns, *above right, create a distinctive frame for a plain passageway. Note how the column theme is repeated in the mantel design.*

Simple, but effective, *is one way to describe the door and wall trimwork treatment in the room at right.*

CHAPTER 2

Elements of Design

Good home design involves selecting elements for a room or entire house that work well together. Architectural trimwork is one such element, and learning to decorate with architectural trimwork requires a basic understanding of the principles of design, such as the concepts of size, scale, proportion, line, rhythm, and harmony. Some of the molding styles and treatments in use today are identical to those found on ancient Greek and Roman buildings constructed over 2,000 years ago. Others have evolved along with more recent house designs. In addition to the basics of design, this chapter will cover some of the key design movements and styles of the last three centuries, including Georgian; Federal; Victorian; Arts and Crafts; and American, English, and French Country styles.

Design Basics

All of the components in a room must relate to one another and to the space itself to achieve good design. At best, you can see when something looks right or if it's out of place. But becoming aware of the fundamental principles of design—size, scale, proportion, line, balance, harmony, and rhythm—will sharpen your eye and help you to make better design decisions.

SIZE, SCALE, AND PROPORTION

Size is relative. A column that looks massive in one space can appear small somewhere else. It is important to choose what is appropriate for your space. Scale refers to the size of something as it relates to the size of everything else. Proportion is the relationship between parts and the whole—the size of the doors and windows in relationship to the room, for example. Even the untrained eye can see when something

The wide crown molding *is in scale with the rest of the objects in this room, including the large chairs and ottoman.*

Large pillars *fit well with the oversized dimensions of this room. Although ornamental, they appear to serve a structural purpose.*

is out of proportion—the windows are too big or too small, for example. But achieving the right scale and proportion can be difficult for the layperson and often requires patience and some experimentation.

Design Drawing. It's easy to experiment with small objects, moving them around or exchanging one object for another. But you can't apply this method to trimwork. In this case, practice on paper. You don't have to be an artist, just take accurate measurements of the space and use ¼-inch graph paper. Each square will represent 1 foot. Using a T-square, draw straight lines and accurate corners. To draw arched doors and windows, use a compass.

Making a floor plan of the room is an essential step in planning a design, but you'll need an elevation (a view as if you are facing a wall, for example) to see whether the molding or trimwork you are considering is the right size for the installation. Again, draw everything to scale, including the trimwork.

Line

Lines convey qualities that affect the perception of space. Vertical lines (a column, for example) imply formality, dignity, and strength. Horizontal lines, like those of a chair rail, suggest repose or a foundation. Diagonal lines express motion. Curved lines, such as in an arched doorway, suggest freedom or softness.

Balance

Balance is the arrangement of architectural components, furnishings, or patterns in a way that creates a sense of rest, poise, and equilibrium. A balanced arrangement can be symmetrical or asymmetrical.

Symmetry occurs when architectural elements are exactly the same on either side of a center point. For example, a decorative passageway with a pillar resting on a podium at each end of the opening represents symmetry. Symmetrical arrangements are formal.

Asymmetry occurs when architectural elements are different on either side of the center point. A decorative passageway with a pillar resting on a podium at only one end of the opening is an illustration of asymmetry. Asymmetrical arrangements have a casual, less structured look about them.

This arch forms a transition *to a sleeping area that contains similar styles of trimwork.*

Rhythm and Harmony

Rhythm relates to visual patterns and how they carry the eye around a room. Harmony works with rhythm to create cohesion by linking all of the patterns and parts of a design. Architecturally, there are five types of rhythm—repetition and pattern; progression, or graduation; transition; opposition, or contrast; and hierarchy.

Repetition and pattern take place when the repeated use of an element of design, such as shape, form, or color, creates a pattern. The width of a series of wall frames and the series of parallel flutes on a fluted pilaster are examples of repetition and pattern.

The sequence of shapes from small to large or large to small represents progression, or graduation. For example, the tapering sequence of profiles on the base of a pilaster leads progressively to the fluted section of the pilaster above it. The way the cap and midsection of the pilaster shift to the fluted section is also an example of progression.

Transition is the way the viewer's eye is led from one point to another. For example, a chair rail can help the eye make the transition from the treatment on the lower portion of the wall to the treatment on the middle section.

Abrupt change that forms an intersecting, recurring pattern is called opposition, or contrast. The intersection of the vertical and horizontal spacing that surrounds each wall frame is an example of opposition.

Hierarchy occurs when elements are grouped together in a way that makes some elements appear more important than others. In a wall-frame treatment, for example, a tall and heavy-looking base molding and a three-piece built-up chair rail will look more important than the wall frames they enclose.

Wide, deep-colored molding *helps bring out the neutral walls and the bright colors used throughout the room.*

A bedroom fireplace wall, *above, is enhanced with crown molding.*

Light-colored furniture, *right, complements the dark molding.*

Simple trimwork, *below, adds distinction to a mirror over a vanity.*

Interior Design Styles

Although you can mix styles to create an interesting and sophisticated interior, it's easier to match a room's trim to the style of the furnishings. The result is typically more unified. But unless you're going for a strict period look, mixing similar styles can work nicely.

Today's most popular decorating styles lean toward traditional features. Few people stick strictly to one look, preferring to combine pleasing elements of more than one related style.

There are two basic "camps": formal and informal. Formal traditional-style decorating may include elements from the eighteenth century's English Georgian period or American Federal period, as well as elements from the formal Victorian style of the nineteenth century. Informal interiors may include a combination of Country styles (typically American, English, and French), informal Victorian, and Arts and Crafts (including Mission- and Stickley-style furniture).

Here's a description of the design styles.

A mixture of styles *in the furniture and architectural treatments lends a relaxed elegance to this traditional-style dining room.*

Classic molding, *a narrow mantelshelf, and the gilt-frame mirror are hallmarks of the Georgian period.*

Georgian

Restrained classical details and symmetry define this elegant style. During the latter part of the period, plaster walls replaced those made of wooden panels. This change eliminated the dark and somber interiors of earlier years. Brightly colored walls also contributed to a lighter and more delicate appearance. Architects began using plaster molding to frame and separate space on the featureless walls. This innovation led to wall-frame treatments constructed of wood molding.

Although it is commonly believed that wall-frame treatments are a less expensive version of paneled wainscoting, designers typically choose one or the other depending on the look they wish to achieve, not because of cost. Wall frames also offer an excellent opportunity to use contrasting colors to manipulate the perception of space. (See Chapter 3, "Combining Color, Pattern & Trim," page 45.)

FEDERAL

During the nineteenth century, Americans inspired by the connection of their new democracy to the first democracy tried to evoke Greek architecture (the Greek Revival style). Completely classical, dignified, and stately, Federal-style furniture accompanied this movement. The legs were always turned and lion's paws were carved on feet. Typical motifs seen in Federal-style furniture and ornament include lyres, sways, festoons, scallops, urns, acanthus leaves, scrolls, spiral carved turnings, and eagles. During the Federal era, there was much interest in archaeology and architecture, and Thomas Jefferson, himself an architect, was an important proponent of the movement.

***Federal-style homes** often had light and airy interiors with high ceilings and large windows and doors.*

VICTORIAN

The Industrial Revolution gave rise to a prosperous middle class in both England and North America. These new consumers, eager to acquire a vast array of home furnishings, crammed their homes with an extravagant mixture of period furniture and pattern. To satisfy the demand, manufacturers began mass-producing home furnishings and wallpaper at a prodigious rate. The resulting creations were both historically exaggerated and sometimes poorly manufactured. Authorities on interior design agree that the Victorian Era was a period that went over the top in its reinterpretations of earlier styles. Taste and beauty were sometimes overlooked in the mad dash of conspicuous consumption.

Despite its decorative excesses, however, the Victorian Era contributed a major design scheme, the tripartite wall. The division of the wall surface into three separate and distinct areas, and the relative proportions of height of each area, mirror the design and proportions of the classical use of a pedestal, a column, and an entablature.

The trimwork *used on the fireplace surround combined with the furnishings creates an authentic Victorian interior.*

Natural wood finishes *and trimwork with crisp, simple joints are characteristic of the Arts and Crafts movement.*

American Country-style interiors *often draw on the classic American farmhouse for inspiration.*

Arts and Crafts

The Arts and Crafts movement was born in England in reaction to the design excesses of the Victorian Era. Proponents regarded the ostentatious display of newly acquired wealth in Victorian England with disdain. Influential figures in the American Arts and Crafts movement were furniture maker Gustav Stickley and renowned architects Frank Lloyd Wright and the Greene brothers. As a group, they established two main goals.

First, they sought to fashion a uniquely American expression of the Arts and Crafts movement by emphasizing simplicity, honesty, and function of design. Craftsman-style and Mission-style furniture are superb examples of the American Arts and Crafts movement.

Second, they maintained that every aspect of a home's design, from landscaping to architecture to interior decor, should be an expression of one dominant style.

Today, Craftsman and Mission furniture have made an enormous comeback. But this style is incompatible with the trimwork found in many new homes. The broad, rectilinear surfaces of the furniture clash with the insubstantial, curved, and beveled molding and trim. If your furniture is representative of this style, you might consider installing your trimwork to make it compatible with your furnishings.

Country Style

Country style reflects comfort, unpretentiousness, and a devotion to nature. American Country style, more rustic than English or French Country, often draws on Colonial history for its context. Furnishings and textiles are simple and homespun. Plain muslin, ticking, or cotton plaids and checks look at home in this decor, as do simple florals. Plain furniture without much ornament fits nicely into an American Country setting, especially if it shows a little distressing in the finish. Homemade quilts, a storage trunk, or other utilitarian decorative touches add charm to the American Country look.

English Country style derives from rural cottage life. Authentic cottages have simple, flat casings, tongue-and-groove paneling, and round-wood beam ceilings. Furnishings and textiles exhibit a look of faded glory; slightly worn fabrics, lived-in furniture, and the casual blending of good-quality antique oak or pine heirlooms with new pieces are characteristic of English Country. Chintz with large floral patterns and lively stripes works well, along with accessories such as vintage china, flatware, and candlesticks.

French Provincial style reflects the colors of earth and sky and uses natural materials such as stone, wooden beams, and clay tiles. A rustic French farmhouse look might use tongue-and-groove paneling, miniprint wallpaper and textiles, and accent pieces such as clay pottery, a large cupboard or armoire, and a massive harvest table in a big, rustic kitchen.

Mixing Interior Decorating Styles

As you think about installing trimwork, you'll want to give some consideration to compatibility of architectural style, trim, and decor. Ask yourself first what style of trim will work best with the historical character of your home. Mixing trimwork from various eras can be tricky. While you can combine style elements of, say, Victorian and English Country, other combinations may clash. The flat, square profiles of Arts and Crafts trim, for example, would be incompatible with an ornate Victorian treatment; likewise, the handsome, classic look of some Federal-style motifs would be too stately for a country room.

Second, be consistent throughout your home. While you can mix past and present attractively, a home that changes style radically from room to room ends up feeling disjointed.

Third, consider not just architecture and trim but also furnishings, fabrics, and accessories. You needn't slavishly stick to one style or era in your choices, but the results will work best if all of the elements are compatible. In the end, your own personal vision is the most important tool you have to pull it all together.

***Most homes** are a combination of decorating styles. This room contains rustic, Country-style elements as well as more refined Federal influences.*

The repeating arches, *chair rail, and wall panels create design continuity in this narrow hallway.*

The molding on the stair, *left, is a distinctive treatment called a shadow railing.*

A fireplace surround, *above, displays the ornamentation favored by Victorian designers.*

Craftsman style, *below left, encompasses trimwork, light fixtures, and furniture design.*

Divided wall surfaces *painted bright colors, below, were introduced in the Georgian period.*

Southern Style
PARIS
At HOME with ART

CHAPTER 3

Combining Color, Pattern & Trim

Although most of this book concerns selecting and installing trimwork, it is important to remember that the molding you choose must work well with the other design elements in the room, including the colors of the walls and ceiling and the patterns and textures created by wallpaper and furniture. Many homeowners lack confidence when it comes to combining colors, but this chapter provides the basics for designing with color and then shows you how to create rooms with distinct character by combining trimwork with paint and wallpaper in a variety of ways. You'll also learn how to choose and apply paints, including some simple decorative paint techniques that will provide you with a custom finish for your walls, and how to select and install wallpaper.

For the sake of design harmony, *it's important to coordinate colors in adjoining rooms that are open to one another.*

Color & Pattern

Remember the adage "The whole can be greater than the sum of its parts"? Apply this to your interior, specifically the walls. For a dramatic effect, use color, pattern, and print to play up the visual tension between the trimwork and the "filling wall," the area between the chair rail and the cornice and crown moldings.

Working with color is not easy for everyone, although some people have a knack for it. Selecting colors and combining patterns can be exasperating at times, and mistakes may be costly. Even professional designers confess that it's a trial-and-error process. But if you undertake the challenge, the result can be rewarding.

How to Work with Color

The best way to overcome the fear of color is to learn more about it. Basically, it works as follows: light reflected through a prism creates a rainbow known as the color spectrum. Each band of color blends into the next, from red to violet. Modern color theory forms those bands from the spectrum into a circle called the color wheel to show the relationship of one color to another. (See "Using a Color Wheel," below.)

Colors (also known as hues) vary in their intensities. Value refers to the lightness or darkness of a color. Tinting with white gives a color a lighter value, creating a tone; adding black gives a color a darker value, creating a shade.

Color Perception. Certain colors are "warm": red, yellow, orange, peach, and cream, for example. Because they energize a room, use them where there's typically

Smart Tip *Using a Color Wheel*

The color wheel is the designer's most useful tool for pairing colors. Basically, it presents the spectrum of pigment hues as a circle. The primary colors (yellow, blue, and red) are combined in the remaining hues (orange, green, and purple). The following are the most often used configurations for creating color schemes.

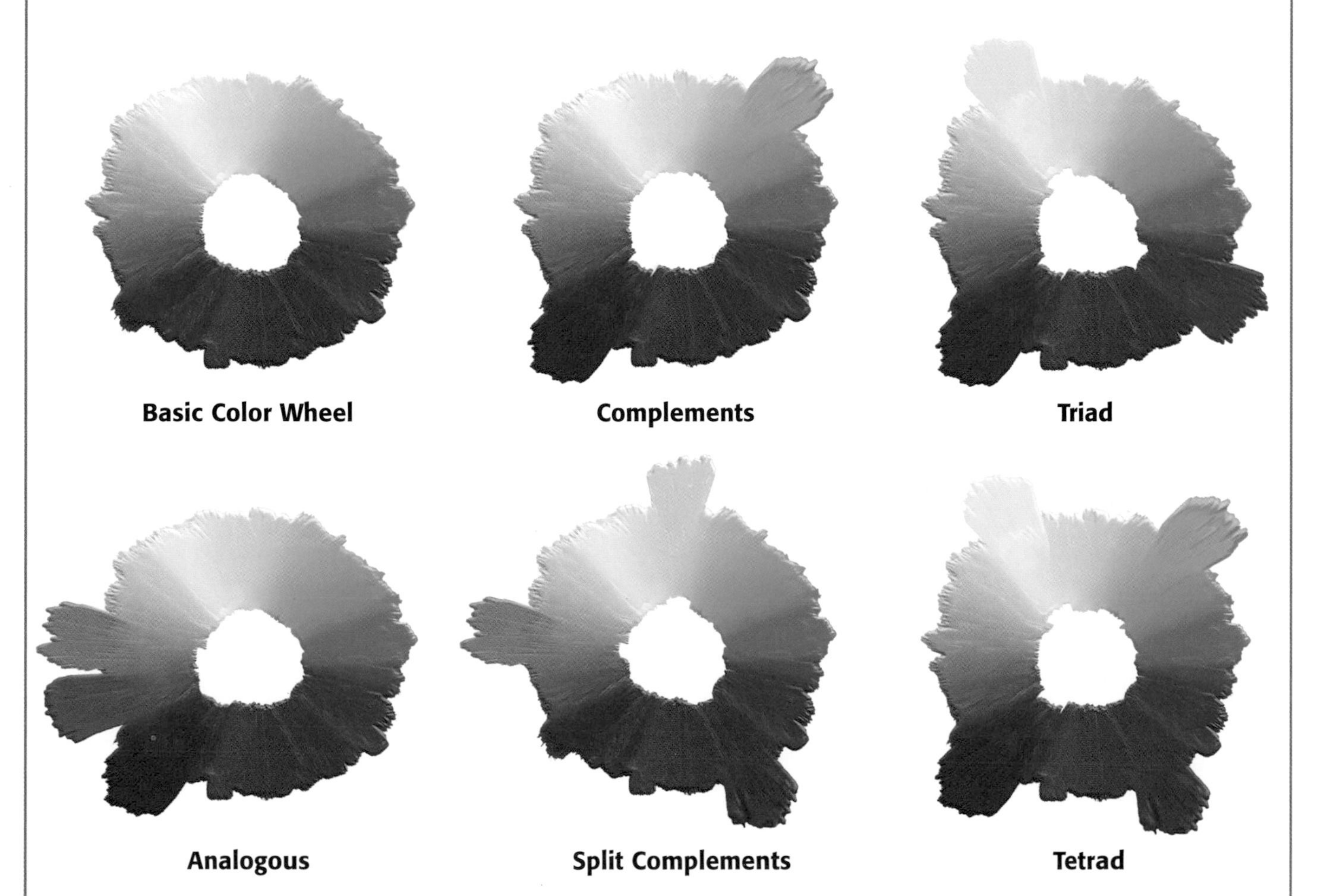

Basic Color Wheel **Complements** **Triad**

Analogous **Split Complements** **Tetrad**

a lot of activity, such as in the kitchen, dining room, or family room. Other colors—blue, green, gray, and lilac—are "cool," and enhance areas intended for rest or relaxation, such as a bedroom or a bath.

Keep in mind that color perception is subjective as well as theoretical, and it can do more for a room than influence mood. Color can affect the way you see the size and shape of space. Because warm colors seem to advance, you can use them to make a large room cozy or to draw attention to an interesting element such as trimwork. Conversely, use cool colors, which appear to recede, to open up a small space or to push something into the background to downplay its importance or to play up an adjacent area or feature.

The before-and-after photographs *of this living room offer convincing proof of the transformative qualities of trimwork. Gold accent paint draws attention to the new crown molding and window cornices, above.*

A layering of crown molding, *a vinyl border, picture rail molding, and sponged-on wall color add drama to this room.*

Theories aside, ultimately choose a color you really like. But be careful about too much of a good thing. Use bold colors only in areas in which you don't spend a lot of time, because saturated hues get tiresome. Reserve the drama for hallways or entry foyers.

Developing a Color Scheme. Selecting colors and patterns that will work together—and with the other furnishings in the room—involves careful consideration. Basically, color combinations fall into two camps: harmonious and contrasting schemes. Harmonious, or analogous, schemes are derived from nearby colors on the wheel (less than halfway around). Contrasting, or complementary, schemes are direct opposites. Harmonious schemes, like soft colors, are comfortable and pleasant. Contrasting schemes are dramatic, but they may be too much to live with in large doses unless you stick to light tones. Otherwise, use contrasting colors as accents in areas rather than as whole-room schemes.

Pulling a Look Together

When you think you've settled on a choice in color and print, it's a good idea to look at color chips and wallpaper samples along with fabric swatches at various times of the day and under different light conditions. Always do this in the room you plan to use them in before making a commitment. Designers often present their designs and color schemes to clients on a sample board that includes swatches of all proposed fabrics, carpeting, paint colors, and wallpapers. A designer may even take the concept a few steps further by creating a scaled-down vertical section of wall. You can make something similar that works just as well.

To make sure *your choices of paint, wallpaper, fabrics, flooring material, and decorative details work together, create a sample board.*

Creating a Sample Board. It's not necessary to build the display to scale, but details, including using thin wood strips to simulate the trimwork, can help you envision the room better. You can use oak tag or poster board, but matte board is best.

Keeping somewhat to scale, cut wood strips to represent the molding, and attach them to the board. Paint all of the parts in your proposed color scheme. Paint suppliers will sometimes mix colors in quarts, so you won't need a whole gallon for each test sample. But even if you do have to buy a gallon, it's still less expensive than having to repaint an entire room later if the color is wrong.

Next, attach samples of the proposed wallpaper with glue or staples. As a standard practice, retailers will provide samples for free or for a nominal charge. But get a sample that is large enough to show what the pattern or print will look like when you install it. If you have to buy a roll, take it home, tape it to the wall, look at it, live with it for a few days—and then decide.

Decorative Paint Techniques

Sponging *is a technique for applying one or more colors of paint to a surface using a natural sea sponge.*

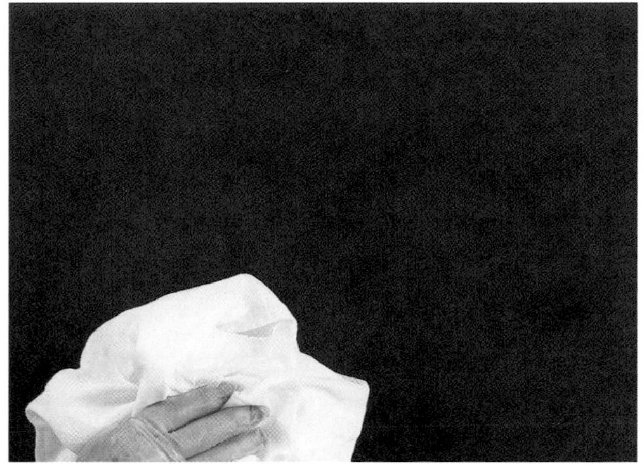

Faux Moroccan leather *gets its subtle yet sumptuous look by blending various glazes with a wadded cloth.*

Combing *techniques often imitate wood. Here a steel-wool pad is used to create the grain.*

Stippling *lends texture to a surface. Two taped-together staining brushes are an ideal tool.*

Decorating with Paint

Paint is typically the least expensive way to finish a wall and add instant style with color. In addition to a standard paint job—applying a solid color with a paint roller or brush—you may want to consider a decorative paint finish. Decorative painting, or faux finishing, involves manipulating wet or partially dry paint with various instruments such as sponges, rags, combs, or specialty brushes to produce special effects. A deft blending of tints, shades, and tones, applied with random or planned strokes, can create the illusion of depth or texture, or even the appearance of natural materials. The simplest of these techniques—sponging, ragging, combing, and stippling—are subtle, while faux wood, stone, or leather finishes are strong. To see what these decorative finishes look like and for easy instructions, refer to pages 57 to 61.

Buy the best-quality paint you can afford. Cheap paint doesn't cover adequately, which means you'll have to apply additional coats, so any initial savings will be lost on the expense of buying more paint. Besides, a high-quality paint reflects light beautifully and yields a rich, lustrous finish. It's also durable and easy to keep clean.

Paint Finishes

Paint for walls, ceilings, and trim comes in a variety of finishes—high gloss, semigloss, satin (or silk), eggshell, and flat (or matte). The lower the enamel content, the less reflective the finish. High-gloss paint contains the most enamel and has the most reflective properties. Flat paint has no enamel; therefore it is not reflective.

The enamel content in any paint may differ from one brand to another. Moreover, different manufacturers will sometimes use different finish terminology. For example, some manufacturers refer to an eggshell finish as "satin," but technically they are two slightly different finishes.

As a general rule, professional designers paint the three different surfaces of a room according to the finishes described in the table "Paint Finish Schedule," page 53. Multiple finishes make room surfaces more interesting and appealing, with each finish performing a separate aesthetic function.

A semigloss finish makes moldings stand out against a matte-finish wall because the eye naturally responds to varying levels of luminance. The more luminous surface appears to advance against the less luminous one. Furthermore, a semigloss finish reflects considerably more light than an eggshell finish.

Four types of paint finishes *in descending order—flat, eggshell, semigloss, and gloss. They range from matte to shiny.*

Average Drying Times

Base Coat	Dry to the Touch	Cured
Interior Paints		
Latex, flat	20 minutes to 1 hour	1 to 3 hours
Latex, eggshell	2 hours	4 to 6 hours
Latex, satin	2 hours	4 to 6 hours
Alkyd, eggshell	5 hours	24 hours ±
Alkyd, satin	5 hours	24 hours ±
Interior Enamels		
Latex, semigloss	45 minutes	4 to 8 hours
Latex, high gloss	2 hours	24 hours ±
Alkyd, semigloss	4 hours	24 hours ±
Alkyd, high gloss	4 hours	24 hours ±

Types of Paint

You have two types of paint from which to choose: alkyd and latex. Alkyd, often inaccurately called "oil-based" paint, contains synthetic resins as its binder. These resins have replaced the linseed oil of yesterday's oil paint. High-quality latex paint contains 100 percent acrylic resin. Moderately priced latex paint contains 100 percent vinyl resin, which is less durable. Alkyd paint cleans up with mineral spirits or turpentine, while latex cleans up with water.

Alkyd paint provides the most beautiful finish for trimwork and until recently was also regarded as tougher and more durable than latex paint. However, new latex paint seems to outperform alkyd paint on those counts. The main disadvantages of alkyd paint are its toxicity and noxious fumes. It's also highly flammable, as are the toxic solvents required for cleanup. Time may be a factor in your choice of paint type as well. Alkyd paint takes much longer to dry than latex, but that gives you more time to work on a decorative finish, for example, which has to be done while the paint is wet or tacky.

Classic Paint Schemes

The three most popular of the classic paint schemes are traditional, monochromatic, and neoclassical. Each one involves a clever use of color to create a particular effect. The result is often attributed to one color's

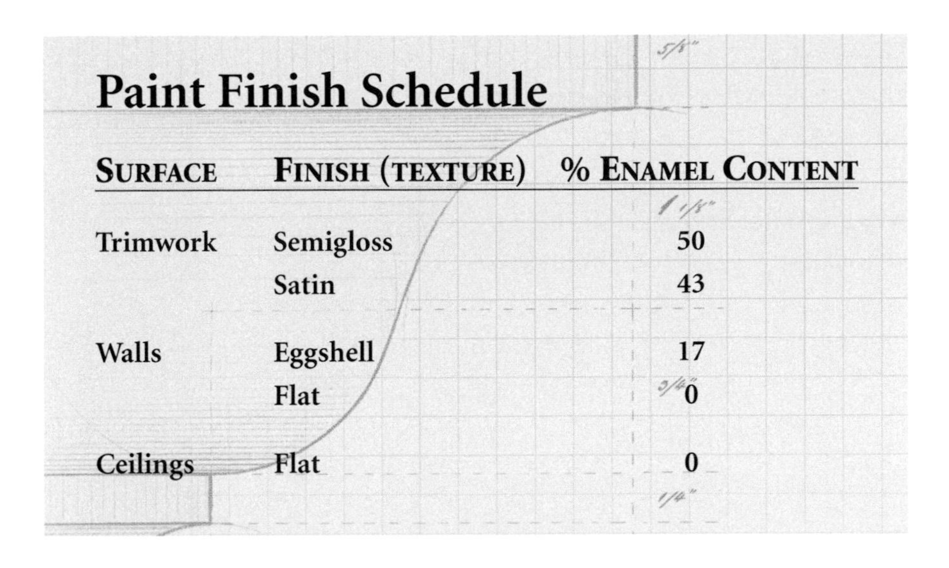

Paint Finish Schedule

Surface	Finish (texture)	% Enamel Content
Trimwork	Semigloss	50
	Satin	43
Walls	Eggshell	17
	Flat	0
Ceilings	Flat	0

***Semigloss paint** helps the doors and trim stand out against a busy print.*

relationship to another. When planning your scheme, refer back to the color wheel combinations on page 47 for guidance.

A Traditional Scheme. A traditional paint scheme involves two colors, usually an off-white for the trim and a moderate to significantly darker value of a harmonious or contrasting color for the walls. Although this scheme is simple, it can be effective. Its strength lies in its ability to highlight the trimwork and its three-dimensional quality.

A Monochromatic Scheme. A monochromatic color scheme consists of different values of the same hue. Most monochromatic schemes can be divided into two groups. In the first, two closely related values of the same color (one on the trim, another on the wall) create a subtle contrast. The finished effect can have an almost dreamlike quality.

Another monochromatic scheme involves painting two sections of the wall in slightly different values of one color, and then coating the trimwork in a tone that is considerably lighter than the first two. For example, if you install wall frames, make the area inside the frames the darkest value. Then use a slightly lighter value on the margins and the surrounding wall, and a still lighter value on the moldings. If you have a chair rail and no frames, make the area above the chair rail slightly lighter than the area below it. Use a much lighter value than that of the first two paints to finish the trimwork. The end result is dramatic and sophisticated.

A Neoclassic Scheme. A neoclassic color scheme is different from both the traditional and the monochromatic schemes because it has no contrasting hues or values. It's just one color, one value. In a neoclassic color scheme, the trimwork and color appear to dissolve into each other, lending a sculptural quality to a room.

Strict rules don't exist, *but there are three classic paint schemes you may want to consider: traditional, top; monochromatic, middle; and neoclassic, bottom.*

Preparing Walls

What You'll Need

- Paint scraper or putty knife
- Utility knife and taping knives
- Palm sander and 120-grit sandpaper
- Paintbrushes
- Eye protection
- Joint compound and primer

PAINT TIP: Poor surface preparation is the number-one cause of paint failure. Preparing surfaces properly may be tedious, but it's important for a good-looking and long-lasting finish.

1 Thoroughly scrape away cracked or flaking areas. Trim tears free with a utility knife, and apply joint compound.

2 Use a wide blade to fill large bare patches with joint compound. Apply several thin coats instead of one thick one.

3 Prime all repaired areas. This prevents joint compound from drying out the paint and making it dull looking.

Painting Pointers

The saying "You get what you pay for" is true of brushes and rollers as well as paint. Better-quality tools make the job easier and yield better results. It's also important to prime new drywall surfaces as well as previously painted walls with a high-quality interior latex primer. Primer performs two functions. It seals both the paper facing and the taped joints of new drywall, and it provides a uniform surface for you to evenly apply the finish coat. Before applying the primer, prepare the walls by going over them lightly with 120-grit sandpaper.

Preparing Moldings for Finish Paint. To hide the grain, you'll have to prime the wood properly. Before installing molding to the wall, apply one coat of primer to the molding. This first coat will make the wood fiber "stand up," leaving the surface rough. Sand the wood smooth; then install the molding. Fill any nailholes with wood filler, and sand them until they are smooth. Then apply the second coat of primer, making sure to paint over the spots thoroughly where you used wood filler or caulked gaps or joints. This essential step in the process will prepare the moldings to accept two coats of the finish paint.

Preparing and Painting Walls. Mask the trim's edges with a quick-release tape that you can remove after the cut-in paint has set up. When masking chair rails and base moldings, use tape that is wide enough to protect the trimwork from any misting or spraying from the roller. When rolling paint onto a wall, keep an eye out for ridges, puddles, and splatters, and make sure that your strokes are even.

If you use flat paint and apply it generously, constantly backrolling it, a single coat will usually do the job. But two coats will provide a better finish. With eggshell paint, use a ⅜-inch-nap roller. Avoid overworking the paint and limit backrolling. Apply two even coats to the surface.

Decorative Painting

Set up the surface for a decorative finish, such as sponging or rag rolling, with a base coat of flat or eggshell latex paint. Many of the techniques acquire their unique character with a wash or a glaze. A wash is thinned-out latex or acrylic paint. A glaze is a paint mixed with a transparent glazing medium and a thinner. The glazing medium comes in both latex and alkyd formulations.

Painting Walls

What You'll Need

- Angled sash brush
- Wide paintbrush or roller
- Extension pole for roller
- Drop cloths and rags

PAINT TIP: Paint won't hide imperfections. Rather, it will make them stand out. So shine a bright light at a low angle across the surface to spot problem areas before painting.

1 Use a trim brush to cut in a 2- to 3-in. strip of paint all around trim and in other areas you can't easily reach with a roller.

2 Start by painting thick vertical stripes. Then roll left and right on the diagonals across the stripes. This spreads the paint evenly.

3 When the original stripes have been spread over a section of wall, roll straight up and down to create a uniform finish.

Sponging. This is the easiest and most versatile decorative paint finish. It creates a dappled finish, a subtle play of color that ranges from delicate to bold. Certainly, the dazzling result is worth the effort. It all depends on the colors you choose and the transparency and glossiness of your glaze.

Because it produces a textured surface with great visual depth, sponging disguises imperfect walls and hides dirt in hard-use areas such as children's rooms.

Choosing a contrasting color *for the molding gives the walls a deep, rich look in this Country-style dining room.*

Sponging On: Two Colors

What You'll Need

- Paint tray
- Sea sponges
- Latex gloves
- Latex paint for base coat
- Two tinted glazes
- Clear top coat (optional)

PAINT TIP: Use this method to apply two coats of light glaze over a dark base coat. Be sure to constantly vary your strokes because a repetitive pattern is more noticeable when you put light glazes over a dark base coat.

1 After the base coat dries, sponge the surface by dabbing on one of the glazes. Avoid creating an identifiable pattern. Reload the sponge as often as necessary. This step covers about 40 percent of the base coat. Let the glaze dry.

2 Repeat Step 2 with the second color, sponging it on so that it covers about 40 percent of the wall. Let it dry.

3 The final finish reveals about 25 percent of the base-coat color. The overlapping light and dark areas create the illusion of depth and texture.

Appropriately, the technique takes its name from the only tool usually used to apply the finish: a sponge. Not just any sponge, however. It must be a natural sea sponge, the only sponge that has the irregular shape and uneven surface necessary to create a mottled texture. Sea sponges come in round and flat shapes and are sold in paint and craft stores.

Rag Rolling. More refined than sponging, rag rolling creates smooth, flowing textures reminiscent of fine materials such as vellum, brushed suede, crushed velvet, and soft leather. Ragging may also go by the names cloth distressing, rag-rolling, and parchment; although they are often used interchangeably, each one refers to a variation on the ragging technique.

Ragging techniques are fairly easy to execute. Soft cloth, usually cheesecloth, is either bunched in the hand or rolled and used to apply or lift off wet glaze. Sometimes newspaper is pressed over the glaze to soften and blend the colors before the cloth is worked over the surface. Other materials, such as old sheets and towels, plastic bags, burlap, carpet padding, chamois, and canvas also create an incredible variety of looks. Experiment a little with different ones.

Sponging Off: One Color

What You'll Need

- Two sea sponges
- Several buckets of clean water
- Latex paint for base coat
- Tinted Glaze

PAINT TIP: After working the technique on a small surface, you can expedite the drying time of an oil-based glaze by using a blow dryer or by adding a dryer (such as terebene dryer, copal medium, or light-drying oil) to the glaze formula.

1 Mix the glaze to the desired color and thickness. Sponge the glaze onto the surface. Make sure each stroke occasionally overlaps the previous stroke. Let about 20 percent of the base-coat color show through.

2 Using a clean, damp sponge, lift off as much of the glaze as possible. Frequently dip the sponge into water and wring it out. Occasionally drag the sponge over the glaze to meld the colors together.

3 The final finish. About 10 percent of the base color shows through, and the entire surface has a delicate, misty appearance.

The finished effect depends on the kind of cloth used and the pressure applied when working it over the glaze, as well as the glossiness and translucence of the glaze itself. Using newspapers instead of cloth to lift off the glaze will affect the look as well. Ragging techniques require two skills not learned with sponging. The first is the ability to bunch or fold the cloth correctly. The second is the knack for working in corners and along edges.

Combine molding and trimwork *with decorative paint finishes. A sponging technique in this room introduces a unique effect.*

Rag-Rolling Off

What You'll Need

- Roller with 1/4" nap or foam cover
- Multiple 6'-long strips of soft cloth
- Latex paint for base coat
- Alkyd-based tinted glaze
- Clear top coat (optional)
- Latex gloves

PAINT TIP: Work with a partner. One person can roll on the glaze while the other lifts it off with the rag in a rhythmic pattern of even, steady strokes.

1 Roll the glaze evenly over a base coat using crisscross strokes: vertical, then across, and then vertical again.

2 Form a relaxed wad with a cloth, and then roll it through the wet glaze, working from top to bottom. Avoid a repetitive pattern. When the cloth starts to put paint on the wall, get a clean one.

3 Overlap sections slightly so you don't produce a recognizable line. Go over the glazed surface a second time with fresh rolls of cloth.

Antique Stippling

WHAT YOU'LL NEED

- 1½- to 2"-wide decorator brush
- Oval sash brush or small stippling brush
- 90-weight cheesecloth folded into pads
- Satin or eggshell alkyd base-coat paint
- Alkyd-based tinted glaze
- Antiquing glaze (optional) and paintbrush
- Latex gloves

PAINT TIP: Antique stippling looks best when it's executed with low-contrast colors.

1 After the base coat dries, brush the glaze over the carved part of the surface, completely coating the area.

2 Using an oval sash brush or other small brush, apply glaze to the rest of the surface with an up-and-down pouncing, or stippling, stroke. Stipple it twice.

3 As the glaze begins to become matted, wipe along the molding with dampened cheesecloth. Keep turning the cloth so you're always working with a clean section of it.

4 If you wish, apply a light coat of the antiquing glaze over the rest of the trim. Feather out the glaze so that just a hint of color shows.

5 The finished trim. So that color subtly fades onto the wall, you can glaze the edge of the molding and lightly stipple it. This is optional.

To create a combed effect, *drag a stiff-bristled brush, steel wool, or a notched tool through wet glaze.*

Top Coats. Complex finishes such as faux stone or wood call for a protective clear top coat. Otherwise, a top coat is optional. There are many top coats on the market that come with water or alkyd bases, and some have a full ranges of finishes—flat, eggshell, satin, semigloss, and high gloss. Choose a top coat based on the amount of shine you want and compatible solubility. If you use an acrylic glaze, choose a water-soluble top coat. If the glaze is an alkyd formula, use a solvent-soluble top coat. Varnish and polyurethane can be water- or solvent-soluble, but only water-soluble polyurethane will not yellow over time.

A chair rail *and wall panels help set off the print of this wallpaper.*

Working with Wallpaper

The power of wallpaper lies in its capacity to grace walls with highly stylized vignettes of color, texture, and pattern. Today's selection of wallpaper patterns is immense, so you have a good chance of finding the right one for your decor. Motifs range from abstract and geometric patterns to florals, stripes, and plaids. Some manufacturers reproduce documentary papers or reinterpretations of historical prints as well as wallpapers that mimic the look and texture of decorative paint finishes, fabrics, or natural materials. Pastoral scenes called toiles, Chinese-inspired chinoiserie prints, Jacobean florals, classical and historical motifs, and faux silk patterns such as moiré or damask look particularly at home in traditional settings that include trimwork. Tone-on-tone patterns are understated and elegant.

Borders and Dadoes. A border is a horizontal strip that is usually about 15 inches wide and runs along the ceiling line below a cornice, at chair rail height, or around the trim of doors or windows. Wallpaper companies typically offer coordinated borders and wallpapers in different colorways to make it easier to match up prints. But you don't have to stick to them if you feel confident enough to make a selection from altogether different designs. Wallpaper installed on the lower half of a wall is called a dado.

Crisp off-white crown and base molding *sets off the vibrant hues in this formal floral-pattern wallpaper.*

Types of Wallpaper

With the exception of rare specialty papers, most wallpaper is not made of paper at all. These are the most common types.

Vinyl Coverings. This is today's most popular wallcovering. It's durable and cleans easily. Fabric-backed vinyl is heavy and usually doesn't come prepasted. It's scrubbable and is most often recommended for kitchens and baths, especially if it contains a mildewcide. Paper-backed vinyl is lighter in weight and prepasted, which takes a lot of the hassle out of installation. It comes in a wide range of patterns. Vinyl-coated paper is inexpensive, but it tears easily and doesn't hold up to dirt and stains.

Flocked Coverings. These first became popular during the eighteenth century. They feature a raised fuzzy pattern that resembles cut velvet. Some flocked papers are prepasted, and some are washable.

Embossed Coverings. These papers have a raised design and a relief background that simulates raised moldings. One type, called lincrusta, is a heavy linoleum-like product that requires professional installation. The other type, anaglypta, is cheaper and lighter and made of cotton-fiber pulp. You can install it yourself. Both originated in the nineteenth century.

Natural Coverings. Grass cloth, hemp, and other natural coverings bring texture to a room. They are expensive and delicate, and require professional installation. However, you can find excellent look-alikes in the vinyl category that are easy to install, washable, and durable.

How to Work with Pattern and Print

In the form of wallpaper, pattern and print can draw attention to a wall or camouflage its flaws. Because pattern is largely a vehicle for color, you

Most vinyl wallpaper, *like the one in the photo at right, are durable and washable. The flocked covering in the middle photo resembles damask. Metallic details enhance the formal wallpaper pattern, bottom.*

REPAIRING WALLPAPER

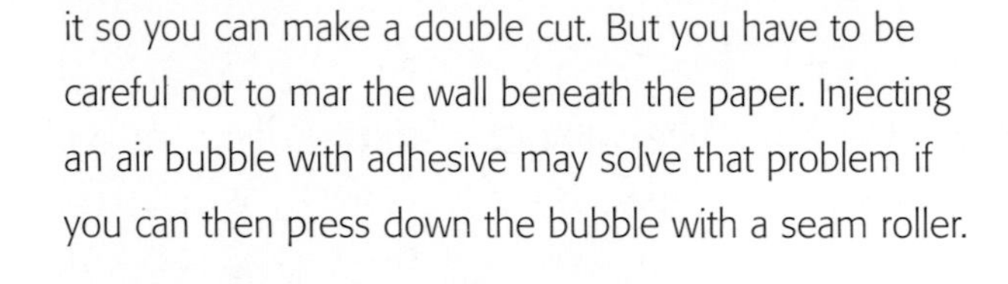

Sometimes it's easier to make spot repairs than to replace existing wallpaper, especially if the wallcovering was expensive. The overall plan is to create a patch piece larger than the damaged area and position it so you can make a double cut. But you have to be careful not to mar the wall beneath the paper. Injecting an air bubble with adhesive may solve that problem if you can then press down the bubble with a seam roller.

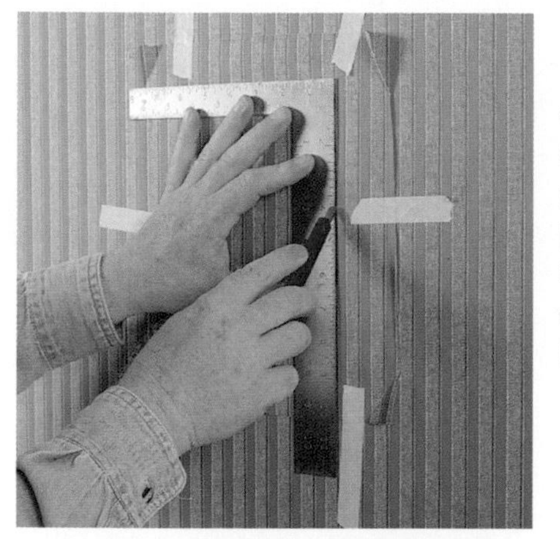

1 To patch a damaged area, align a patch piece over the pattern; tape it down; and cut through both layers.

2 Remove the patch and the damaged piece from the wall; the cutout part of the patch should fit in the hole.

1 To fix an air bubble, make a small puncture hole in the bubble with a razor knife.

2 Use a special syringe to inject adhesive so that the bubble can be rolled flat with a seam roller.

can apply many of the same rules to guide your selection. Large-scale patterns are like warm colors in that they appear to come toward you, while small-scale patterns appear to recede the way cool colors do. But a large pattern can also transform a small, insignificant space into something special. In general, use strong patterns the way you would bold colors—in places where you don't linger. The exception: in a room that lacks furniture, "fill up" the empty space with a bold print.

Mixing Patterns. It's not complicated to mix more than one print if you find links in color, scale, or motif. For example, use the same or similar patterns in varying sizes, or develop a theme that focuses on florals, geometrics, or period prints. The most effective link is

color. Shared colors or hues that are the same level of intensity will work together successfully. In addition, you can find manufacturer-coordinated lines through wallpaper books and in-store design services.

Wallpaper Preparation

Make sure a wall is clean and smooth before installing wallpaper. With existing walls, repair minor cracks and spot-sand raised areas. Major

The print in this wallcovering *is subtle enough to coordinate with the other patterns in this room.*

Hanging Wallpaper

What You'll Need

- 2' level and chalk-line box
- Wallpaper, tray, and sponge
- Scissors and smoothing brush
- Paste brush, adhesive, and bucket (for unpasted papers)
- Cutting guide and utility knife
- Seam roller

TRIM TIP: Use liner paper to smooth out a damaged wall and to provide uniform support for expensive paper.

1 Use a level or chalk-line box to mark a plumb line where the seams will fall. Plan the layout of strips before you paste.

4 Position the paper on the wall, making sure it's aligned with the plumb line. Leave a slight amount of excess at the ceiling.

5 Smooth out the strips with a brush, starting at the top corner near the guideline and moving down and across.

damage requires replacing the drywall entirely. Wash dirty and greasy walls with a solution of equal parts of warm water and ammonia, and let them dry for several hours before applying a primer-sealer. Don't confuse this with a primer intended for paint. A wallpaper primer-sealer is meant specifically for use under wallcovering to protect the drywall. There are different types, but pigmented acrylic primer-sealer, also called a universal sealer, does a good job of protecting the drywall from surface damage during future removal, and it cleans up with water. Use a special stain-killing primer-sealer on spots that don't come off with simple washing, or they will bleed through the new wallpaper.

Although it's best to remove existing wallpaper, you can paper over it if the first layer is sound. However, if any portion of the old paper is loose, and you don't make the necessary repairs, the new wallcovering will not adhere.

The right combination of wallpaper, paint, and trim can provide an elegant backdrop for the rest of your home's furnishings. By choosing each of the components with care and properly preparing all of the surfaces for application, your work will yield excellent results.

2 Dunk prepasted wallpaper in a pan of lukewarm water; unpasted papers have to be treated with adhesive that's spread on with a brush.

3 Fold the soaked roll onto itself to make it easy to carry, and place the strip on the wall.

6 Trim away excess paper at the top and bottom with a guide and a utility knife.

7 Near corners, you can overlap seams by double-cutting through both strips for a perfect match. Finish edges with a wallpaper roller.

COLOR IN DECORATION
The Town House

Bright white molding, *left, creates a frame for the lively colors of the walls and furniture.*

Dark wood trim *works well with some of the colors contained in the pattern of the wallpaper shown above.*

Trimwork painted a solid color, *below, is the best way to counter a colorful wall treatment.*

NAILS
NAILS
EB14B
14.4v

CHAPTER 4

TOOLS FOR TRIMWORK

Using the right tool for the job won't necessarily guarantee success, but it will allow you to spend time concentrating on the work rather than trying to compensate for an inadequate tool. When purchasing tools for a trimwork project, stay clear of cheap, entry-level models. For example, cheap cutting tools won't hold a keen edge, and throwaway brushes will litter a finish with bristles. But you should also avoid top-end professional tools. They certainly won't hurt your results, but most amateur woodworkers don't need the capacity or power that professional-grade tools deliver. A heavy-duty router may pay off for a cabinetmaker who uses the tool five days a week, but it's overkill in most home shops. As a rule, you'll do fine (and save money) using midpriced tools that do one job well.

Basic Hand Tools

Do-it-yourselfers today are faced with an array of tools in a wide range of quality and price. There are so many that once you start collecting them, the urge to acquire more and more can be irresistible. But for most trimwork (and other how-to jobs around the house) you need only a small toolbox of basic equipment.

***A tool box** helps to keep your hand tools organized. Some have removable caddies and storage for small parts.*

Basics. The hand-tool starter kit includes a comfortable hammer, trim saw, block plane, and everyday items such as rulers, screwdrivers, a utility knife, nail set, and square. There are endless fine points to consider about each one, but it works to buy them as you need them and to stick to midrange quality—a "better" tool in the familiar marketing range of good-better-best. With chisels, for example, the cheapest may have weak handles, while the most expensive may have cutters made of exotic metals that are difficult to sharpen.

Metal Quality. Pay attention to the quality of striking tools and to tools, such as a plane, that must have a true surface to perform well. The main difference in quality is in the metal manufacturing process. Inexpensive metal tools often are cast (poured into a form) and then painted in part to conceal the process. Higher-quality metal tools are drop-forged (pounded into shape). This process removes more air bubbles from molten metal and makes the tools stronger. In general, when manufacturers take the time to drop-forge a tool and then machine-grind its surface, they leave the fine-grained metal unpainted.

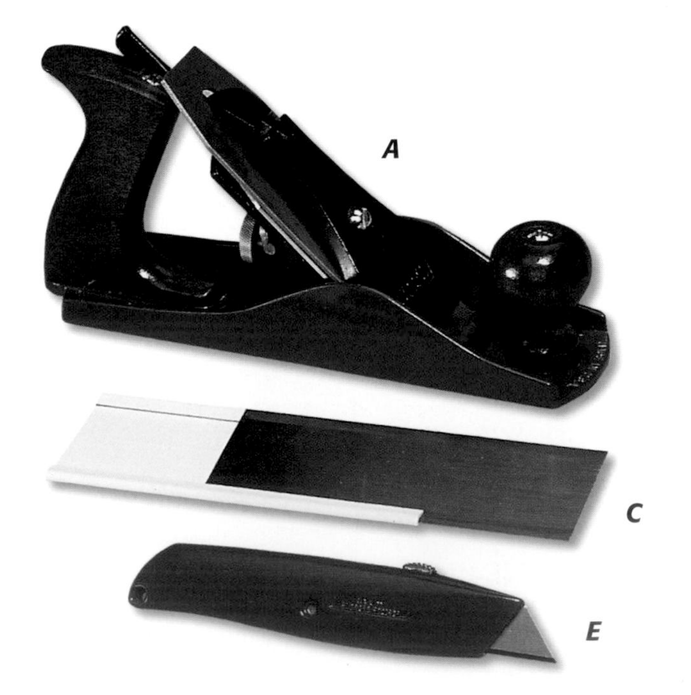

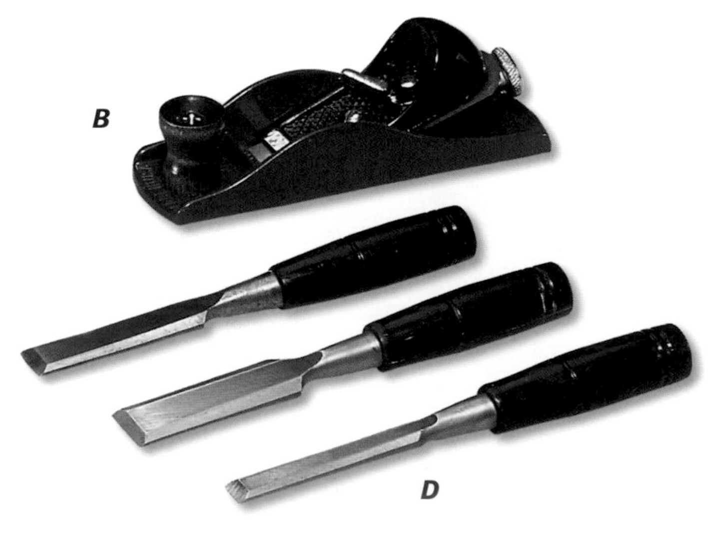

***A**—bench plane; **B**—block plane; **C**—cabinet scraper; **D**—chisels; **E**—utility knife*

Measuring and Layout Tools

Measuring and layout work is straightforward. But it's easy to make a mistake that can complicate a project and waste wood. That's why it pays to follow the adage "Measure twice and cut once." To reduce the chance of duplicating an error, measure length by height the first time, then the other way around on your double check. It also helps to use the most efficient measuring tools and techniques for the situation at hand.

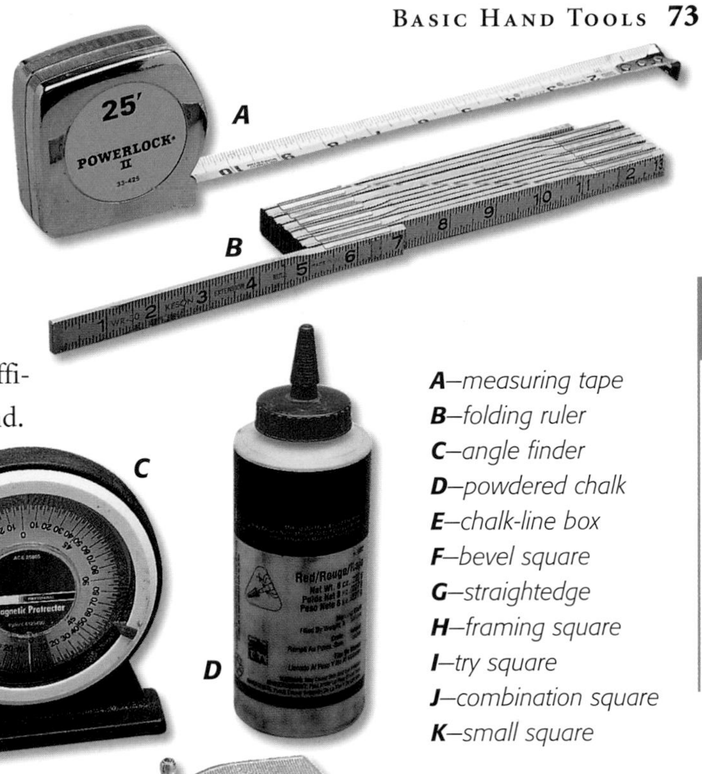

A—measuring tape
B—folding ruler
C—angle finder
D—powdered chalk
E—chalk-line box
F—bevel square
G—straightedge
H—framing square
I—try square
J—combination square
K—small square

Initial-Point Measuring. Many measuring operations are repetitive—for example, to keep framing modular so that you can nail trim into studs every 16 inches. But each time you measure from one stud to another there is a margin of error. Each miscalculation may be small, but the combined effect can create a significant error. You can defeat this problem by periodically measuring overall distance from an initial point. If you are installing a series of evenly spaced trim pieces, for example, it pays to periodically check your layout from the corner where you started.

Cut-Line Marks. Even pros sometimes waste a board with a miscut when they forget which piece is the good end and which piece is the scrap. The simple way around this common problem is to get into the habit of putting an X on the scrap side whenever you mark a cut.

Trim Measurements. To lay out tight trim joints, you should fine-tune your measurements down to the sixteenth marks on a ruler—and get rid of those stubby pencils. It may seem like hairsplitting, but you also have to allow for the thickness of a saw blade. A typical crosscut blade on a circular saw has splayed teeth that can carve a path ⅛ inch wide through wood. A backsaw, on the other hand, often has no set and makes a minimal kerf. Even at this fine scale, stick with one cutting procedure, such as cutting just a hair outside your pencil line.

Using a Laser Level

WHAT YOU'LL NEED

- Rotary laser level and tripod
- Measuring tape and pencil

TRIM TIP: Pick a central location for the laser from which the projected beam will reach all the walls involved in the project. This is the easiest way to check existing floors and ceilings for level.

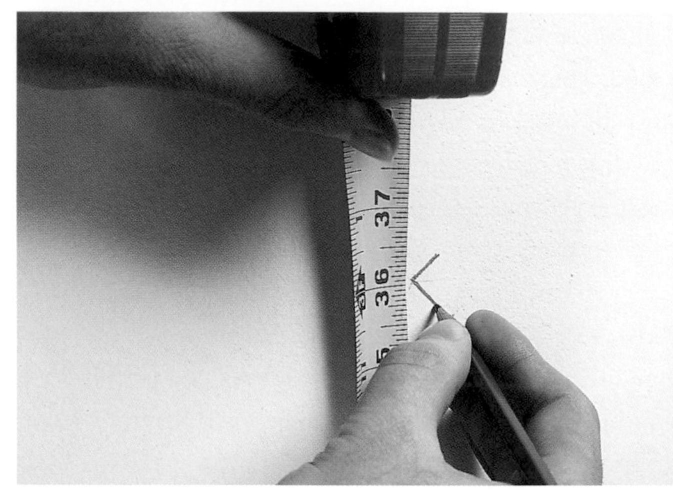

1 Pick a midrange elevation point on your project—the top of the chair rail, for example—and mark it on the wall.

2 Set up the rotary laser so that it is approximately level with your mark, and adjust the beam to meet it exactly.

3 With the laser mounted in a central location, you can duplicate your original mark on the projected beam.

LEVELING

In a perfectly plumb and level room, you can make a precise layout. But in many houses, you have to make a compromise instead. If you dead-level a chair rail, it may look out of kilter with the baseboard. If you dead-level a cornice, it may create gaps against the slightly sloping ceiling. So no matter how precisely you plumb and level trim components, remember to step back and see how they look in the overall framework of surrounding walls, floors, and ceilings.

The tool most often used for leveling is a 4-foot spirit level. Shorter models sometimes are handy in tight spots, but the margin of error increases when you use a short level to extend a line across a long wall. You can extend the readings from a 4-foot level by holding it firmly on a straight 2×4.

To be more precise, particularly over long distances, consider a water level or a rotary laser level. A basic water level consists of a clear tube filled with tinted water. Hold up both ends (any distance apart), and the water at one end will be dead level with the water at the other end. A laser level works by projecting a level beam of light that you can read and mark on any surface in sight of the tool.

Rasps and Coping Saws

Many do-it-yourselfers are familiar with a coping saw, the U-shaped saw with a thin blade that is sometimes called a jigsaw. It's essential equipment for cutting intricate molding shapes in coped joints. But only the most experienced carpenters can get a tight fit the first time around on complex cope. With practice, you can use the coping blade to shave off a bit more wood here and there. But most people have more success shaping the final fit with a rasp. These often are sold in sets that include several profiles. It's also handy to have a file card that removes scrap wood from the file teeth and helps them bite in more cleanly.

A—large files
B—minifiles
C—file card
D—coping saw
E—specialty scraper
F—carbide-tipped scraper
G—small scraper
H—C-clamp
I—lightweight bar clamp
J—spring clamp
K—quick-release clamp

Scrapers and Paint Removers

When you need to remove and refinish existing moldings, you may encounter many layers of old paint. You can remove paint in many ways, but first you should test it for lead. It's possible to have at least one layer of lead-based paint in any house built before 1978. You can use an inexpensive swab-test kit that's available in most hardware stores and home centers for detecting lead, which poses no threat unless it is ingested or inhaled. Some risk exists if you scrape, sand, or otherwise disturb the surface. But you should wear a dust mask or respirator when scraping and sanding down old paint, in any case.

You can scrape off layers of paint fairly easily if you're working on flat boards. The job becomes more difficult on intricate moldings where the paint is nestled into crevices. In those cases, consider a chemical stripper (used with caution according to manufacturer's guidelines) that softens paint so you can scrape it out of tight spots.

Power Tools

MITER SAWS

Two basic types of power miter saws are available. The simple version cuts miters or bevels but in separate steps. The more versatile version, called a compound miter saw, can handle both operations in one pass.

You also may be interested in an offshoot of the basic design: a compound miter saw with rails that allow the motor and blade to slide across the work, called a sliding compound miter saw. This design allows you to make accurate cuts across wide stock. Some newer models are cordless. They cut more quietly and with less dust than plug-in models.

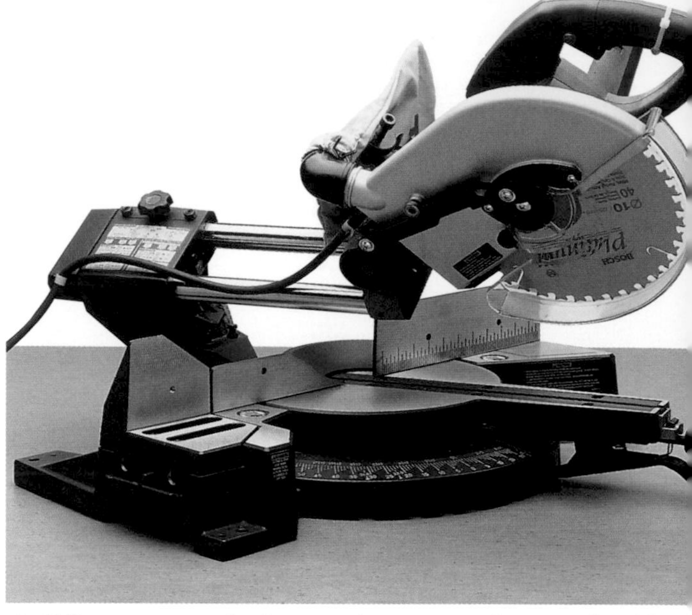

A sliding compound miter saw *increases cutting capacity with rails that allow the motor and blade to glide across the work.*

Cutting Capacity. Two main factors determine the overall cutting capacity of a power miter saw. One is blade size, listed in inches of diameter; the other is slide capability. The smallest miter saws, with a 7½-inch blade, limit the work you can do. The more common sizes are 10 and 12 inches. A 10-inch model will handle many jobs, including compound miter cuts required for a 3½-inch cornice, 90-degree butt cuts in 1×6 boards, and even up to 45-degree bevel cuts in 1×6 boards. A 10-inch compound miter saw is a good choice for most homeowners, although a 12-inch model offers more capacity.

The advantages of the sliding feature are most evident in small saws. For example, a sliding model with an 8½-inch blade can't match every capacity of a regular compound miter saw with a 12-inch blade, but it can bevel-cut a 1×12 board at 90 degrees, which a 12-inch compound miter saw can't do. The main drawback is that sliding compound miter saws are the most expensive type by far.

Cutting Stands. When you're working on long lengths of wood, it's essential to support the molding and keep it flat. That's where a stand comes in. You can buy one with many handy features, such as wheels, tool drawers, and portable extension stands. But it's easy enough to make a rigid extension platform that you can move around and clamp to a pair of sawhorses.

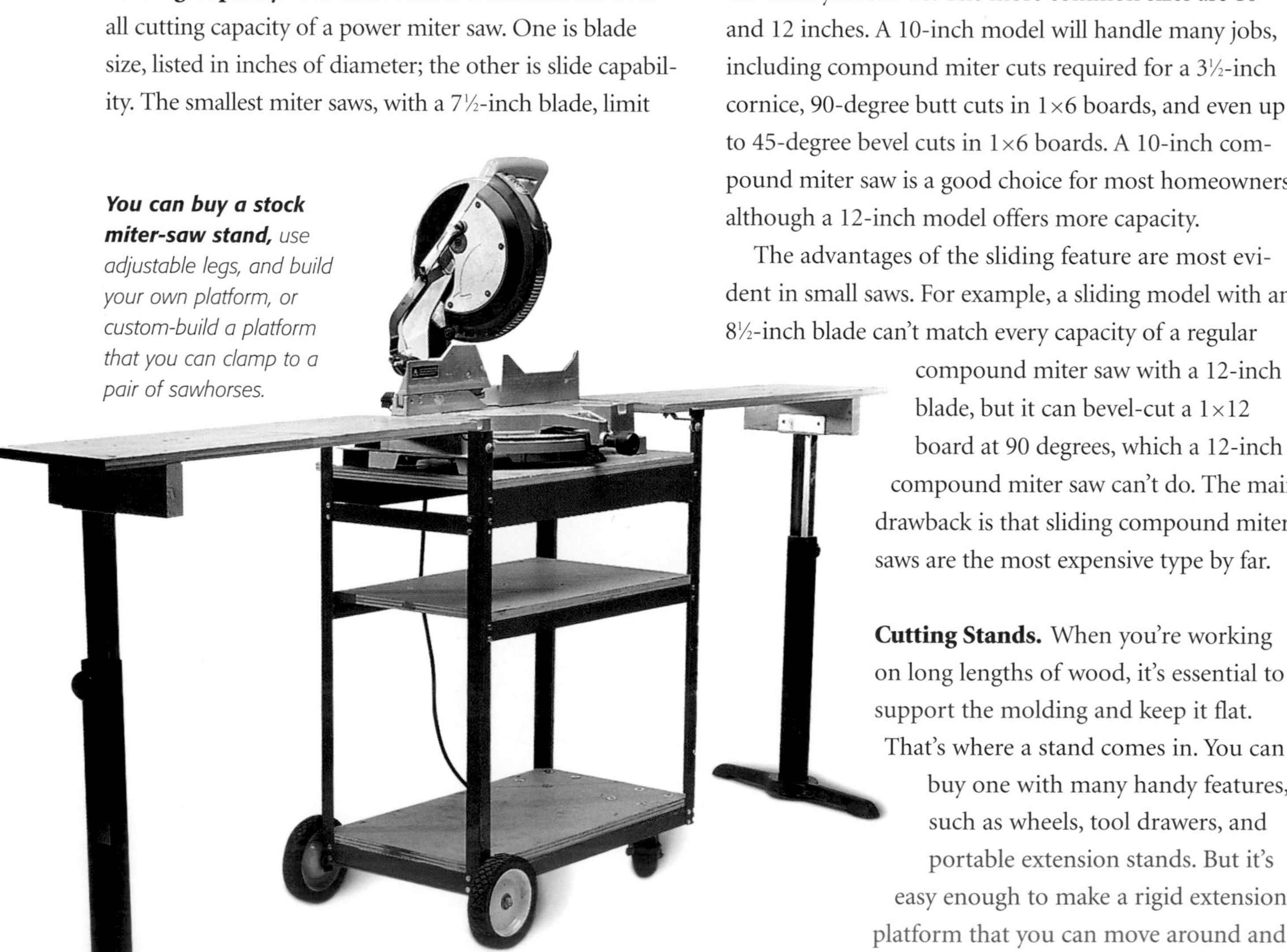

You can buy a stock miter-saw stand, *use adjustable legs, and build your own platform, or custom-build a platform that you can clamp to a pair of sawhorses.*

Saber Saws

A saber saw has a straight, vertical-cutting blade that generally is used in freehand work, such as cutting curves or making small cutouts. In trim carpentry, you'll need it to make neat cutouts in base molding that is formed around a heat register and to cut wall paneling around electrical outlets and switches.

There are two types of saber saws. One features a barrel grip that you rotate to control the direction of the cut. With the more common type that has a fixed top handle, you turn the entire saw to guide the cut.

Most do-it-yourselfers especially appreciate variable speed control among the saw's many handy features, because it offers extra control in tight corners.

Versatile saber saws *offer easy-changing blades, variable speed, and control of the blade-cutting angle.*

Circular Saws

Among the variety of circular saws available, the 7¼-inch model (blade diameter) is appropriate for most homeowners. But try hefting it in the store to see if you can manage the weight with one hand. Look for a tool with good balance that is easy to adjust for blade angle and cutting depth. The handle position should let you push rather than drag the saw through the work. Also consider two safety features. One is an automatic brake that stops the spinning blade as soon as you release the trigger. The other is an arbor lock that prevents any rotation when you change blades.

Circular saws *with comfortable main handles and an auxiliary handle up front help make your cuts more accurate.*

Table Saws

You won't make most molding cuts on a table saw. But it's the tool of choice for ripping boards accurately, a job you may need to do again and again on custom installations where stock sizes won't fit. You could rely on a friendly neighborhood lumberyard to cut lumber to size for a fee. But on large trim projects, having your own saw will be valuable. You could spend top dollar for a large-capacity machine with huge extension tables. But for trim work (and many projects around the house), a 10-inch benchtop model will do. The weak link sometimes is a slightly shaky rip fence. Check this feature in the store to see how firmly and squarely it locks in different positions.

A benchtop table saw *is easy to move around the work area and stable enough once you clamp it in place.*

Compressors

A compressor is essential if you want to use air tools, but unnecessary if you stick with standard power tools. There are two basic types: oilless and oil lubricated. Compressors that have to be lubricated generally will last longer than oilless compressors, but the oilless models are much improved, compact, and very convenient. Even a small unit will do for trimwork, but you may want to compare capacities that are rated in CFMs (cubic feet of air delivered per minute). Larger compressors will make less of a racket. Because they can store more air under pressure, they don't have to run as often to replenish the supply when you're nailing off a piece of molding.

A compressor supplies air *to drive labor-saving brad and finish nailers that are used to fasten trimwork.*

Biscuit Joiners

A biscuit joiner, also called a plate joiner, is the power tool part of a system for joining pieces of wood. Here's how it works: you position the boards—for instance, at a right angle—and draw a pencil line across the joint. Then you use that line as a reference mark to line up the joiner. Pull the trigger, and it makes a semicircular cut into the edge of the board. (You can adjust the cutting height for different lumber.) With corresponding cuts made in both boards, you apply glue; insert football-shaped wood wafers; and clamp. The wafers bridge the seam and expand to make a very strong joint. The alternative (dowel centering) is much more difficult.

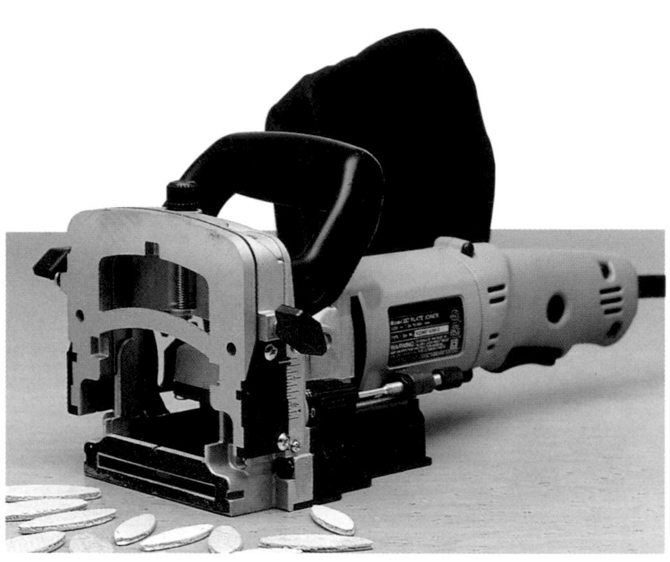

A biscuit joiner *cuts slots into the edges of boards so that you can join them securely with wood wafers and glue.*

Cordless Drills

Professionals and homeowners alike have become used to the convenience of cordless tools. And modern versions have overcome the shortcomings of early models, namely, not enough power. Although battery capacity continues to increase, a homeowner tackling trim projects will do fine with a midrange 1/4-inch drill. You don't need a larger 3/8- or 1/2-inch drill, or top-line batteries, which make the drill less maneuverable. Useful options include a variable-speed trigger, a keyless chuck, and an extra battery so that one is always recharging and ready to go.

A complete drill package *includes a plug-in charger, an extra battery, and a set of drill-drive attachments.*

Using a Nail Gun

What You'll Need

- Compressor
- Air-powered nailer
- Nail clip

TRIM TIP: Trimwork is an ideal application of pneumatic nailers because the tool barely contacts the wood, which can be fragile at some joints.

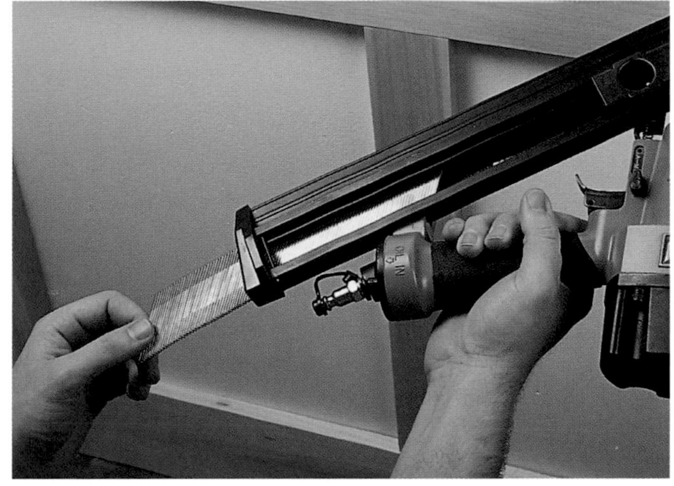

1 Pneumatic nailers use long clips of glued-together nails that load easily into the gun.

2 You can use the tools in almost any position, but the firing head should be perpendicular to the work surface.

3 Most pneumatic nailers have a built-in safety and won't fire unless you first set the tip firmly against the work.

Nailers

The big advantage of air tools is that pneumatic pressure provides the driving force. You simply position the tool and squeeze the trigger. Once you get the hang of it, you'll be able to drive nails faster and more accurately. While brad and finish nailers are small and light, construction nailers are a lot heavier than hammers. But you'll never hit your thumb or damage a piece of molding with missed hits. And the tools are safe if handled properly. Check into the safety-head feature, which forces you to set the head against the work before the trigger will fire a fastener.

Nail clips, *which you buy by the box, are quickly loaded into brad nailers, left, and finish nailers, right.*

ROUTERS

In a professional cabinet shop, molding profiles are formed by large cutting bits with replaceable blades mounted in powerful shaping machines. The home work site equivalent is a router. With a basic selection of bits you can fashion many decorative shapes in stock boards and basically create your own molding designs. It's also a good tool for making rabbets and dadoes.

There are two types of routers. With a fixed-base router (the most common and affordable), the base and motor housing are locked in position. To increase or decrease the depth of cut you need to turn an adjustment collar. With a plunge router, the motor housing and cutting head can slide up and down on rails connected to the base. This makes it possible to start routing in the middle of a board and to stop routing—say, to create flutes on a pilaster—before you reach the edge of a board.

A fixed-base router is best for most casual woodworkers because it's lighter and easier to control than a typical plunge router. For trimwork (and most other how-to projects) you'll do well with a tool that takes bits with ¼-inch shanks. Bits with larger shanks are considerably more expensive.

Setting Up a Router

WHAT YOU'LL NEED

- Router
- Bits
- Locking wrench
- Safety gear for cutting

TRIM TIP: It's important to wear safety glasses or goggles when you use a router because the high rpm of the cutting bit can shoot off wood chips at great velocity.

1 Cutting bits have shanks like drill bits and mount in a sleeve, called a collet, directly under the motor.

3 To adjust the depth of cut, some routers have a ring around the motor, while others have a depth knob.

4 On plunge routers, you need to adjust the mechanical stop that limits the depth of the plunge cut.

A basic router setup *includes a rip fence with extension guides, straight-cutting bits, and molding profile bits.*

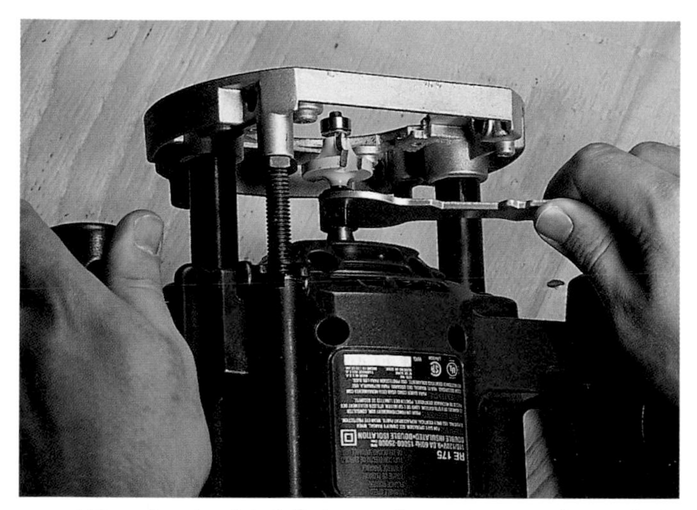

2 When the shank is fully inserted, use the wrench supplied with the router to tighten the collet.

5 It's wise to check the depth and results of your setup on a piece of securely clamped scrap lumber.

BASIC ROUTER BITS

3/8-Inch Corner Beading Bit

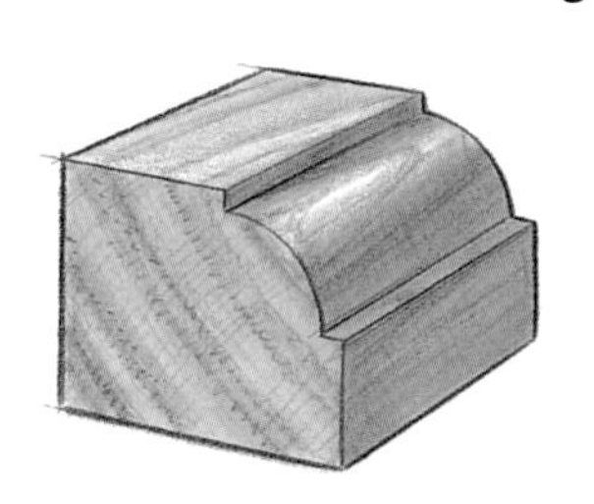

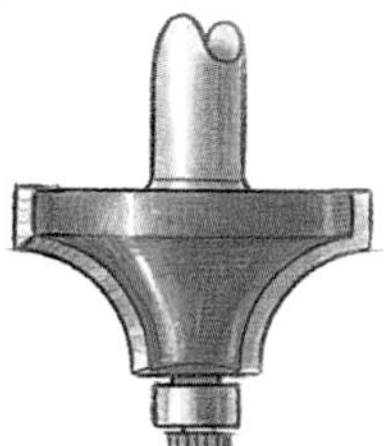

3/8-Inch Beading Bit

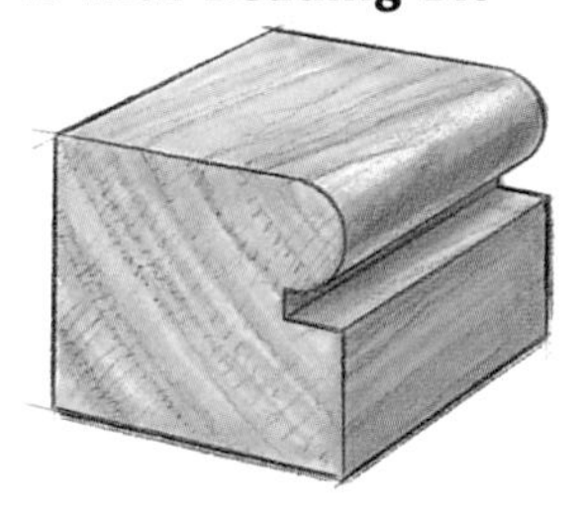

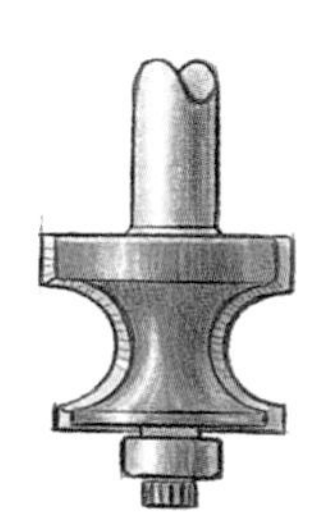

3/4-Inch Ogee Bit

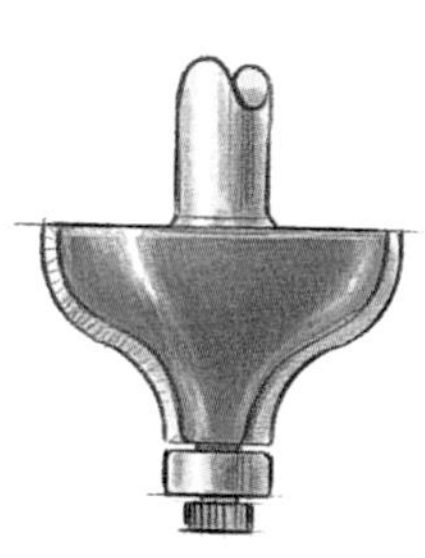

3/4-Inch Core Box Bit

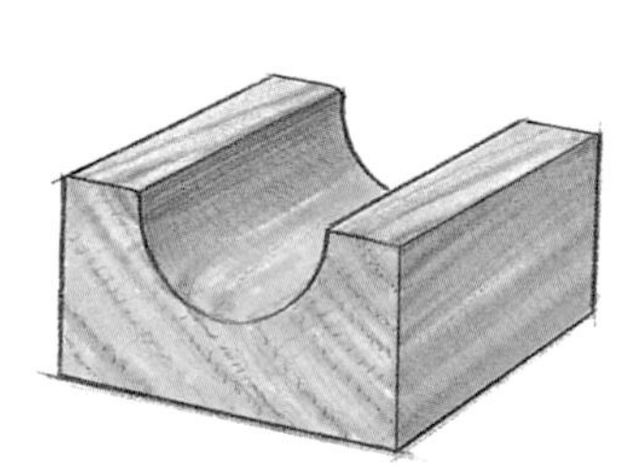

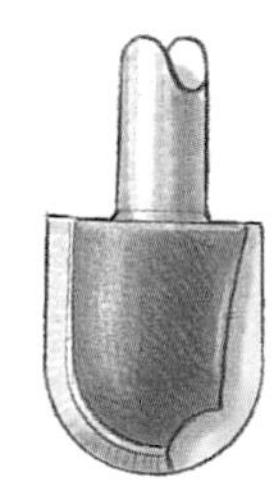

3/4-Inch Straight Bit

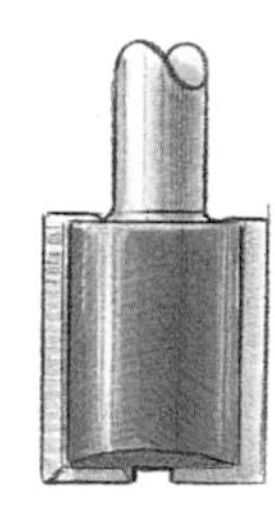

TYPES OF SANDERS

Belt Sanders. These are the workhorse sanders designed to remove a lot of stock with a minimum of effort. That's possible because they have two drums that turn a continuous sanding belt (normally 3 or 4 inches wide) across the work. You can use belts with rough grits to remove a lot of surface blemishes in a hurry, and progressively finer grits for finishing. But remember to keep the belt sander moving whenever you pull the trigger. If it stays in place even for a moment, the powerful rotation will make the belt dig into the wood.

Random-Orbit Sanders. These are the midline sanders that will remove stock and handle a lot of finishing jobs. Many woodworkers prefer them to sheet sanders because the pad rotates with a constantly shifting center point. The eccentric motion allows the tool to erase most or all of its swirl marks, even if you're working in a small area. If you're buying only one sander, this is the one to get.

Sheet Sanders. These sanders are good for finishing with the grain and are easy to operate with one hand. A quarter-sheet model is fine for most home projects, although half-sheet models are handy on larger jobs.

Belt Sander

Random-Orbit Sanders

Sheet Sanders

POWER PLANERS

A power planer is like a very compact and portable jointer. A 3¼-inch model does the same type of shaving and smoothing work, but you simply guide the tool instead of providing the cutting force the way you have to with a plane. Before these power tools were common, carpenters often used a block plane for touch-ups, a larger bench plane for general edging work, and a long (sometimes 24-inch) smoothing plane to edge stock. You'll want a fence accessory to guide the planer along the edge of a board.

Power planers *can clean up board edges and remove thin shavings to create a perfect fit.*

Jointers

A benchtop jointer is another pint-sized version of a large, heavy-duty machine found in professional cabinet shops. It has a large flat bed with a slot in it where a cutter rotates at high speed. As you slide a board on edge along the table (nestled against the back fence for support), the cutter shaves off any high spots but misses the low spots. You can set the cutter height to bite into the wood or barely skim the edge. In either case, after a few passes the edge of the board is flat and true. This allows you to make reliable glue joints and tight connections between moldings.

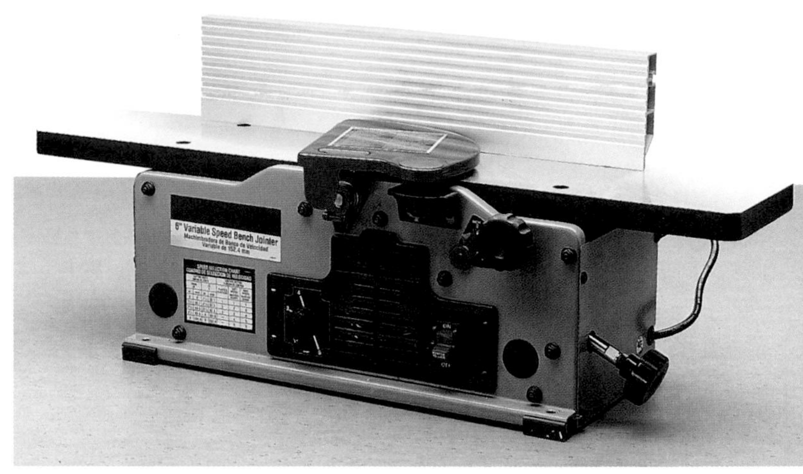

Under the red safety guard *on this benchtop jointer is a cutting wheel that puts true edges on uneven boards.*

Thickness Planers

A thickness planer is like a jointer, except the cutting blade is wide enough to trim wood from the board faces in addition to the edges. It's not essential for most trimwork because stock moldings generally have a uniform thickness. But it will clean up the faces of older boards and does a good job removing table-saw blade marks from boards that have been ripped to make stiles and rails. With benchtop models of jointers and planers, a good approach is to use minimal cutting depths and remove wood a bit at a time with several passes.

Smart Tip *Safety Equipment*

Trim work is not very dangerous, but there are two areas where it pays to be cautious. The first is with power tools, particularly saws. You should check the manufacturer's operating instructions and follow the rules for safe operation. The second is with wood chips and sawdust. You should guard against injury by wearing safety glasses or goggles, and in some situations, by wearing a dust mask or respirator. Also, you'll find gloves handy for sanding and finishing work, and knee pads a comfort when you're installing baseboards and wainscoting.

A*–rubber gloves;* ***B****–work gloves;* ***C****–knee pads;* ***D****–safety glasses;* ***E****–safety goggles;* ***F****–particle mask;* ***G****–respirator;* ***H****–ear protectors*

CHAPTER 5

INSTALLING TRIMWORK

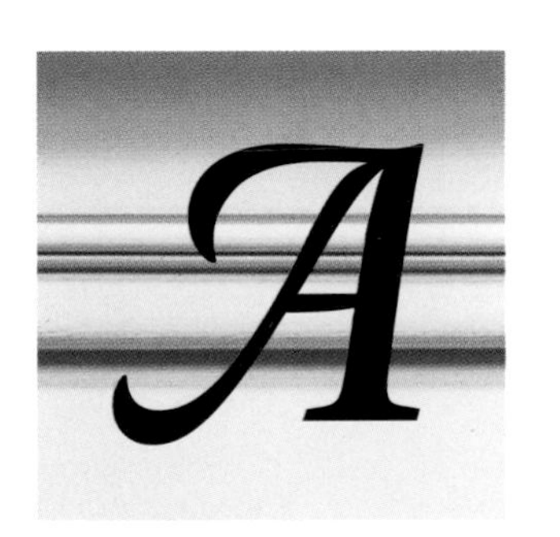

dding trimwork to a room provides the finishing touches to the design. You will find that what was once an empty box becomes a well-appointed space that has a definite style. Replacing stock "builder's trim" with more distinctive moldings and casings makes a room more attractive and adds perceived value to the space. As you will see, some trim projects can be very elaborate and best attempted by an experienced woodworker. But you will be surprised at what you can accomplish with more modest projects that require only some basic tools and techniques. This chapter covers those basic techniques. Novices who will do the work themselves will find the material here invaluable. Experienced woodworkers will benefit from the review of basic techniques covered here.

Lumber for Molding

Most do-it-yourselfers use molding that's available at local lumberyards and home centers, even when it's not in the best condition. There are other sources, of course, where you can special-order hardwoods and exotic carved moldings, among other items. But this kind of service is costly; you have to plan the complete materials order ahead of time; and it may take a while to get the wood you need on-site.

One alternative is to make your own molding. Professional wood shops use large and extremely heavy-duty planers, shapers, and jointers to form and dress molding. Few amateur woodworkers have those special power tools in their home shops.

But there are benchtop-model versions of these tools that are within many do-it-yourself budgets and are solid enough to handle edging and similar work on a project scale as opposed to a commercial scale.

Prepping Lumber

Even without these benchtop tools, you can improve stock boards, such as 1×6 pine and other molding components, that often come from the lumberyard with a few defects.

Even when boards are true but just a little dingy or stained, you should take the time to clean them up with a belt sander and fine sandpaper. Remember to keep the sander moving once the belt is turning to prevent dig marks.

If some of your lumber isn't straight, you can true up the edges with a hand plane, power plane, or table saw. Trimming very rough edges can become a problem if you need to match the width of other moldings. You may remove the trouble spots but leave a board that's too narrow.

The best way to guard against this type of problem is to select your lumber carefully. Look for the straightest boards that are free of knots and splits, and bypass pieces that are twisted. Even if you can wrestle them into position on the wall, chances are that they will pop their nails or split from the strain.

***Blades for circular saws and power miter boxes** come in several shapes and sizes, but blades with more teeth and carbide tips generally produce the cleanest cuts.*

Truing Lumber

What You'll Need

- Table saw
- Sander

TRIM TIP: On some ripping work, particularly with wide boards, it helps to have a partner separate the two sides of the cut (well past the blade) to prevent binding.

1 Sight with one eye along the edge of a board to reveal high spots, low spots, or an overall curve, or crown.

2 Turn the adjustment wheel on the front of the table saw to set the depth of cut of the blade.

3 To make the smoothest, most efficient cuts, allow only the tops of the blade teeth to protrude above the board.

4 Set the straightest edge against the fence, and feed the board into the blade. (The guard is removed for clarity.)

5 Even a sharp blade may leave some marks along the edge of the board, which you can remove by sanding.

Saw Setup

WHAT YOU'LL NEED

- Power miter saw
- Secure saw mount to bench

TRIM TIP: If you're using a new saw, it's tempting to plug it in and start cutting. But you should take the time to read the owner's manual, including the safety precautions.

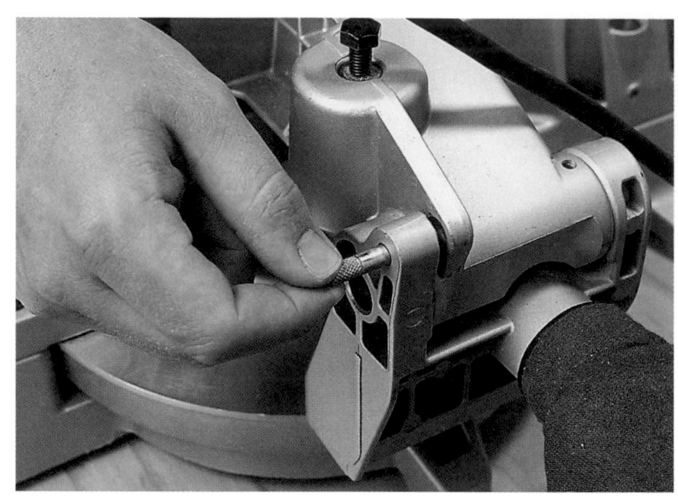

1 Most saws have a spring-loaded locking button that you need to release in order to free the saw arm.

4 Release the handle to swing the saw left or right along the front miter scale. Most handles are screw-type.

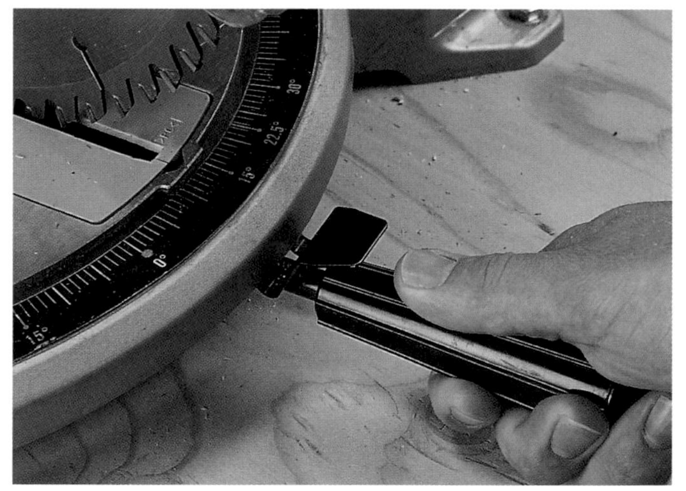

5 When you reach the desired degree setting, screw the handle tight to lock in the position.

Mitering Basics

A miter is the most basic joint used in trimwork. It's a 45-degree cut used where two boards join at a right angle, such as at the corners of a window. It's the type of joint you see on picture frames and most other trimwork in the house.

Instead of a butt joint used on some molding where the square end of one piece joins the flat edge of another, both pieces of a mitered joint are cut at 45 degrees and join in a right-angle, 90-degree corner. With a miter, the decorative surfaces and patterns of the molding are aligned and flow smoothly from one board to the next.

You can cut miters with handsaws held in a guide, or use a special miter box with the saw blade built in. There are other tools, too, such as the very precise guillotine-style cutter generally known by its trade name, Lion Trimmer. But the tool of choice for pros (and for amateurs tackling large projects) is a power miter saw. With a sharp, fine-toothed circular blade, you can make quick cuts at 45 degrees for miters because the saw is built with detents that allow you to lock in the correct angle. It also adjusts to cut irregular angles.

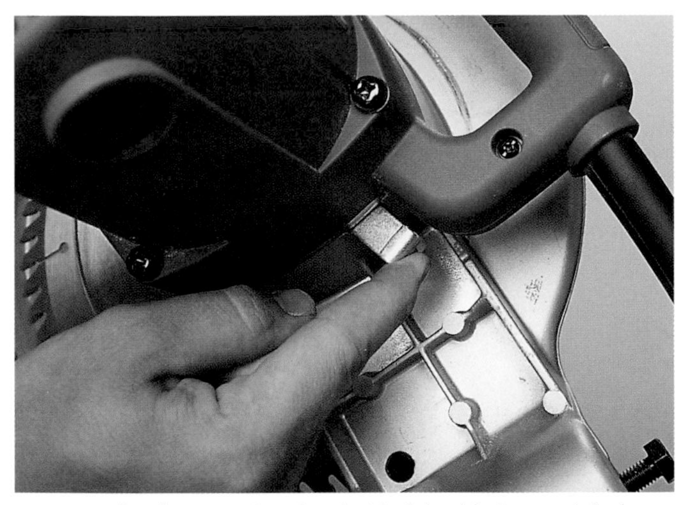

2 Another button, often just behind the blade guard, locks the blade so you can safely change it or tighten it.

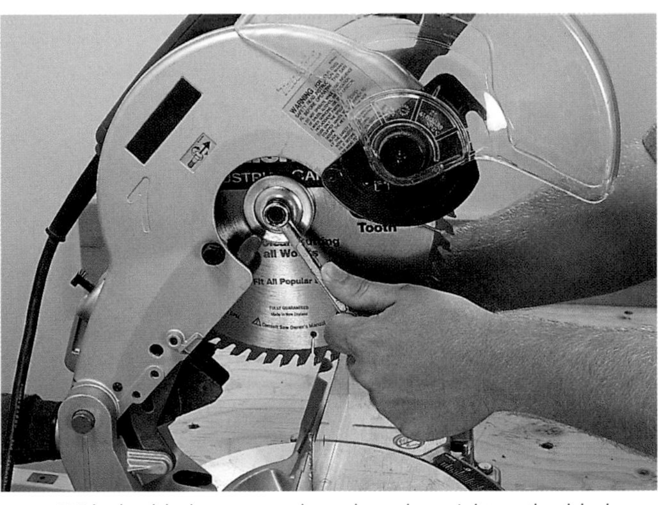

3 With the blade mounted on the arbor, tighten the blade-holding bolt with the wrench supplied with the saw.

6 Typical saws have a lockout button (under the thumb, here) that you must depress before you can squeeze the trigger.

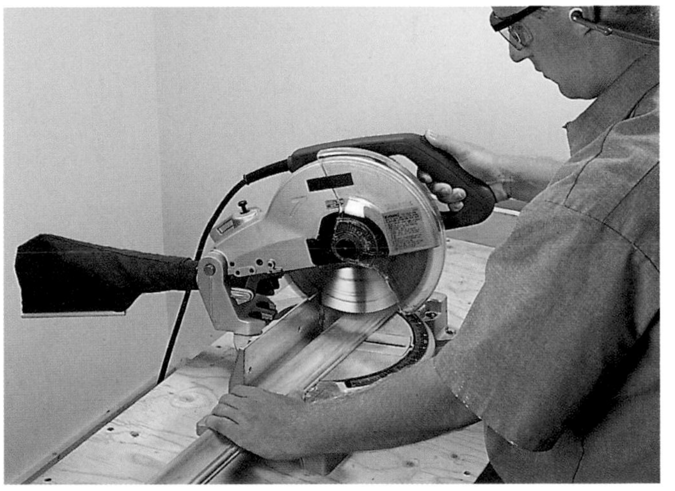

7 Plug the saw into an adequate and grounded power supply; put on your safety glasses; and start cutting.

The scale *on the front of a power miter saw is calibrated so you make a straight crosscut at the 0-deg. setting. The degree numbers increase on both sides of the 0 mark so you can set the saw to cut 45-deg. miters (and other angles) to the right or left.*

Using a Hand Miter Box

What You'll Need

- Hand miter box
- Secure mount to bench

TRIM TIP: Because hand-powered miter boxes generally are much lighter than electric-powered models, you need to clamp them securely to a workbench to avoid shifting that could alter the cut.

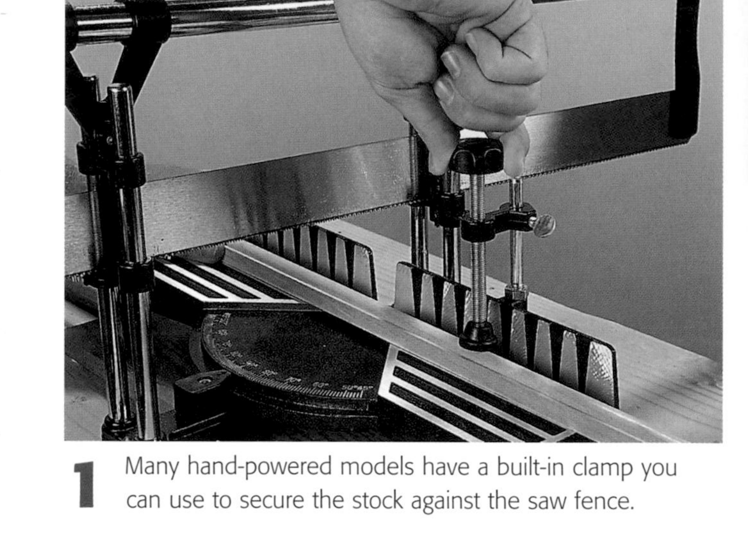

1 Many hand-powered models have a built-in clamp you can use to secure the stock against the saw fence.

2 Like power models, hand miter boxes can swing and lock to cut angles left or right of the 0-deg. central setting.

3 The thin, fine-toothed blade built into this miter box travels smoothly back and forth on a pair of guides.

Other Mitering Options

If you don't have a power miter saw, you can do very well making cuts on trimwork the way they've been made for centuries: by hand. There are several hand-powered tools that are up to the job. And although it may take you a bit longer using muscle power, these tools may offer more control and make finer cuts than a typical power miter saw.

To form neat joints with any hand-powered mitering tool, you need a saw blade with fine, sharp teeth. You could use a 10-point carpenter's saw, which means the saw has 10 teeth per inch. More teeth generally mean a slower but finer cut, while fewer teeth mean a faster but rougher cut.

Also check the blade for a characteristic called set. This term refers to the amount of sideways bend or play in the teeth. A saw with a lot of set cuts a wide kerf, while a saw with only a little set cuts a narrower and generally cleaner-edged kerf. Some trim saws have no set at all and make extremely fine cuts.

But a full-sized finishing saw is a bit of a handful on trim joints. A better option is a backsaw, also with no set in its 12 or 13 teeth per inch. It makes clean-edged

Using a Miter Trimmer

What You'll Need

- Miter trimmer
- Secure mount to bench

TRIM TIP: Most pros who use this type of tool hold the molding by hand close to the fence. But watch those fingertips: the blade is extremely sharp.

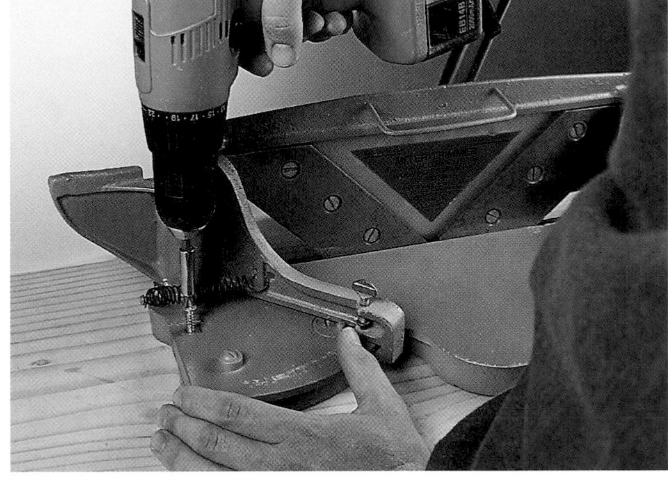

1 If a clamp will get in the way of the fence or the ratchet arm, use screws to fasten the box to a stable bench.

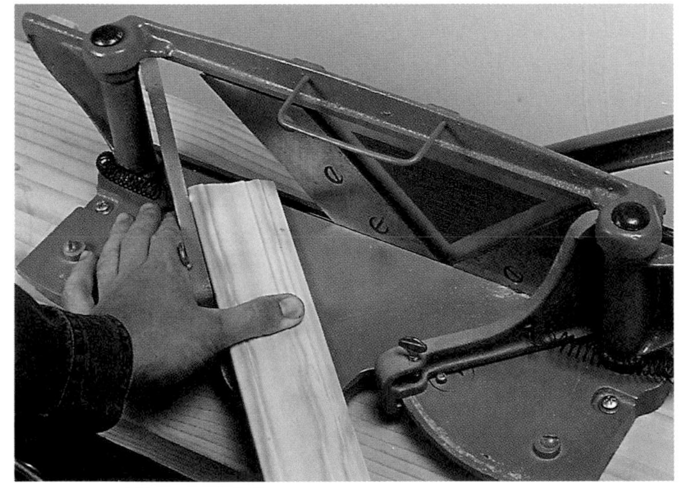

2 Once you set the piece against the 45-deg. fence (one on each side), draw the blade across the end of the board.

3 Power comes from pulling or pushing on a long handle that ratchets the blades back and forth.

cuts and is easier to control because the blade is reinforced and more rigid than that of a conventional saw.

With any handsaw, of course, you'll need to use a miter box to guide the cuts. There are many types, from basic wooden boxes with guide slots cut at 90- and 45-degree angles that will do for occasional work, to professional-quality boxes with a built-in saw you can swivel and clamp accurately at any angle.

This type of box (shown on the previous page) is the muscle-powered version of the electric-powered miter saw. The good ones have an accurate scale on which you can slide the saw mount and lock up the position before cutting a 45-degree miter or any other angle. Because these tools are lightweight, you need to fasten them securely to a workbench to minimize movement while cutting.

Another hand-powered option is the miter trimmer shown above. There are several manufacturers, but this tool generally is known by one of the trade names, Lion Trimmer. The tool has large blades attached to a sleeve that you ratchet back and forth, and adjustable fences for positioning the wood. The blades simply slice off wood from the end of a board, including very thin shavings so you can trim for a perfect fit.

Drilling & Joining

Most trimwork is attached with a hammer and finishing nails. So why would you need a drill? There are several situations (one shown below) where you'll use a drill to screw trim in place. But you'll use a drill even more to make pilot holes.

You need pilots to prevent narrow and thin pieces of molding from splitting, particularly near the ends. Pilot holes also help you get nails going at the correct angle and prevent bent nails, which can mar molding.

A pilot bit should be about half the diameter of the fastener. You can mount one in a power drill or a handy pin drill with a ratchet mechanism that turns the bit as you push down on the handle.

To join pieces of trim, you can use glue and nails. But on large frames, the tool of choice is a plate joiner. It's like a miniature circular saw that cuts shallow slots in the edges of boards. Specially shaped wafers made of compressed wood fit into the slots to bridge the joint. When you add glue, the wafers swell, which greatly increases the strength of the joint. With the wafers in place, you just fit the boards together and clamp them in a square position until the glue sets up.

Using Wall Anchors

WHAT YOU'LL NEED

- Power drill
- Combination countersink/counterbore bit
- Ruler, level, and marker
- Wall anchors and fasteners
- Screwdriver and hammer
- Dowel and wood glue
- Chisel and sandpaper

TRIM TIP: Where a pilaster doesn't fall over a stud, use a combination of construction adhesive and an anchor-type fastener.

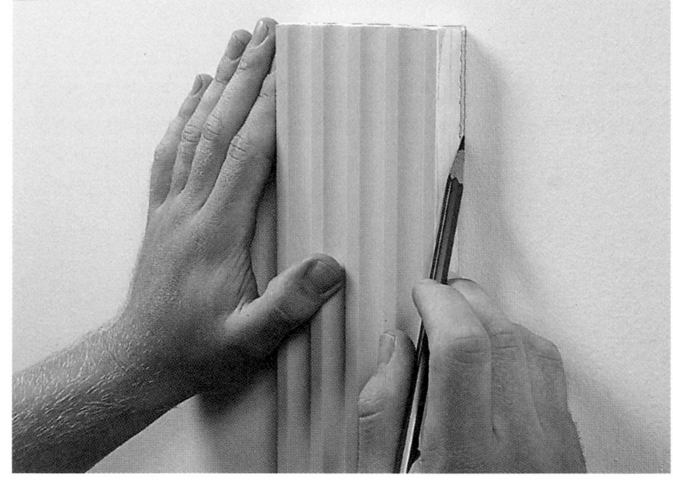

1 Once you cut the pilaster to length and check its position for plumb, mark the outline with a pencil.

4 Remove the pilaster, and drill a pilot hole in the drywall as required for the type of anchor you're using.

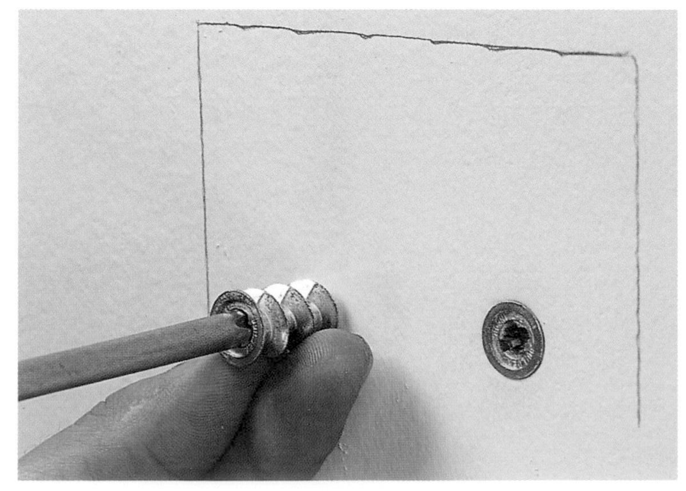

5 Insert anchors in the pilot holes. These anchors have wide threads that grip the edges of the drywall.

A plate joiner *has a horizontally mounted blade that cuts matching grooves in the edges of boards you want to join. Glue and wood wafers bridge the gap to make a strong connection.*

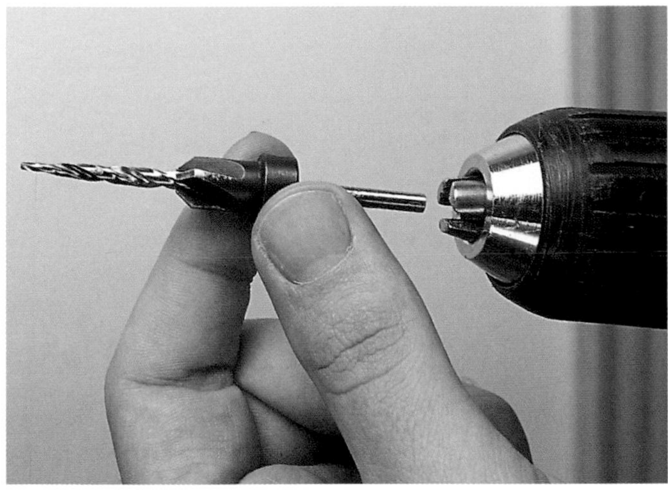

2 Use a combination bit to drill a pilot hole, countersink, and counterbore through the pilaster.

3 The combination bit leaves a hole you can plug later and a mark on the drywall underneath the board.

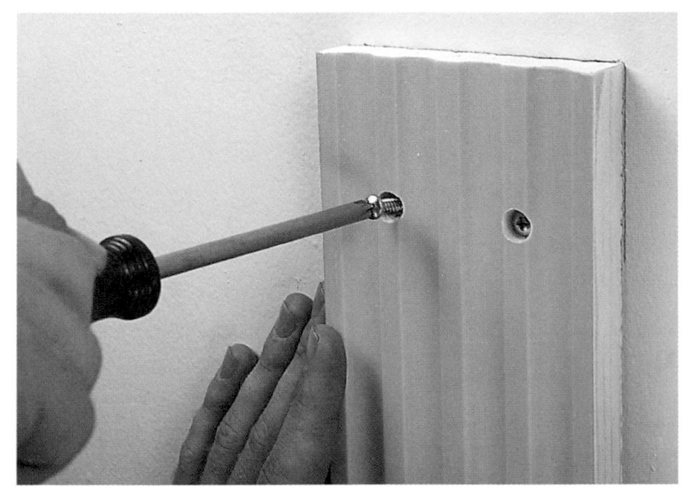

6 Reposition the pilaster using your marks as a guide, and drive screws through the board into the anchors.

7 Use a piece of dowel stock (with glue) to fill the hole; trim off the excess with a chisel; and sand to finish.

CLEANING UP EDGES

Even if you don't have a home shop full of stationary power tools such as jointers and planers, you still can prepare trimwork. It just takes a little longer using hand and portable power tools. Use a belt sander, right, to smooth surfaces and to provide finishing touches on the edges of boards. Use a power planer, below left, to reduce the width of boards in a hurry. Make a final pass with the rotating blade set to trim just a hair off the edge. Of course, you also can use muscle power and a hand plane, below right. Long planes are best for smoothing and straightening edges.

A belt sander *has two drums that spin and guide a continuous belt of sandpaper over the work.*

A power planer *has a small rotating blade that you can adjust to remove a little or a lot of wood.*

A hand plane *with an adjustable blade and a long bed can true up and clean the edge of a board.*

Sanding Basics

Some boards and stock moldings come from the lumberyard or home center ready to install. But that's more the exception than the rule these days due to a general decrease in lumber quality. As a practical matter, you often need to prepare your wood before you can cut and install it.

In professional shops, rough boards are cleaned up with a trip through large wood surfacing machines. The do-it-yourself equivalent is planing (in the case of very rough edges) and a lot of sanding. This is one area where you want the assistance of power tools, because sanding by hand is difficult, time consuming, and not as accurate as power sanding.

The most efficient tool for cleanup work is a belt sander. It works like a floor sander, spinning a sandpaper belt over the wood. Working in line with the grain, use a medium-grit belt to remove material and a fine-grit belt to remove dirt and small surface scars. On smaller jobs, the best tool is a random-orbit sander. Its swirling motion erases most sanding marks and allows you to use the tool across joints where you can't always work with the grain.

Using a Belt Sander

WHAT YOU'LL NEED

- Belt sander
- Sanding belts

TRIM TIP: Always adjust the belt-tracking control before contacting the wood. If a belt strays, the exposed edge of a roller could scar the wood.

1 Sanders have a mechanism (often a lever as shown above) that releases tension on the front wheel.

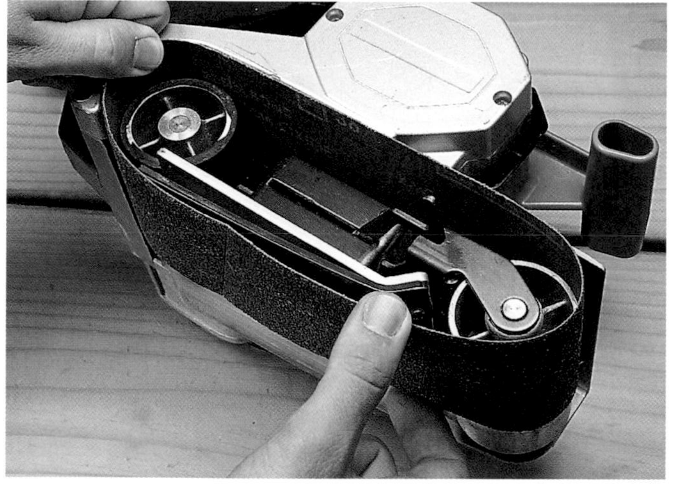

2 With the front wheel compressed, you have room to slide a belt over the sander wheels and base plate.

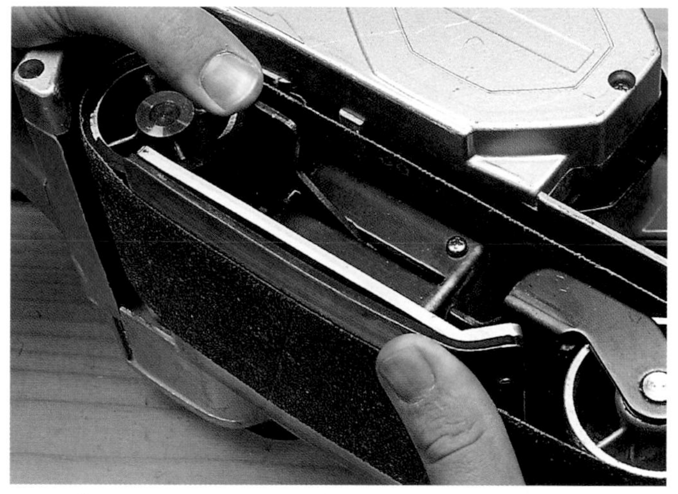

3 The next step is to extend the front wheel and apply tension to the sanding belt. (This lever locks to the left.)

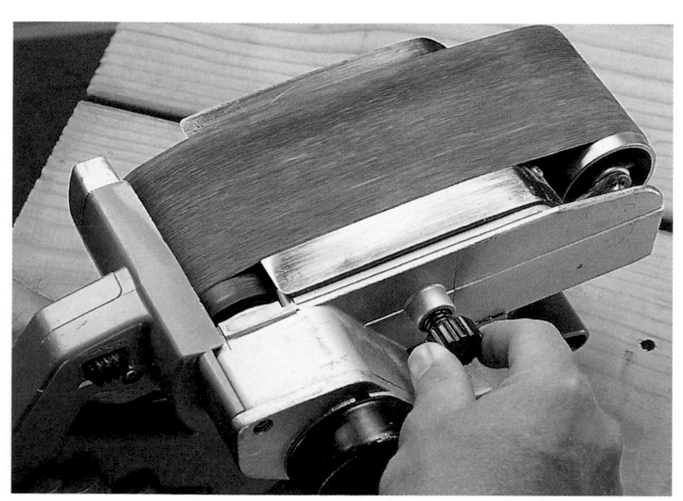

4 Center the belt; turn on the sander; and adjust the tracking control to keep the belt centered as it spins.

5 Keep both hands on the sander, and keep the sander moving with the grain to prevent dig marks.

CHAPTER 6

CASINGS FOR WINDOWS & DOORS

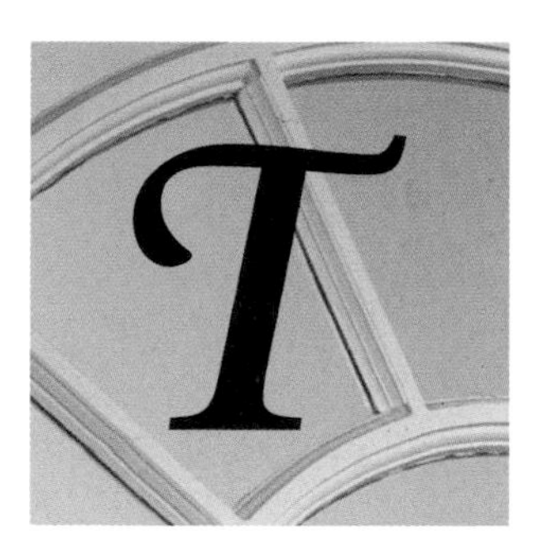

Trimwork contributes to the overall design scheme of a room, and the casing you select for doors and windows is a good place to set the tone for that scheme. You have much to choose from in this area, including wide trim with flutes and carved corner blocks that would work well with a Victorian or Federal-inspired decor or simpler casings that would be more at home in a Country-style room. In most cases, you will use the same style trimwork around doors that you selected for the windows, but there is no reason to use the same casings throughout the house. One tact is to splurge on the doors and windows in the more public rooms, such as living rooms and entry halls, and use simpler, less formal casings in the other parts of the house.

Door casings *can be built up with molding, including an outer strip of backband molding, showing multiple reveals.*

Types of Casings

There are two basic types of window casings: tapered and symmetrical. Tapered casings are thinner on the edge closest to the window or door and thicker on the outside edge. Stock Colonial and clamshell casings are tapered casings. When you form corners with tapered casings, you must miter the joints.

Symmetrical casing is the same thickness on both edges and has a uniform pattern across its face. This type of casing rests on top of a plinth block or window stool and joins corner blocks or headers with square-cut butt joints. These casings often look more decorative than stock Colonial-style casings, and they are easier for most do-it-yourselfers to install because you don't have to miter symmetrical casings.

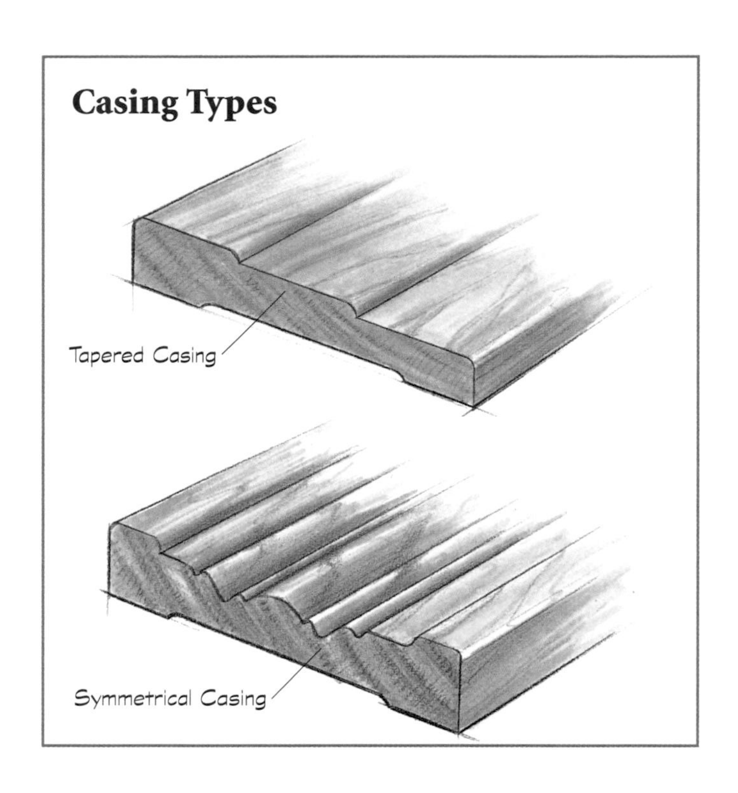

Casing Reveals

The edge of a doorjamb is flush with the surface of the adjoining wall, and there is usually a narrow gap between the jamb and the nearby drywall. Casing has to bridge that gap. Typically, the door side of the casing covers most but not all of the jamb, leaving a narrow edge called a reveal. This helps to add definition to the molding and avoids an unsightly seam where the edge of one board lines up directly over another.

When you're working on a new jamb, you have to establish the reveal and stick with it to maintain a uniform appearance. If you're replacing existing trim, you may need to clean up the edge of an old jamb with a sharp scraper and a sander even if you duplicate the old reveal. Although there are several varieties of door treatments, they all share this detail—a slight setback of at least ⅛ inch from the edge of the jamb. If you install plinths or corner blocks, which are slightly wider than the casing, you may need to experiment with their exact placement to maintain the reveal.

A typical reveal *between a doorjamb and casing creates a handsome transition at cased openings.*

Large windows *often look best trimmed with a stool and apron that support the side casings.*

Window Stools

The main difference between adding molding around a door and a window is that a window has a fourth side to trim. You can handle this lower section of molding in several ways. Your choices depend mostly on what type of casing you're using.

When large casings were in fashion, most windows were trimmed out with two pieces: a window stool and an apron. A stool, which most homeowners recognize as a sill, extends past the jamb into the room like a small shelf and runs onto the wall on each side to give the bottom ends of the vertical leg casings a surface against which to butt. An apron is a board that sits just under the stool, generally cut flush with the outside casing edges. This approach still works.

Symmetrical casings often look best when they rest on a 1-inch-thick window stool or when they run all the way down to plinth blocks resting on the floor. Without a stool, the casing goes right past the bottom of the window. So to complete the frame, you need to add a flat board with a bead detail between the leg casings on the window jamb's lower reveal line. You wind up with a squared-off A-shape that extends the window casing trim to the baseboard and can make a window look taller. (See the illustration on page 117.) It generally doesn't look right to run symmetrical casings around all four sides of a window using corner blocks.

Planning Window Stools

The section at each end of the stool that extends onto the wall is called a horn. If you're installing large, thick casings, the horn may be too small to support them. For good looks and sufficient strength, the horns should extend about 1 inch beyond the outside edge of leg casings and fully support their bottom edges.

If you need to install a new stool, you have a couple of options. The stool may be available as a stock item that you can cut to fit, but these boards usually are only 11⁄16 inch thick. A window stool made from 5⁄4 stock, which is actually a full 1 inch thick (or slightly more, depending on the mill that made the lumber), will look much better with large casings. You can buy this 5⁄4 stock and ease its edges with a router to finish it.

By selecting a router bit that duplicates or at least closely resembles the profile of existing trim in the rest of the house, you can make the new molding details blend in.

You can finish the horn in several ways—for example, by leaving the extension with a square return to the wall or forming a slight curve that makes a graceful return. You may want to use a router to finish the exposed edges of the molding—with a slight roundover, for instance.

Replacing an Existing Stool

A window stool usually has a rabbet on the back bottom edge that joins it to the window jamb. As you remove an existing stool, save a section and crosscut it to expose the profile. After ripping a piece of 5⁄4 stock to the required width for the new stool, use the section of old stool as a template to form the rabbet on the back edge of the new piece.

You can do this with two or more passes on the table saw. (You may want to make these cuts in a scrap piece and test the fit.) Then cut the stool to length, and use a saber saw to form the corner cutouts for the horns.

The horns of a window stool *extend beyond the casing.*

Creating Jambs

On some installations you may need to start the project by building a jamb to line the opening. This is not difficult work for most do-it-yourselfers and often is not necessary because many doors and windows come complete with jambs. Doors may be prehung and include hinge hardware and locks.

If you buy this type of unit, it will probably come with at least one diagonal brace applied by the manufacturer across the edges of the jamb sections. It's wise to leave the brace on during the installation as it helps to keep the jamb square and prevents racking as you fasten the door or window into position.

If you are casing a room opening or passageway, you'll have to make a site-built jamb. First, take the time to face the jamb stock (or at least to sand it) when the boards can be clamped securely to a workbench. If you have a jointer or planer (or a smoothing plane), you also may want to clean up the edges of the boards even though most of those surfaces will be covered by molding. Truing the edges will help you to get a tight fit between the jamb and the casing. In any case, you should avoid simple butt joints between jamb pieces and create a rabbet where the top piece joins the sides.

Typical Jamb Joints

3/8"
3/4"
Rabbet
Side
Top

Assembling a Jamb

What You'll Need

- Drill, router, or circular saw
- Hammer or nailer
- Clamps, combination square, chisel
- Glue and nails
- Jamb stock

TRIM TIP: Once you've established the depth of cut, make the first cut on your guideline very carefully. Then you simply run the saw through to clear the rest of the wood.

3 To control the rabbet cut, firmly clamp a guide board and the jamb to a stable bench.

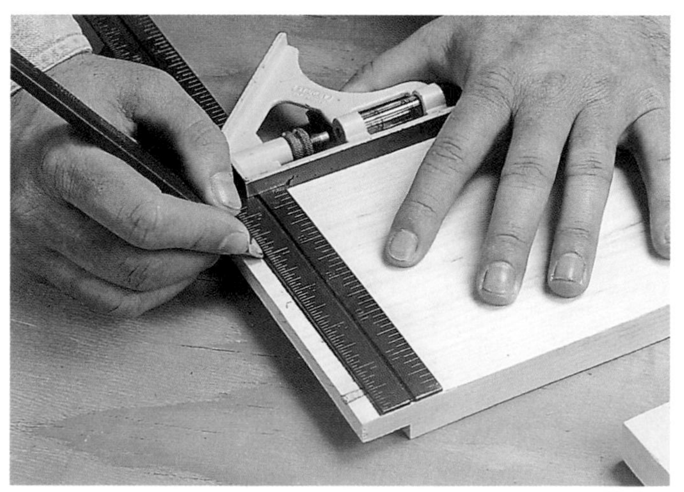

6 When the rabbet is cleaned up and ready for assembly, mark a nailing line on the outside of the joint.

1 Cut the head jamb to length, and mark the joint outline with a square for a 3/4-in. jamb leg.

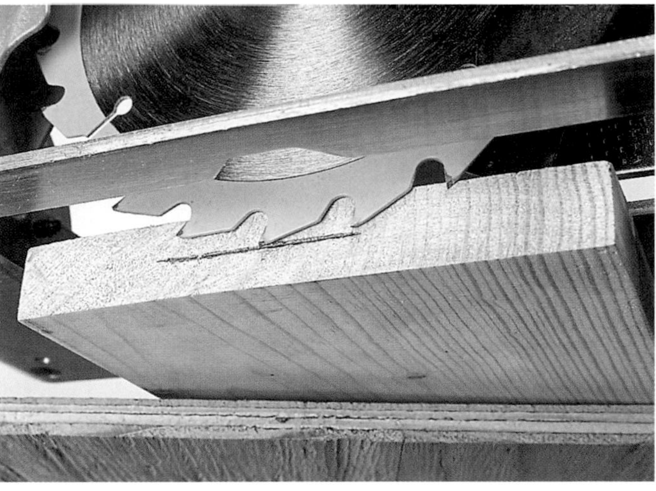

2 Set the blade depth on a circular saw to reach halfway (3/8 in.) through the thickness of the board.

4 Make the innermost cut with the saw along the guide. Then make multiple passes to kerf the remaining wood.

5 You can use the saw to remove all the wood, or clean up the thin strips between kerfs using a sharp chisel.

7 Add glue to the mating surfaces of the jamb parts just prior to assembling them.

8 Square up the jamb frame before fastening. You may want to set the pieces around a square block for support.

Installing Jambs

As a general rule, the newer the house, the more likely it is to have room openings finished only in drywall rather than cased out with trimwork. Creating drywall-only openings is the least expensive way to build, but it can create an unfinished look. Trimming out these openings is often the first step in an overall effort to build architectural detail into your home.

Side Jamb Length

To trim the opening, you'll have to install a jamb before the casing. Start by establishing a level reference line that spans the opening on one face of the wall. (See the photos on the next page.) Measure from your line down to the floor on each side of the opening, and mark the dimension on the wall. Then measure up from the reference line to the top of the opening on each side to see whether one side is lower than the other. Take the shorter measurement, subtract enough space for shimming (at least ¼ inch, and more on irregular openings), and mark this height on both sides, along with the other dimension you marked.

Figure the length of each side jamb by adding the measurement from the reference line to the floor and the height dimension you just determined. The side jambs run the full height of the opening, while the head jamb generally sits in ⅜-inch-deep rabbets cut into the sides. (See the photos on pages 102 to 103.) You also could copy the method used on most prefabricated jambs, where the head jamb sits in a dado.

Basic passageways are transformed *with a surrounding of trim that ties into baseboards and chair rails.*

HEAD JAMB LENGTH

Measure across the opening at several elevations to see whether it has a narrow point. If it does, subtract at least 1 inch from the smallest measurement. This inch accounts for the wood that will be left in the rabbeted side jambs, plus shimming space. You may want to hold the board in place to be sure of your cut marks.

OVERALL JAMB DEPTH

Using a combination square or a ruler, check several points on all three interior surfaces of the opening, noting each measurement. If the numbers vary by more than ⅛ inch, you'll need to adjust the width of the jamb pieces to account for the thicker parts of the opening. Another option that's worth a try is to use a hammer and a block of scrap wood to compress the wall. Just slide the block along the wider parts of the opening, hitting it firmly with the hammer. If that doesn't work, try removing some of the corner bead on one or both sides of the opening.

Once you come up with a consistent depth measurement for the opening, it's wise to confirm it by building a template. Rip a short length of 1×6 to the width you think will match the opening depth. Mark reveal lines on

Preparing a Passageway

WHAT YOU'LL NEED

- Measuring tape and level
- Combination square
- Hammer, finishing nails, and nail set
- Scrap block
- Jamb stock and shims
- Utility knife

TRIM TIP: If the edges of an opening are not true, you can strip off the corner bead and use shims to build supports for plumb jamb surfaces.

1 The best way to determine side jamb length is to work from a level reference line marked on each side of the opening. Measure from the pencil line down to the floor and up to the header.

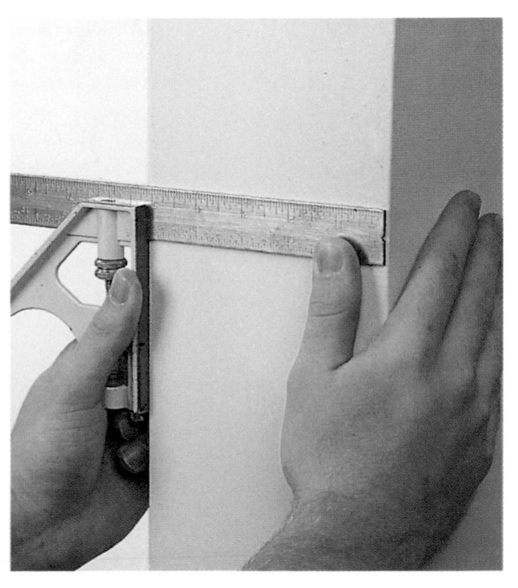

2 You also need to determine the depth of the passageway. Check it at several points to be sure that your jamb stock will fully cover the interior faces of the opening.

3 If you find only small bulges in the wall edges, try to reduce them by hammering firmly on a wood block, or strip off the corner bead and use shims to make the opening plumb.

Sequence continues on next page

Continued from previous page

4 Check your measurements and layout with a jamb template. It should slide smoothly along the opening.

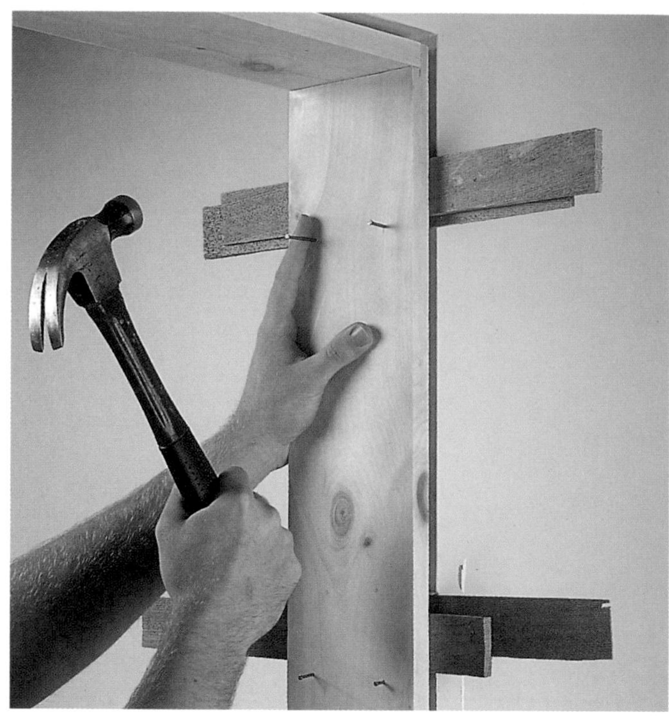

5 You can tack nails below shims to hold them up, but the tight fit from overlapping generally makes this unnecessary.

both edges of the board with a pencil and a combination square. Cut two pieces of the casing you plan to use, and attach them to the ripped 1×6 along the reveal lines.

Slip the template over the edge of the passageway wall, and gradually slide it all the way around the opening. It it's too tight in several spots, try again with a slightly wider template. If just a couple spots are tight, work on those high points with a hammer and scrap block. Remember that a U-shaped casing assembly can bridge small gaps where the wall is slightly concave, while high spots may prevent the outer face pieces on the walls from joining squarely with the piece on the inner surface of the passageway.

ASSEMBLING THE JAMB

Once you find the perfect width, rip all three jamb boards down to that dimension, allowing for some sanding or planing to smooth the ripped edges. Then cut the lengths you determined previously (page 104). Using a router and rabbeting bit, cut a ¾ × ⅜-inch rabbet into the top end of the faces of both side jambs. Another option is to cut the rabbet with a circular saw (held against a guide) with the depth of cut set to ⅜ inch. (See the photos on pages 102 to 103.) Repeated passes will produce a clean joint.

To assemble the three jamb pieces, set them down on a flat surface, and spread carpenter's glue into one of the rabbets and the corresponding end of the head jamb. Insert the end of the head jamb into the rabbet and nail the joint together. Shoot or drive three nails into the outer side of the leg jamb through the rabbet joint and into the end grain of the head jamb. Fasten the other end of the head jamb the same way. To keep the assembly square as you join the pieces, you may want to set each side and head connection around a square block of wood tacked to the work surface.

ATTACHING THE JAMB

To keep the three-piece frame square (and reduce joint stress) during the installation, install a brace near the bottom. Then set the frame in the opening, and make sure the top edge is in line with the height line mark.

6 As you check for plumb, adjust the shims by hand to start, and then tap on the thick ends with a hammer.

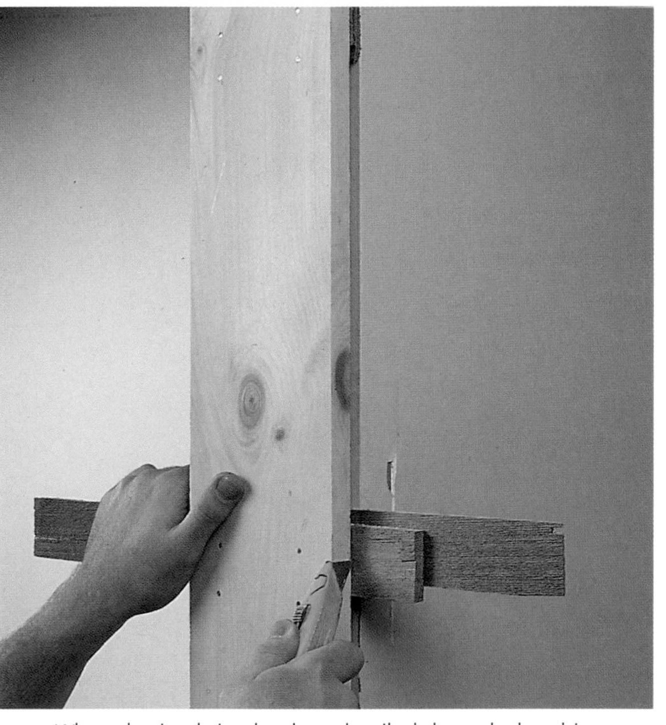

7 When the jamb is plumb and nailed through the shims, trim off the excess with a utility knife.

To hold the assembly in place at first, you'll need to set a few pairs of overlapped shims. Then you can start checking the margins against the opening and use a level to check for plumb. Continue by inserting pairs of shims at the midpoints of the jamb pieces and then halfway between the midpoints and the tops and bottoms of the jamb stock. This is a process of gradual adjustment in which you need to be checking constantly with a level, adjusting the shims, and checking again for plumb and level.

To finish the installation, drive and set nails through the jambs and the shims. Then you can use a sharp utility knife to trim the protruding sections of the shims flush with the edges of the jamb.

SMART TIP *Bracing the Jamb*

Once the glue has set on the rabbeted joints of the jamb, you can maintain the bond and prevent racking by fastening a temporary brace across the legs. Leave the brace long on both sides to help position and hold the jamb assembly in the opening. When you're finished with the shimming and nailing, simply remove the screws and brace.

***Fasten a brace** across the jamb legs with screws to keep the assembly square during the installation.*

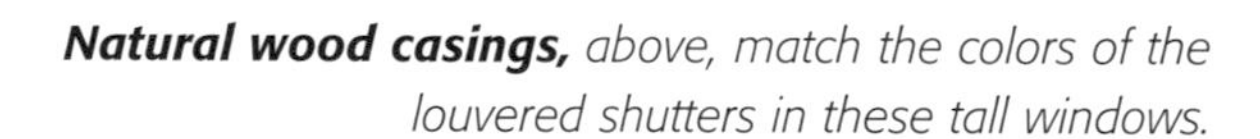

Natural wood casings, *above, match the colors of the louvered shutters in these tall windows.*

The simple casing *that surrounds the oval window at right helps turn this section of the wall into a focal point.*

Although not door casing *in the traditional sense, the trim treatment shown below adds an interesting touch to this door.*

Door casing *with solid butt joints, above, forms a transition between a kitchen and a mudroom.*

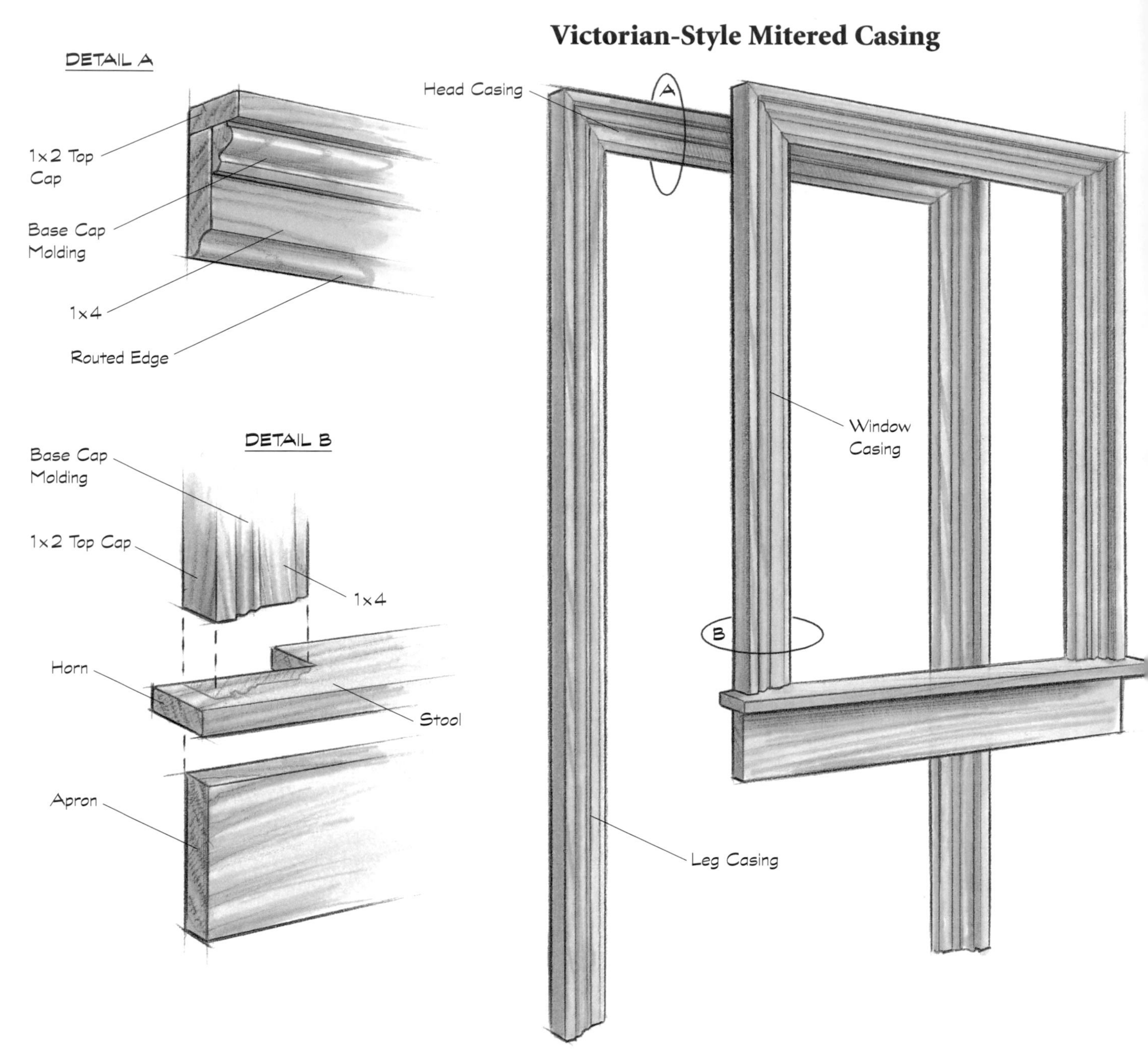

Three-Piece Victorian-Style Casing

Although three-piece built-up casing looks large compared with most stock Colonial casing, its scale actually is about halfway between the scale of modern molding and the overwhelming trimwork of the Victorian era. Finished with a clear sealer, it may be a little heavy in modest-size rooms with standard 8-foot ceilings. Finished with paint that complements the wall color, it will add decoration and detail to any room.

The easiest approach is to prepare built-up lengths of this casing on a workbench in three basic steps: sanding, routing, and assembling.

Sanding. Clamp the 1×2 and 1×4 boards to a workbench one at a time, and sand them with a random-orbit sander loaded with 120-grit sandpaper. Sand just the face side of the 1×4s. Sand both sides and the good edge of the 1×2s, but don't tip the sander and round the edge too much. You should ease the edge slightly with a few quick strokes of fine sandpaper.

Routing. Mill a ¾-inch ogee detail onto the bottom edge of the 1×4. You can do this yourself with a router or a router mounted in a specialized worktable, or look around for a small woodworking shop that will perform this work on a shaper with an automatic feed. Working on your own, clamp the stock securely to the bench, and make at least two passes: one to remove about two-thirds of the depth, and a final pass at full depth. Of course, you can rout another shape if you don't happen to have the right-sized ogee bit.

Remember that there is no one correct combination of moldings, as long as you pay attention to basic design principles. You may like the idea of a complex shape built up from different components. Or you may prefer a simpler approach, such as installing a wide casing trimmed on its outside edges with a backband.

Assembly. Start by attaching the 1×2 top cap to the edge of the 1×4. Clamp the 1×4 to the top of the bench with the milled edge down and away from you. (Even two 2×4s spiked together and laid across sawhorses can serve as a bench for this job.) Spread glue along the edge of the 1×4, and nail the top cap to it. Keep the back edges flush. Work from one end to the other, adjusting the free end to keep the surfaces flush.

Release the clamps, and flip the casing over to apply the base cap molding. Apply glue to the back of a length of molding; set it in place; and nail it off, continually pushing it into place as you work from one end to the other.

Built-up Colonial moldings *add great depth and detail compared with smaller and plainer stock casings.*

Installing the Casing

Mark a ⅛-inch reveal line along the edges of all three sides of the window or door frame. Then square off the bottom of the leg casings, and stand one leg casing in place. Make a mark on its inside edge at the point where the inside edge of the leg casing intersects the reveal line on the head casing. Repeat the same process for the other leg casing before mitering at the mark. Then tack the components into place.

Cut and fit the head casing next. If the profiles line up, you can pull the casings off the wall and install them permanently using glue and nails. Use carpenter's glue between the casing and the jamb and in the miters, and dots of panel adhesive between the casing and the wall. When mitering large casings, clamp the casing firmly so that it won't move during the cut. It's difficult to get perfect miter joints with large casings, so you may have to fill some gaps with caulk.

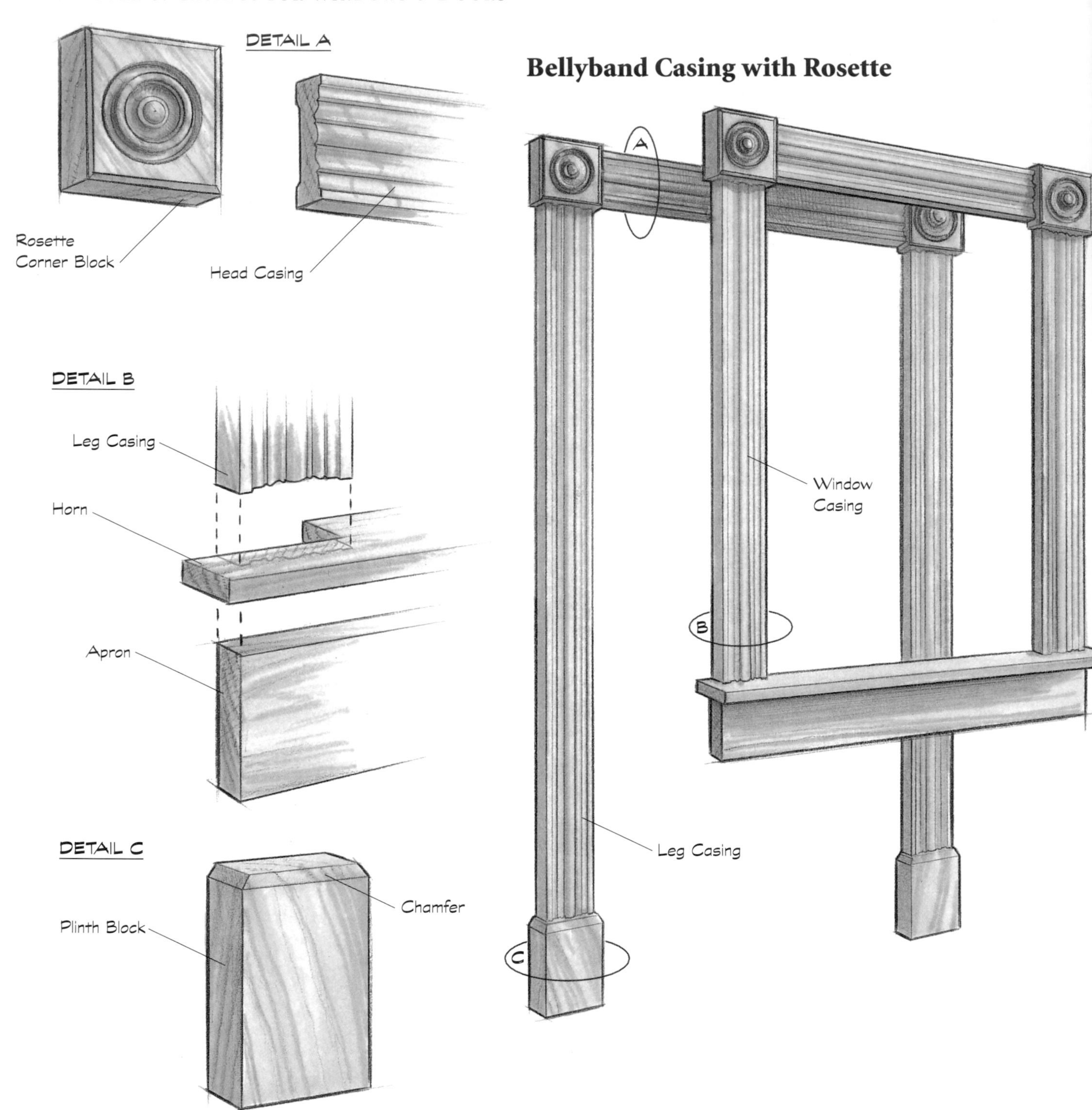

Victorian Bellyband Casing

Victorian bellyband casing is the hallmark interior detail in many older homes. It still looks good today and offers a major benefit that novice do-it-yourselfers will appreciate: no mitering. Due to the distinctive rosette blocks used at the corners of the casings, you can install this style of molding simply by butting the casing legs against the blocks. You still need to make a careful layout and allow for reveals. They can be a little tricky on corner-block jobs because the casing legs are always slightly narrower than the blocks.

Installation Details

One layout approach is to use a combination square to draw reveal lines on the jambs. The inside edges of the

CORNER JAMB

Note that the rosette block below interrupts the reveal and is flush in the corner of Victorian bellyband casing, while the reveal runs uninterrupted around the perimeter of Neoclassical fluted casing, right.

Victorian Bellyband Casing

Rosette Flush to Inside Jamb Corner

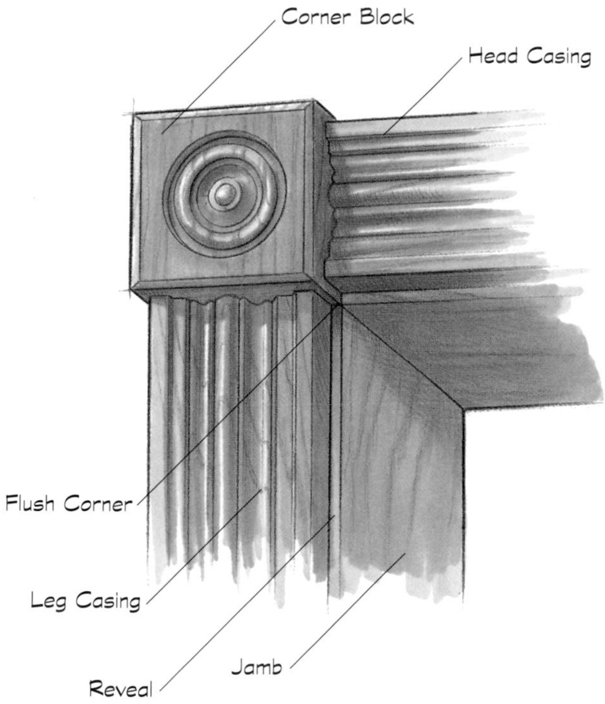

Neoclassical Fluted Casing

Continuous Reveal on Crosshead and Leg

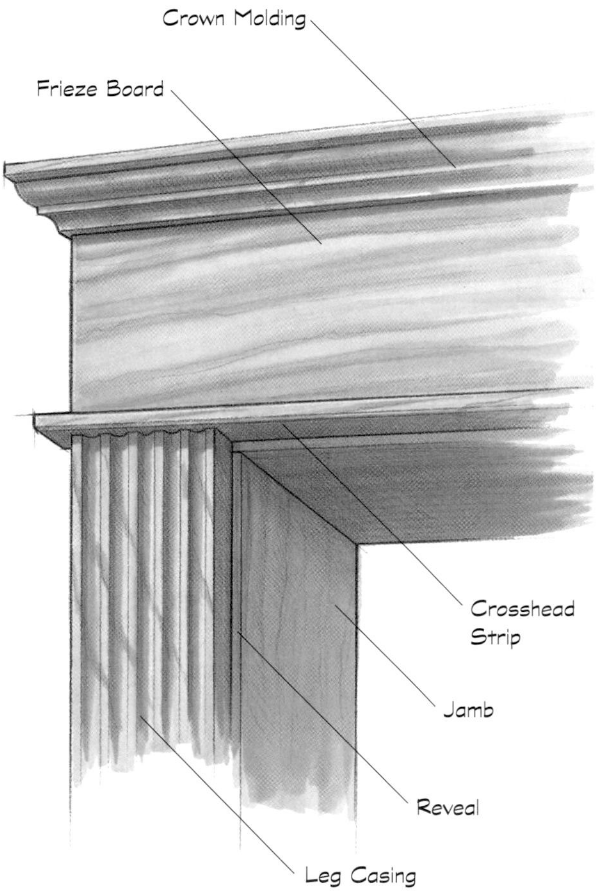

casings will follow these lines. You should set each corner block with its lower inside corner flush with the corner formed by the side jamb and head jamb. This arrangement is easy to lay out and install, but you should check that the casing follows the reveal on the jamb and is centered on the corner block. To be sure about this part of the layout, you might want to tack the blocks into position first and center the narrower casings on the wider blocks to establish the reveal along the jamb.

Be sure that you have square cuts on the ends of the leg casings so they close against both the top corner blocks and lower trim detail, which can be plinth blocks on the floor for doors or a stool at sill level for windows. Nail the pieces with glue in the joints and dabs of panel adhesive on the back of the casings.

Remember that the height of the plinth blocks must reflect the total height of the base treatment. (The base treatment used with this style of casing should be at least 6⅞ inches tall.) If the plinth blocks have a tapered or decorative top edge, then the total height of the base treatment should be slightly lower than the height of this edge.

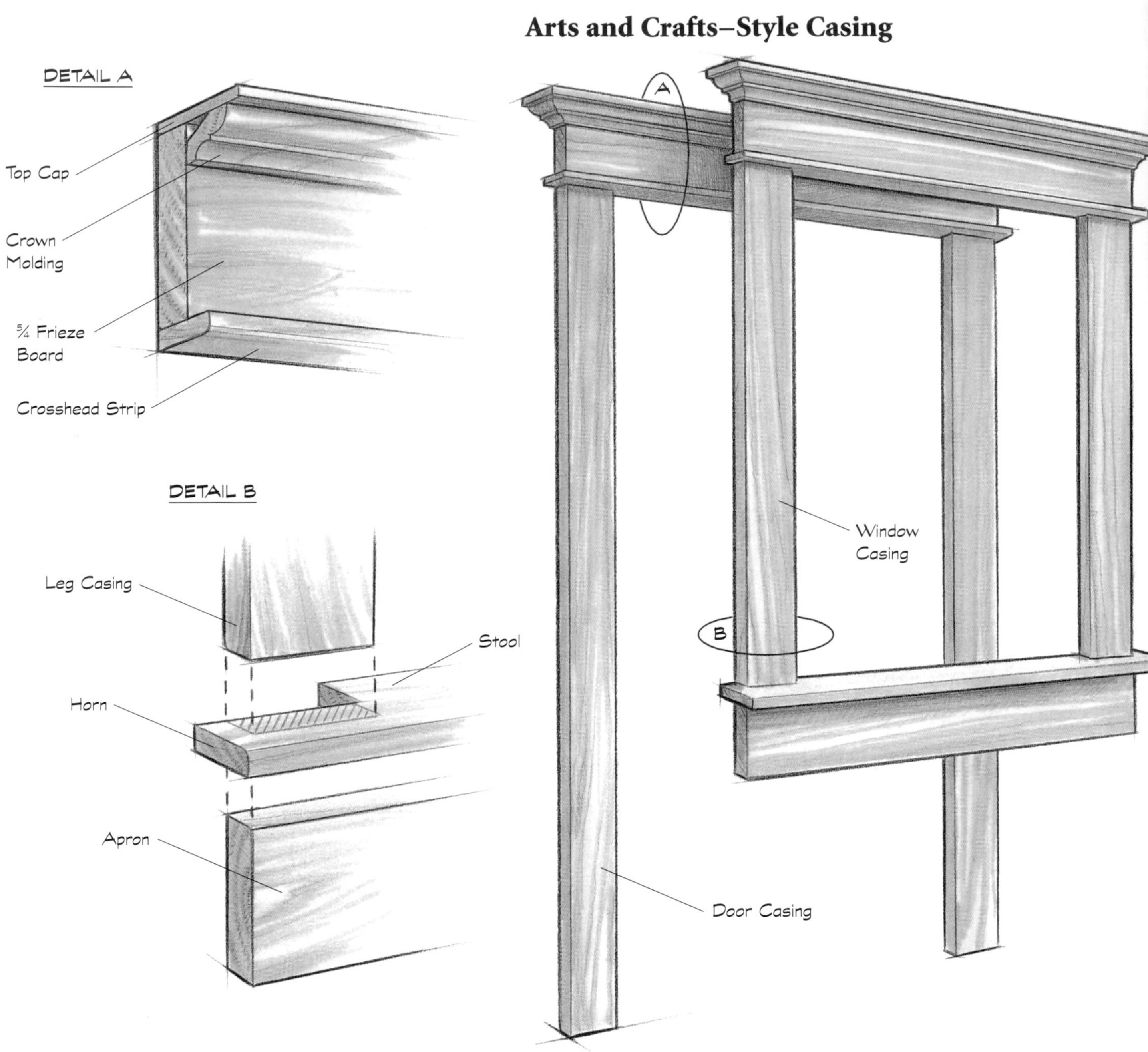

Symmetrical Arts & Crafts–Style Casing

A hybrid approach to trimming openings resembles the Arts and Crafts style in some respects but blends with a simplified version of the Neoclassical approach. The leg casings are not fluted, of course, because Arts and Crafts detailing calls for a flat profile and a sometimes almost rugged-looking use of lumber. The idea of this style is to avoid fussy details and use wood more in its natural state with simple joints. In some cases, Arts and Crafts leg casings may be stock boards, with the same material laid across the top of the opening and overhanging the legs by an inch or so.

You can use the facsimile shown above with or without simple plinth blocks at the base of the leg casings, and make other alterations to suit the style of your house. For example, if you want to stay closer to pure Arts and Crafts style, you may want to dispense with elaborate cornice molding with end returns at the top of the assembly and use something more basic, such as strips of backband molding.

Building Decorative Crossheads

A crosshead is simply a narrow strip of wood that runs horizontally across the top of the opening. It adds depth to the molding treatment and allows you to use basic butt joints on the leg casings.

Depending on the scale of the casings and other moldings you're using, you could select a piece of lattice to use for the crosshead or one-by lumber or even 5/4 material. The larger size used below may look better if you're planning a fairly elaborate cap treatment above the opening. (See the illustration opposite.)

Basic Installation

Start by measuring the distance between the outside edges of the leg casings, and cut the 5/4×6 frieze board to this measurement. Cut a length of 1½-inch-wide bullnose stop molding ¾ inch longer (for a ⅜-inch reveal) as the crosshead strip. Next, cut a strip of crown molding 6 inches longer. Center the length of crown molding on the top edge of the board, with 3 inches hanging off each end. Mark the ends of the crown on its bottom edge. These marks represent the short points of the compound miter cuts that form the outside corners at each end of the crosshead cap. This detail allows the crown molding to return to the wall on both ends of the frieze board.

Making these outside corners is identical to turning outside corners with crown molding on a ceiling. (See "Cutting Crown Molding," page 134.) When making the small return pieces, cut the miter onto a piece of molding at least 12 inches long. Remember that to work safely you should never hold small pieces of wood against the fence of a power miter saw.

When you have cut the returns, predrill them to avoid splitting; then glue and nail the molding to the face of the board first, and attach the returns. Now you can make the top cap. If you're using lattice, a typical reveal is ⅜ inch. Measure the distance between the outside edges of the returns, and add ¾ inch. Cut the lattice; then center and fasten it over the crown moldings.

You can build *the complete decorative crosshead assembly, above, on a bench. Clamp it in place on the jamb reveal line, right, as you fasten it to the studs.*

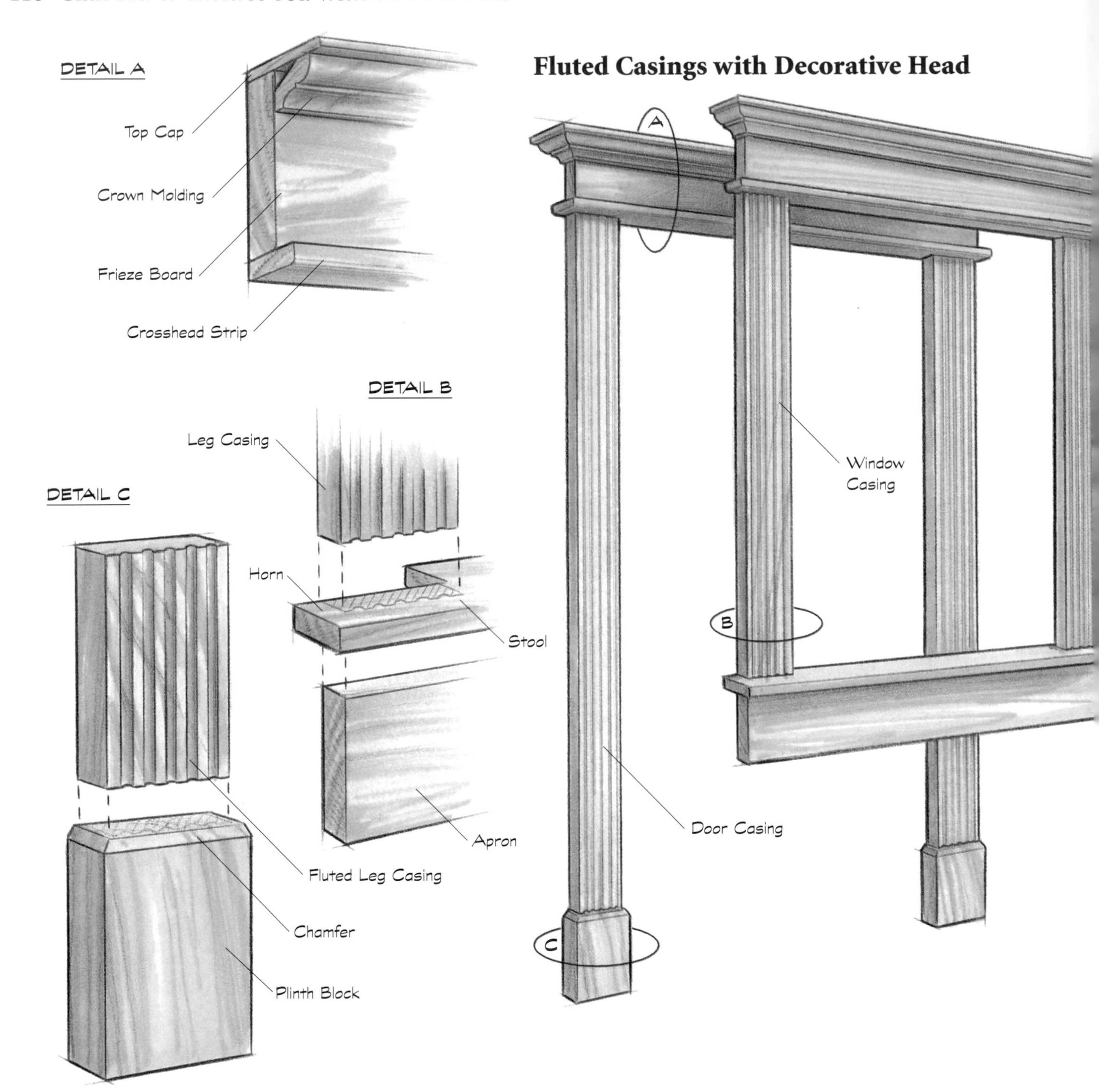

Neoclassical Fluted Casing

Many people can picture flutes as a feature of great stone columns on public buildings. But this design motif, which looks like a series of shallow troughs in the material's surface, is widely used in wood.

You're likely to find that stock fluted casings are too small and special-order casings are too expensive. So you may want to make your own or have a local woodworking shop make them for you. Pros have an easier time than amateurs creating boards where the fluted pattern gradually diminishes near the ends.

With this design variation, the troughs become increasingly shallow and finally disappear, leaving several inches of unfluted wood just before the casing joins the top blocks and bottom plinths. This feature takes a lot of planning and some nifty router work so it is best left to experienced woodworkers.

Alternative Window Trim

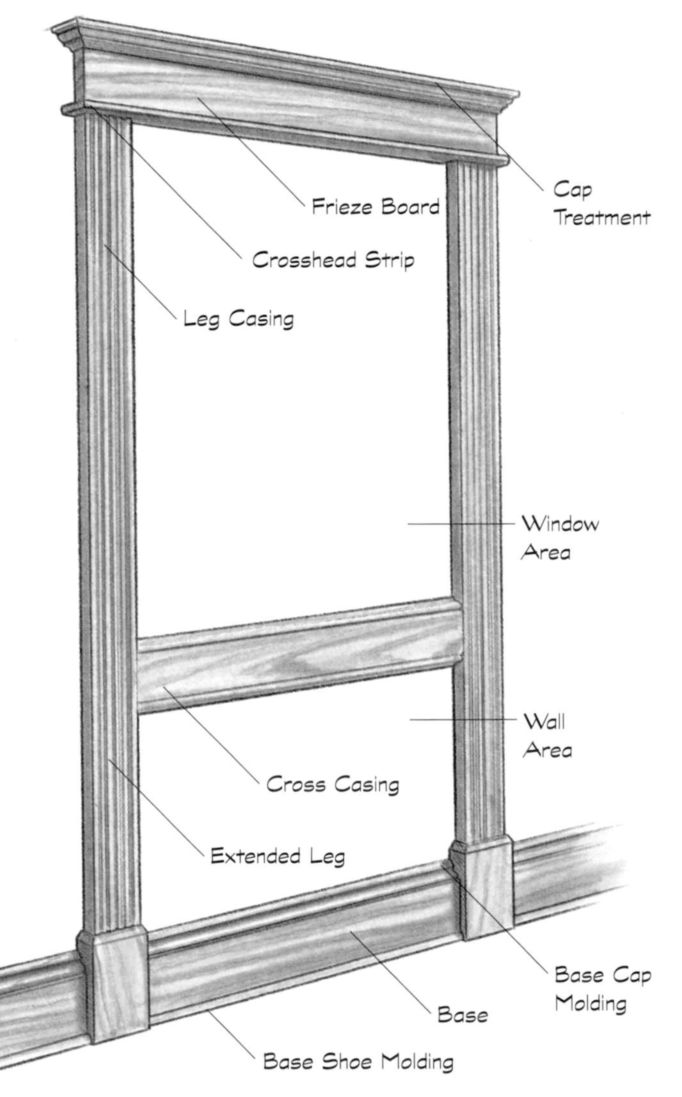

INSTALLATION

Using a combination square, establish reveal lines along all three sides of the jamb, and install the plinth blocks flush with the inside edges of the leg jambs. This approach calls for some additional planning because you need to accommodate the plinth blocks in your base-trim treatment.

Next, square off the bottoms of the leg casings. Position one of the leg casings on top of one of the plinth blocks, and mark the spot where the reveal line on the head jamb hits the casing. Then square-cut each leg casing to length, and install it. Measure from the top outside edge of one leg casing to the top outside edge of the other leg casing, and use this measurement (plus an allowance for a small overhang on each side) to build a decorative crosshead over the opening.

On windows, you have a couple of options. You can stop the leg casings at a window stool or run them down to plinth blocks on the floor. This second approach takes more wood and more time. But it can make short windows, and the room in general, look more expansive. If you run leg casings down to plinth blocks on the floor, you'll need to trim the bottom of the window along the reveal mark on the lower jamb with a piece of cross casing.

A plinth block *at the edge of a passageway is chamfered on the side and top edges to provide a transition between the block and the fluted casing above it.*

This passageway trim *with a decorative top cap provides a handsome entrance to an elegantly trimmed room.*

Decorative molding above openings *can include a main crosshead trim piece, a frieze board, and a decorative cap.*

DECORATIVE CAPS

Using decorative caps is another area of trimwork in which you have a lot of design leeway. Once you're finished with the basic installation of leg casings, you can design many different types of crosshead decorative caps for the top of the opening.

In rooms with standard ceiling height, you may want to stick to a modest design. For example, you could install a bullnose stop and a 1×4 over the crosshead, cap it with a 1×3, and add a piece of 2½-inch crown molding. (See the illustration at right.)

In rooms with higher ceilings, of course, you can use larger stock boards, such as a 1×6 or 1×8, over the crosshead and build up more elaborate caps with combinations of trim. With both large and small caps, however, you must always create mitered return pieces at each end.

In rooms with very high ceilings and double doors, you might add a large frieze panel made of a pine board or a piece of medium-density fiberboard suitable for painting and decorate it with bands of molding. Many designs and types of molding will work, including stock Colonial casing.

You assemble the components of a decorative cap using the same basic tools and techniques used on casings and crossheads. Use carpenter's glue on the wood-to-wood joints, and drive all nails into studs.

Decorative Cap Detail (Cross Section)

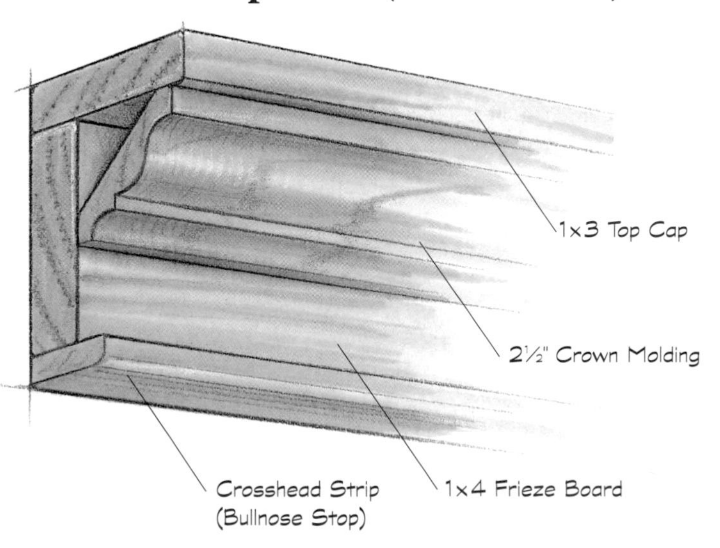

Flat casing, *above, accentuates the unusual shape of the opening. Note the width of the jamb.*

Ornate window casing, *above left, adds an air of formality to a living room window.*

Molding around French doors, *above, draws attention to the view outside.*

Trimwork painted white, *left, frames a view of a mantel and artwork in an adjoining room.*

CHAPTER 7

Crown Molding, Chair Rail & Baseboard

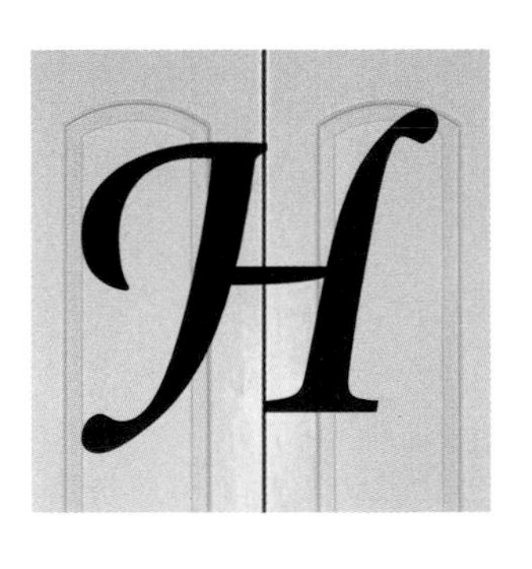

orizontal trimwork extends across the walls of a room and helps to tie different parts of the space together. Crown molding—along with other cornice treatments—chair rail, and baseboard trim are the most common types of horizontal trimwork, and each is available in a number of styles and profiles, so you should have no trouble finding the trimwork that best suits your home. But there are others that you can include in the room's design. A strip of picture rail molding installed a few feet below the cornice creates a wall section called a frieze. In traditional design, a frieze usually receives a wall treatment that is different from the lower wall area. Chair rails are often used alone, but they can be teamed up with wall panels or wainscoting to create a distinctive design element.

Basic Joinery

When you install door and window casings, much of the joinery is straightforward. In the majority of cases, the most complicated joints you'll have to assemble are simple miters at the corners of the windows and doors. But working with base trim, chair rails, and cornices can be more complicated because the molding often must wrap around corners. You can handle most of those transitions with coping cuts on inside corners and miter cuts on outside corners. These cuts allow the molding profiles to continue uninterrupted from one wall surface to another. Miters (and copes) used on cornices, where the molding is angled, are more challenging and require compound miters. Experiment with these cuts, testing your skills and tools on scrap wood. (See "Crown Molding," pages 134 to 139.)

The cornice *above is built up with crown molding over Colonial base. Picture rail molding runs below the cornice.*

The built-up chair rail *above combines a backer piece with a narrower chair rail; a subrail runs beneath.*

This base trim *is built up using base cap molding on top, a 1x6, Colonial base (and backup nailer), and shoe molding.*

Types of Molding Cuts

The two basic molding cuts are miters and bevels. A miter is an angle cut across the wood grain on the face of molding. This is the cut you see at the corners of door and window frames. A bevel is an angle that runs through the thickness of molding. A bevel also forms a miter joint where two vertical moldings meet, as in a baseboard outside corner. When a joint is mitered and beveled—for example, where a sloped cornice molding forms an outside corner—the cut is called a compound miter.

The ideal miter joint makes a nearly invisible connection between two pieces of molding. But when floors or ceilings aren't level, you may need to follow them with baseboard and cornice moldings to avoid gaps, which can throw off some of your cuts. But on most projects, you can create a square and plumb assembly that looks right with the room as a whole.

To handle all the cutting, most trimwork professionals use a power miter saw with a fine-toothed blade. It's the tool of choice, although you can handle many projects using a table saw, a radial-arm saw, or hand tools. There are two main types of power miter saws. The more basic type cuts miters or bevels in stock that's set flat on the saw table or flat against the fence. The more complex and versatile compound miter saw lets you cut a miter with a bevel in a single stroke. (To do this with a basic power miter saw, you must hold the molding upside down against the fence at an angle.) Some compound miter saws have rails that allow the motor and blade to slide forward. This costly feature provides more cutting capacity using a smaller blade.

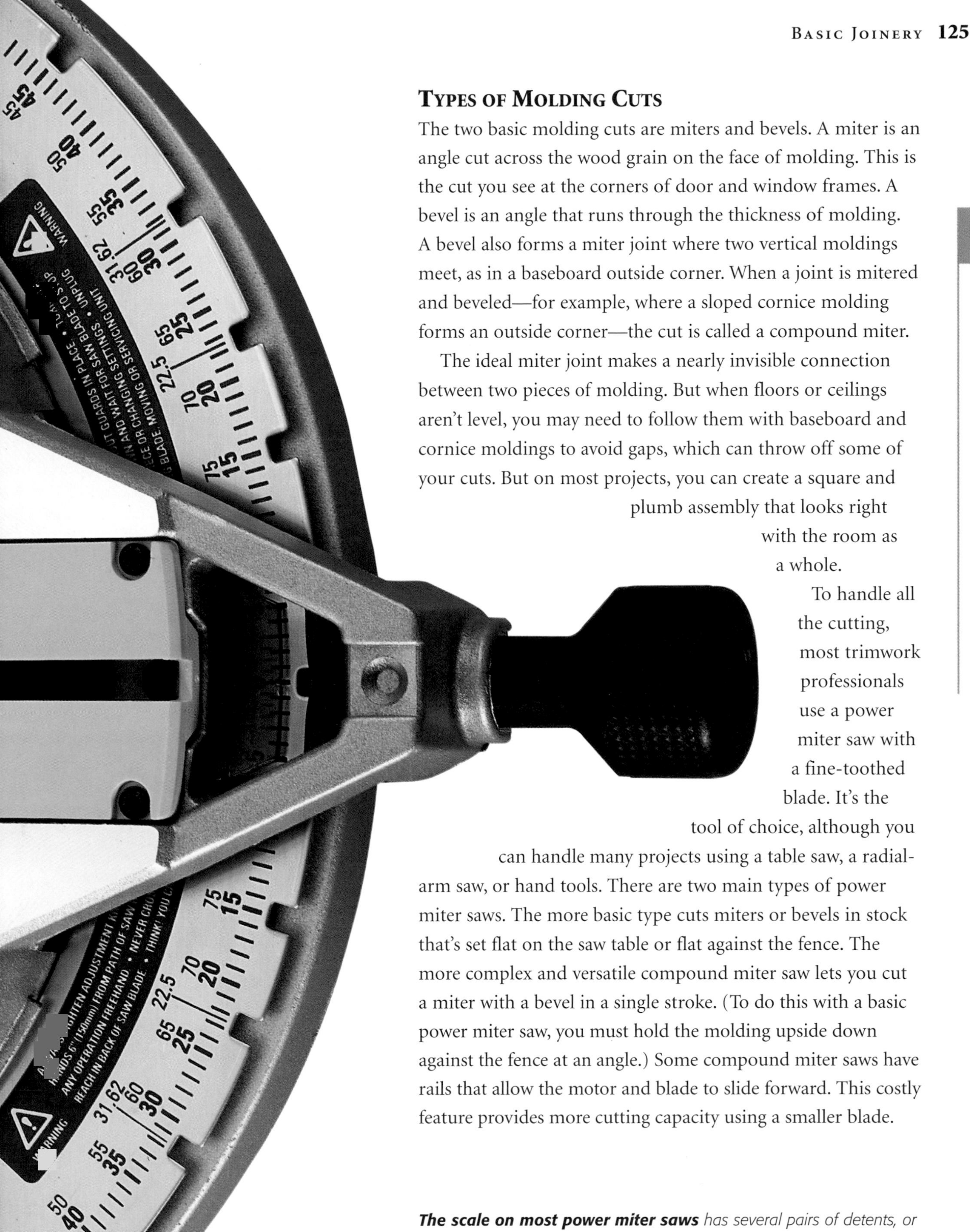

The scale on most power miter saws *has several pairs of detents, or automatic stop positions for the most commonly cut angles. You'll feel them as you swing the saw across its full range of cut. For every detent right of the 0 deg. mark there is a corresponding position left of 0 deg.*

POWER MITER CUTS

If you're new to power miter saws, make some scrap cuts to become familiar with the operations and safety procedures. Most models have detents where the saw will align easily—for example, at 45 degrees, left and right of center. But operating within the sweep of the blade can cause confusion because the scale mounted in front of the saw is calibrated from 0 to 45 degrees, left of center, and 0 to 45 degrees, right of center.

When you set the blade at 0 (the midway position), it will cut a 90-degree angle across molding that is seated along the fence. As you rotate the blade toward the fence, the actual cut angle decreases, even though the angle numbers on the miter scale increase.

Cuts of 45 to 90 Degrees. To rotate the blade to cut a specific angle—66 degrees, for example—on a piece of molding, remember that you need to subtract that number from 90 to find the correct setting on the miter scale. In this case, you subtract 66 from 90, which leaves 24.

Until you become used to the calibration system, you may want to make approximate layout marks on some scrap pieces, set the saw to cut in line with your marks, and see whether the pieces make a rough fit.

Painted cornice molding *turns inside and outside corners without showing any trace of the cut joints.*

Making a Saw Bench

WHAT YOU'LL NEED

- 2x4s and ¾" plywood
- Power drill with screwdriver bit and screws
- Construction adhesive and caulking gun
- Pencil, lag screws or lag bolts, nuts, washers, and socket wrench
- Clamps

TRIM TIP: Most power miter saws have a lock button that safely secures the blade head when you move the saw.

3 Cut a piece of ¾-in. plywood; set it on the adhesive-coated frame; and secure it with screws.

6 Reposition the saw; insert bolts and washers; and tighten the bolts at each corner using a socket wrench.

1 Make a strong and stable saw bench by framing the support platform with 2x4s on edge.

2 Increase stability of the assembly by adding construction adhesive to the top edges of the 2x4s.

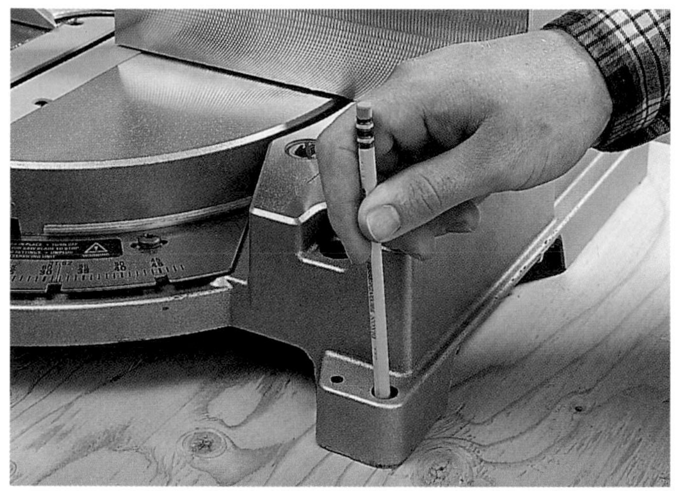

4 Set your saw on the center of the platform, and mark the bolt-down locations with a pencil.

5 Drill bolt holes through the platform. If the holes fall on the 2x4 frame, you can use lag screws instead of bolts.

7 Screw a molding support board to each end of the platform so that the top edge is level with the saw table.

8 Set up your saw bench near the work area, clamping it firmly to stable sawhorses.

Making Mitered Returns

WHAT YOU'LL NEED

- Measuring tape and pencil
- Chair rail molding
- Power miter saw or miter box and backsaw
- Power drill and predrill bit
- Wood glue and brush
- Hammer, finishing nails, and nail set

TRIM TIP: Cut the small return piece from a substantial board that you can hold safely and securely against the saw fence.

1 Mark the end of the dead-end piece about an inch back from the end of the wall.

2 Cut a standard 45-deg. miter on the dead end of the molding. Cut it so that the mitered edge will face the wall.

3 Drill pilot holes into the molding to avoid splits, and attach it with finishing nails. Sink the nailheads with a nail set.

4 Cut the return from a piece large enough to hold safely and securely against the saw fence. Apply glue to both surfaces.

5 You can set a small finishing nail in the return, or simply clamp the return piece until the glue sets.

Outside and Inside Corners

On house walls with perfectly square corners, you can cut molding at exactly 45 degrees to make tight joints. You have to improvise a bit where the corners aren't exactly true, which is most of the time.

One approach is to measure the corner angle with a sliding T-bevel (sometimes called a bevel square) that can capture any angle. You can use the tool setting to make slight adjustments on the power miter saw.

Another approach on corners that are very close to square is to back-cut the molding. This old carpentry trick involves shaving a hair off the back edges of the mating faces with a block plane so that the molding surfaces you see close first.

Dead-End Moldings

Not every piece of molding joins another. For example, you may want to stop a piece of chair rail short of a passageway between rooms.

One option is to leave a square cut. But this exposes rough end grain and often looks unfinished. Another is to cut a 45-degree angle across most of the exposed edge. This looks more finished, but still exposes end grain that can soak up extra stain or paint and look different from the rest of the molding.

A third way is to create a return. You cut a miter on the dead-end piece and a corresponding miter on a small piece of molding that covers all the end grain. (See "Making Mitered Returns," opposite.)

RETURN OPTIONS

One easy way to finish the end of exposed molding is to cut a bevel. (See the photo below, left.) This system is similar to the old-fashioned method of chamfering hard edges. The idea is that cutting an angle (not necessarily 45 degrees) will soften the appearance and look better than leaving a hard 90-degree edge. You may find this bevel method acceptable, particularly if you plan to paint the molding. This way you can sand and fill the grain before priming and painting. On clear-sealed or stained molding, it generally looks better to cut a small return piece. This detail continues the molding profile around the corner and back to the wall.

Beveling the exposed end *of a piece of molding helps to create a finished look at the very edge of a wall. This is best if you plan to wallpaper above or below a chair rail.*

Mitering a return piece *creates a finished look by wrapping the molding profile back to the wall. The chair rail stops short of the end of the wall, however; you must either paint or wallpaper the entire wall.*

Suggested Cutting Sequences

Rectangular Room

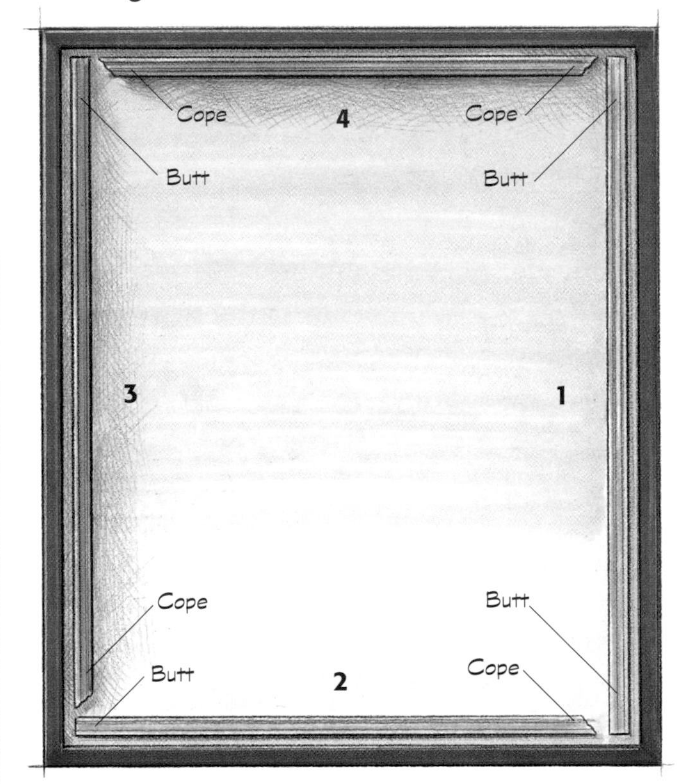

Room with Scarf Joints

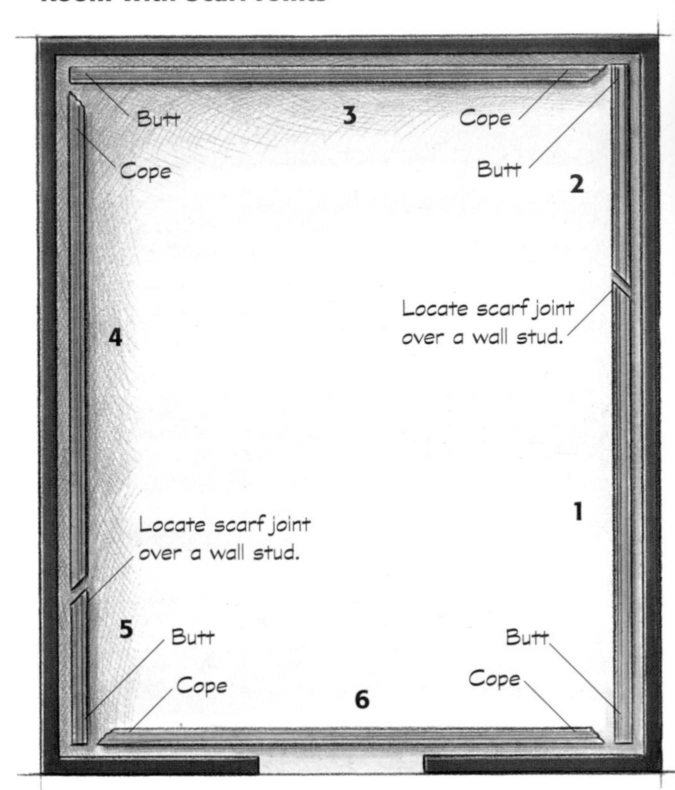

L-Shaped Room

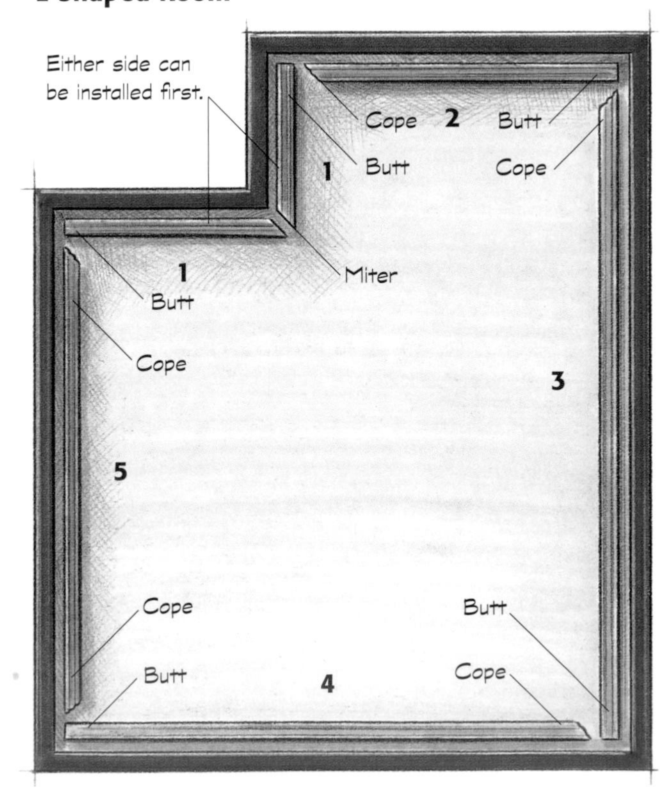

Double L-Shaped Room

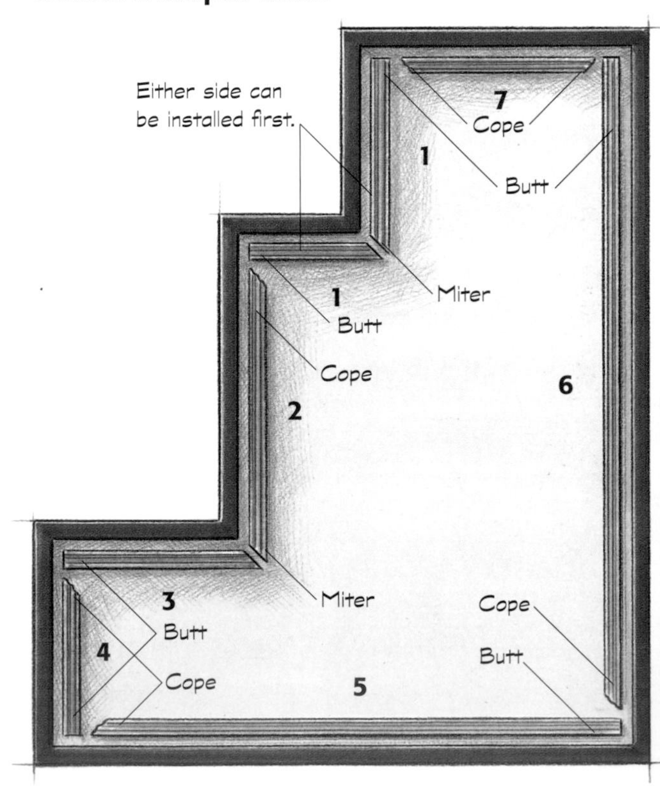

Room with Bay Window

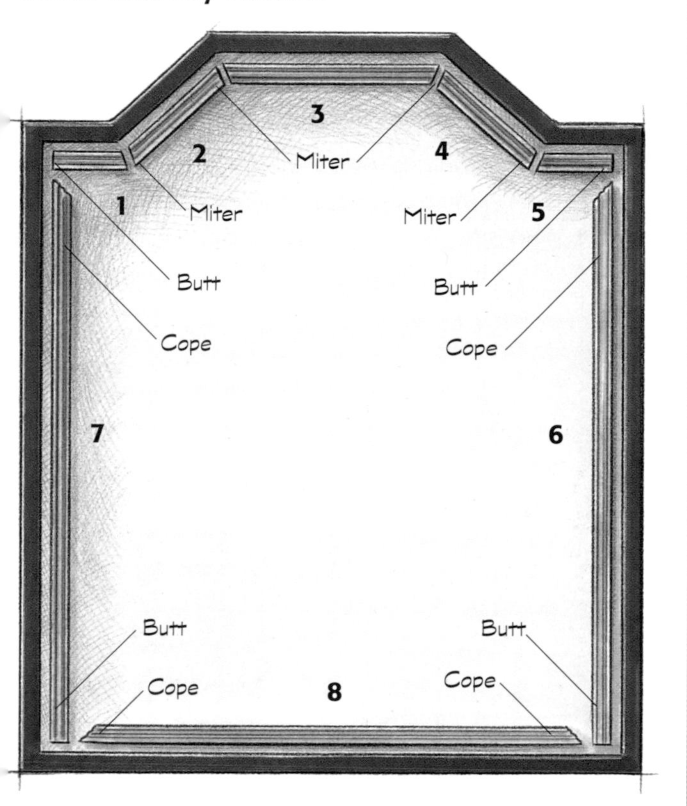

Room with Alcove

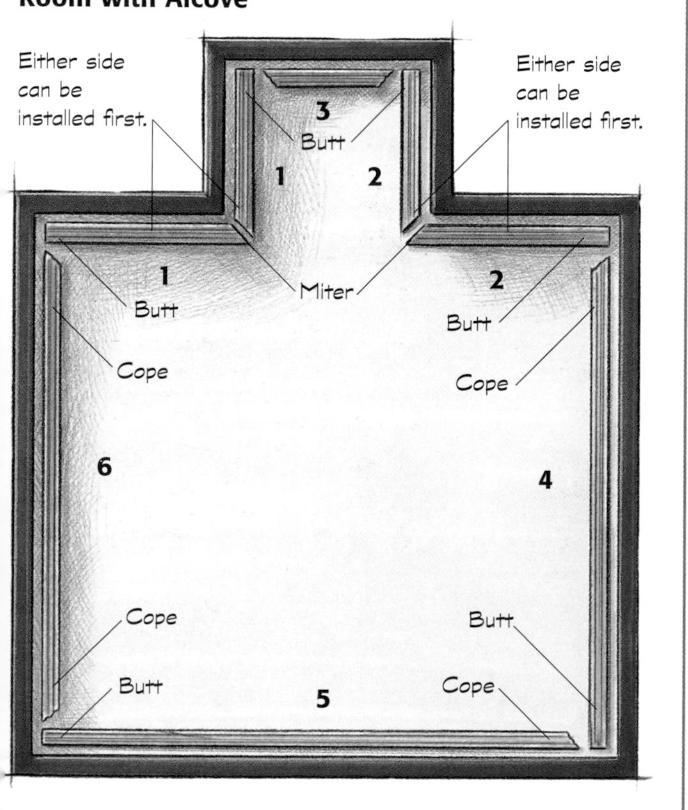

Planning Cuts

On large projects, it pays to sketch out a plan view of your moldings and plan ahead for each type of cut. This helps you to organize the job and make an accurate lumber order. You should also make rough cuts to approximate length before you work on corner joints. Pros may not need to take this extra step, but leaving a few extra inches of length is a hedge for mistakes that novices might make in cutting.

Most do-it-yourselfers find it easy to handle simple miters where two 45-degree cuts form the joint. Use the detents on a power miter saw, and the cut edges should meet cleanly. The most challenging operation is coping a joint.

Coping an Inside Corner. For many do-it-yourselfers, coping is one of the mysteries of molding. But it's worth learning about because coping is virtually always used to create inside corners, particularly on intricate, high-profile trim. Unlike a miter, where two cut faces meet in the middle, a coped joint is one-sided. First you make a straight cut on the end of one piece of molding and fasten it in the corner. Then you shape the end of the second piece to nestle against the profile of the first.

Why bother? First, as you nail the pieces of an inside corner against the wall, the boards tend to separate. (On an outside corner they tend to close.) Second, gradual shrinking of the wood can expose a dark gap line along a mitered joint. But with a coped joint, structural movement and wood shrinkage expose only more wood of the base piece.

Coping takes patience and practice. One approach is to use a compass to scribe the profile of one piece of molding on the end of another. Then you cut the shape with a thin-blade coping saw. The most common approach is to cut a basic miter first and follow up by trimming the profile along the mitered edge. With either method, it's helpful to back-cut (or undercut) the coped piece so that the adjoining surfaces meet and close before the bodies of the two pieces make contact.

Joining Pieced Moldings

On straight runs in large rooms, you may not be able to buy stock molding long enough to reach wall to wall in one piece. In this case you have to join the lengths, creating additional joints. The easiest solution is to make two square cuts and butt one piece against the other. But shrinkage may cause a noticeable gap, as it can at inside corner joints.

The best approach is to cut an overlap between the pieces, called a scarf joint. Simply slice 45-degree cuts through the thickness of both pieces so that the surface of one covers the cut section of the other. Should the seam open a bit over time, you'll see more wood instead of a glaring gap.

Making Scarf Joints

What You'll Need

- Power miter saw or hand miter box
- Baseboard and shoe molding
- Wood glue and wood filler
- Power drill and bits
- Hammer and nail set
- Sanding block and sandpaper

TRIM TIP: If you need lengths of trim that are larger than your vehicle can handle safely, buy shorter lengths and cut scarf joints to join them.

Long runs of molding, *such as the crown molding along this ceiling, often consist of multiple pieces joined by scarf joints.*

3 Test-fit the scarf joint (without glue), and predrill through both pieces at the joint.

6 Fill the nailholes with wood filler. You may need to wait and fill the holes again: some fillers shrink as they set.

1 Start by making a square cut (or miter if you plan to cut a cope) on the far end of the board you need to piece.

2 Cut both of the 45-deg. miters that will form the scarf joint. (Locate the scarf over a wall stud.)

4 Apply wood glue to both sides of the joint. (You will need to wipe off some excess after nailing.)

5 Drive finishing nails through the predrilled holes, and set the heads just below the wood surface.

7 Clean up any traces of glue and filler around the joint with sandpaper before finishing the wood.

8 To further disguise the joint, consider nailing a shoe molding to the bottom of the baseboard.

BASIC MITER SAW CUTS

Inside Corner, Left Side Cope. *Place the molding bottom up on the saw's table. (Note that the cove detail is at the top.) Position the molding so that the excess will fall to the left.*

Inside Corner, Right Side Cope. *With the molding bottom up, reposition the miter gauge to the left 45-deg. mark. The excess falls to the right.*

Outside Corner, Left Side Miter. *With the gauge set on the left and the molding bottom up, cut so that the excess falls on the left.*

Outside Corner, Right Side Miter. *Move the gauge to the right. Turn the bottom of the molding up, and cut so that the excess falls on the right.*

Crown Molding

Cornices provide a decorative transition between wall and ceiling that can improve the appearance of almost any room. The most popular cornice is crown molding, a thin length of wood installed diagonally.

To minimize problems with expansion and contraction of the wood, consider stock that is primed on both sides, or prime it yourself, including the back. It also helps to store molding in the room for a few days ahead of time and to fasten all joints with glue and nails.

Where rigid stock won't conform to slight variations along the wall or ceiling, use an adhesive caulk to seal the visible seams prior to painting.

CUTTING CROWN MOLDING

Crown molding is installed at an angle to the wall. For this reason, the cuts needed to form corners are more complicated and require a compound miter. You can make this joint using hand tools, of course. With a basic power miter saw you need be careful about how you set the molding against the fence. With a compound miter saw you can set the molding flat.

Cutting with a Basic Miter Saw. If you are using a basic power miter saw, remember its limitations. When you lay a piece flat on the table, you can only miter or crosscut it; when you stand a piece up against the fence, you can only bevel or crosscut it; and you can

COMPOUND MITER SAW CUTS (See text at bottom of page, and make test cuts!)

Inside Corner, Left Side Cope. *Tilt the saw to the correct angle, and set the miter gauge to the right. Place the molding so that the top faces the fence and the excess falls to the right.*

Inside Corner, Right Side Cope. *With the saw tilted, set the miter gauge to the left. Place the molding so that the bottom faces the fence and the excess falls to the right.*

Outside Corner, Left Side Miter. *With the saw tilted, set the miter gauge to the left. Place the molding so that the bottom faces the fence and the excess falls to the left.*

Outside Corner, Right Side Miter. *With the saw tilted, set the miter gauge to the right. Place the molding so that the top faces the fence and the excess falls to the left.*

only make bevel cuts along a vertical 90-degree axis.

Because you can't adjust the blade to make a compound miter, you need to adjust the molding. Place the molding bottom up and face out on the saw table, with the top side resting squarely on the table. In this position you can make compound miter cuts at any settings on the scale, left or right of center.

To cut the left side of an outside corner, set the miter gauge to 45 degrees to the left and cut with your piece to the right of the blade. To form the right side of an outside corner, set the miter gauge to 45 degrees to the right and cut with your piece to the left. To avoid confusion, it pays to make test cuts on pieces of scrap molding and keep them handy for reference.

Cutting with a Compound Miter Saw. With a compound miter saw, you can cut the molding set flat on the table. Most crown moldings form a 45-degree or 52-degree angle with the ceiling. (See "Where to Nail?" page 136.) Determine your crown molding's angle before tilting the saw and setting the miter gauge.

- To fit 90-degree corners using 45-degree crown molding, set the saw tilt left at 30 degrees and the miter angle (left or right) at 35.3 degrees.

- To fit 90-degree corners using 52/38-degree crown molding, set the tilt left at 33.9 degrees and the miter angle (left or right) at 31.6 degrees.

Smart Tip: Where to Nail?

With most molding installations, you can nail into wall studs to make solid connections. On some cornice installations, however, upper nails will reach into ceiling joists every 16 inches only if the joists run perpendicular to the wall. Where joists are parallel with the wall, you need either nailing blocks or a continuous nailer for support. You may want to install the blocks for extra support in any case.

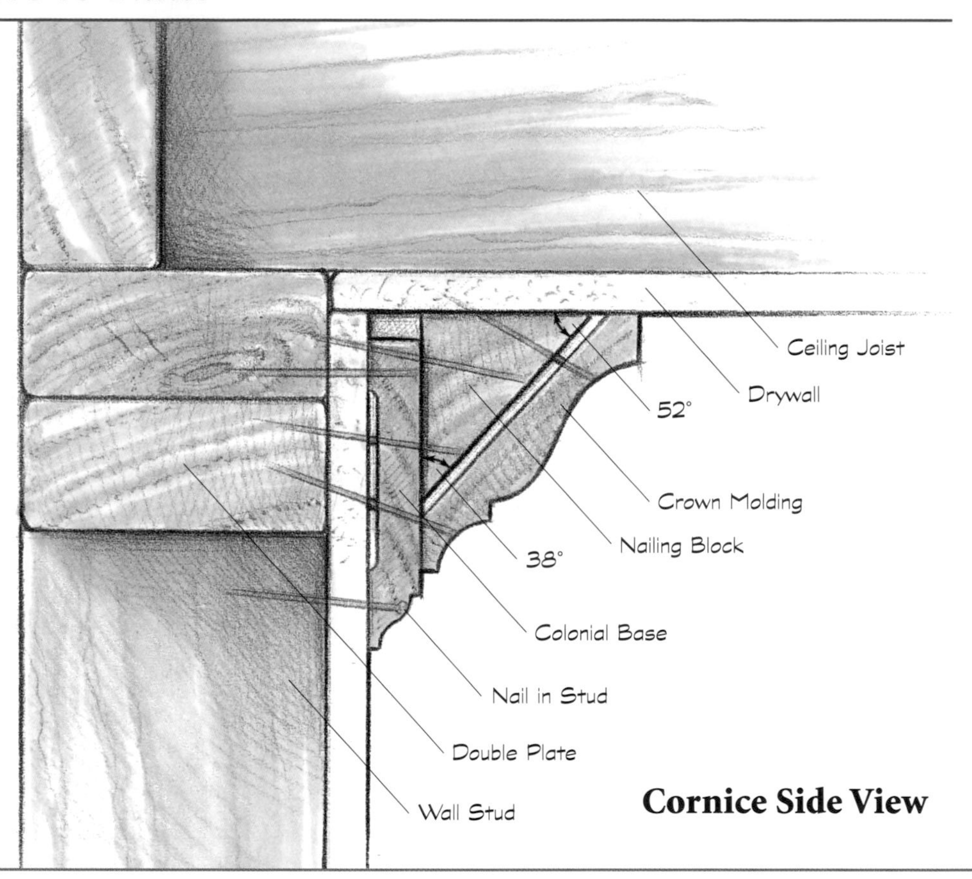

Installing Crown Molding

To calculate the rough lengths of molding you'll need, start by measuring all the walls about 2 inches below the ceiling. If the adjoining surfaces are true, simply follow the wall and ceiling lines. (You can test for bumps and depressions using a long, straight 2×4.)

Install the crown with glue and nails driven into wall studs. You can drill pilot holes through the top of the molding and drive 16d finishing nails into the top plate of the wall frame or into the ceiling joists.

If the wall and ceiling aren't true, you can do one of two things. The first is to force the crown into position using a wood block and toenails. This may work when the ceiling is fairly flat with only a few shallow depressions. The molding itself won't be straight, however, which may magnify the problem.

The second thing you can do is to test a scrap piece

This large-scale cornice treatment *consists of several stock moldings built up on a standard one-by board.*

of molding at several locations to find the lowest point of the ceiling. Then level that low point along the walls where you'll be working, and strike chalk guidelines. Install the molding along the guidelines, and fill any gaps between the top of the molding and the ceiling with joint compound or caulk. This tends to flatten out the crown molding, though.

Installing Corners

In most cases, the best approach is to install all outside corners before inside corners. But you need to plan the installation carefully, and allow at least an inch or so of extra wood in case you make an error and need to recut coped joints at inside corners.

When two outside corners are separated by an inside corner, save the piece coped at both ends for last. In rooms with walls longer than your molding stock, of course, you'll need to piece the lengths together with a scarf joint.

Once you've cut the cope on inside corners, create a tight fit by adjusting the position of both corner pieces and by sanding or filing the cope as needed. To adjust the tacked-in-place square-cut piece up or down for fitting, tap it with a hammer and block.

Installing Crown Molding

What You'll Need

- Chalk-line box and measuring tape
- Crown molding and nailing blocks
- Power miter saw and coping saw, files
- Power drill and bits
- Hammer, finishing nails, nail set
- Wood glue, caulk, and caulking gun

TRIM TIP: Test for the direction and location of ceiling joists with a stud sensor, by tapping with a hammer to hear the sound of hollow or solid areas, or by tapping in test finishing nails.

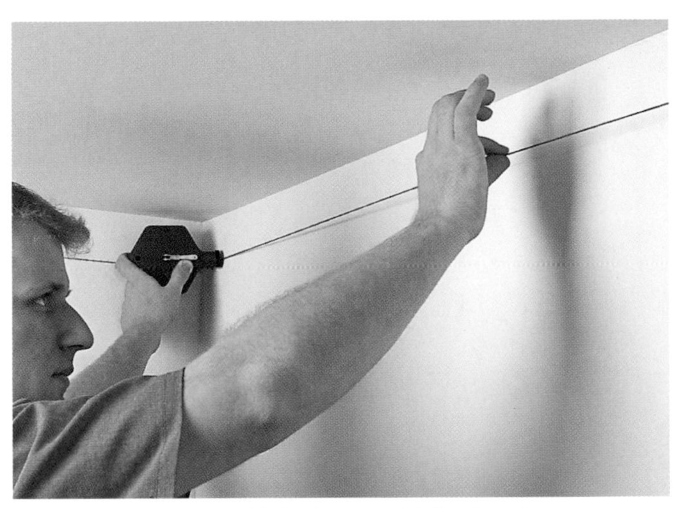

1 Once you've established your guideline location, snap a chalk line for the molding.

2 Match the angle of the molding installation to the angle of the nailers, and cut them on your power miter saw.

3 Nail or screw the support blocks to wall studs and the wall top plate every 16 inches.

Sequence continues on next page

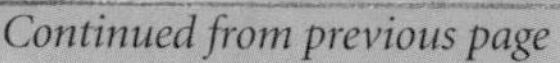

Continued from previous page

4 Install the full-length square-cut cornice, fitting it into the corner. Don't nail within 3 or 4 ft. of the corner yet.

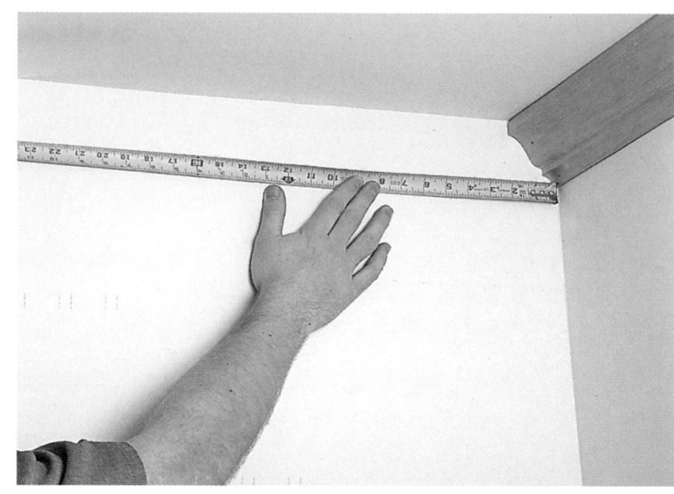

5 Measure out from the corner (plus an extra couple of inches) to find the rough length of the coped molding.

8 Rotate the saw as needed to maneuver the thin blade along the profile of the miter.

9 Use an oval-shaped file (or a round file in tight spots) to clean up curved sections of the profile.

12 Double-check your measurements, and trim off any extra wood from the rough measurement.

13 Adjust and fit the pieces; support the coped piece in place; and drill near the coped end to prevent splitting.

6 Cut the coping miter on another board, and transfer the dimension from Step 5, measuring from the miter tip.

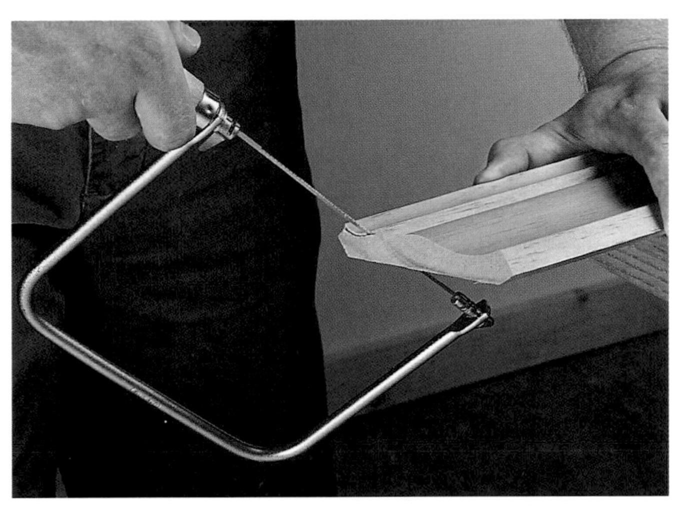

7 Use a coping saw to start the profile cut. Angle the saw to back-cut the coped piece.

10 Use a flat rasp as needed to clean up the upper section of the coped cut or to increase the back-cut angle.

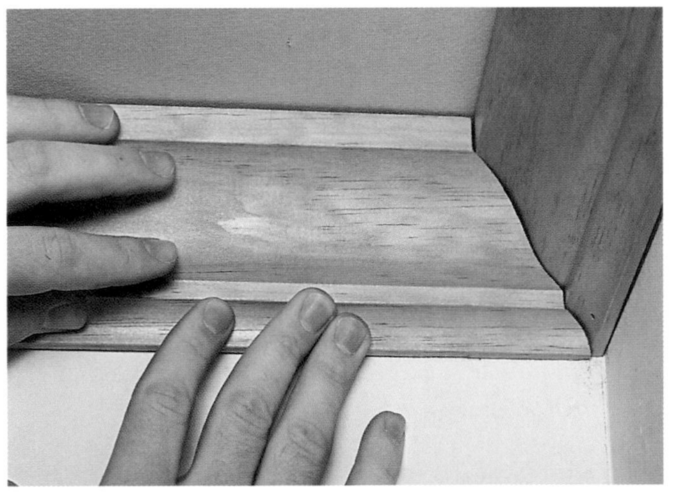

11 Test-fit the coped piece in place, supporting the other end to be sure the board is level.

14 Apply wood glue to sections of the coped end that will make contact with the square-end piece.

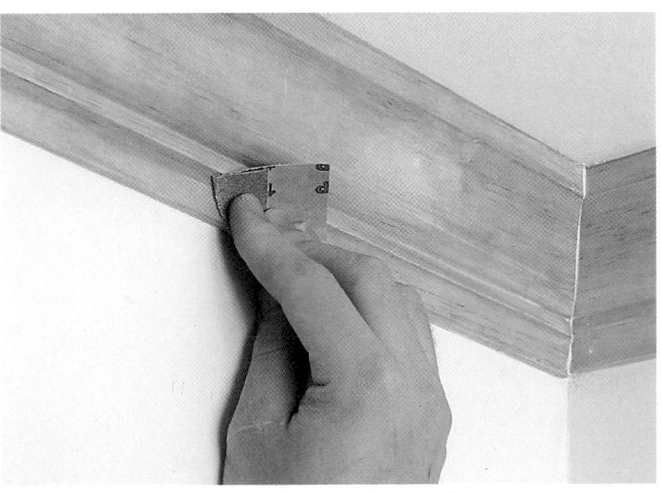

15 To finish, drive and set finishing nails to secure the corner pieces, and sand or caulk the joint as needed.

Installing Plastic Molding

WHAT YOU'LL NEED

- Hand miter box or backsaw
- Pencil, sanding block, and sandpaper
- Caulking gun and construction adhesive
- Hammer, finishing nails, and nail set
- Drywall taping knife, paintbrush, and paint
- Joint compound and crown molding

TRIM TIP: Foam trim is best cut with a backsaw. Power miter saws with fine-toothed blades also work. Larger-toothed blades tend to tear the foam unevenly.

1 With a section of molding held in place, mark guidelines along the top and bottom.

2 After cutting and test-fitting the trim pieces, lay a bead of adhesive just inside your guidelines.

3 Press the molding into the adhesive, and attach it with finishing nails. Sink the nailheads just below the surface.

4 Use a small taping knife and some joint compound to fill any gaps in the corner and to cover all nailheads.

5 After the joint compound, apply a coat of primer. When the primer dries, follow with one or two finish coats.

Nonwood Moldings

Purists may shudder at the idea of using plastic instead of wood. But the truth is that modern synthetics are a very reasonable alternative to wood, as long as you plan to paint. Several companies offer a variety of moldings, including some that are very detailed and complex. The pieces are lightweight, are easy to cut with a saw, and will not shrink or warp the way some wood does. Many firms also offer corner treatments that eliminate complex coping cuts. And in many catalogs, you'll find ceiling medallions and other pieces that are copies of moldings used in historic houses.

All of the moldings *in the photograph at right are made of polyurethane foam, which is easy to cut and install.*

SMART TIP Using Decorative Corner Blocks

Coping and mitering can be difficult, especially in older homes where framing may not be square. An attractive alternative is to use corner blocks like these. The moldings and blocks are polyurethane foam, but wood corner blocks are also available. This system also uses blocks, instead of scarf joints, between pieces in long runs of molding. Be sure to plan where your blocks will fall, and space them evenly along the wall.

Molded fittings *can be used to cover corners where you would have to cope a wood joint.*

Decorative fittings *that complement the molding can also serve at corners instead of compound miter joints.*

Cornices for a Bay Window

As complicated as cornice joints can be in a four-cornered room, they are even more intricate at a bay window. That's because bays introduce angles greater than 90 degrees that require special attention. There are different styles of bays, but many have 135-degree angles, a measurement that is reserved with a detent stop (at 22½ degrees) on the scale of most power miter saws.

On existing windows in old and new houses, you may find some odd angles that are several degrees off the detent stops. Use a sliding T-bevel to capture the angle and transfer it to your saw setup. You can test for a discrepancy using two pieces of scrap and then make minute adjustments to the saw setting, if needed. When you install new windows, you often can find the angle on a measured plan of the unit. If you're careful not to change the angle during window installation, you may find it practical to use the miter-saw detents, which almost automatically result in tight joints, and then use caulk or joint compound to take up any small discrepancies between the molding and the wall.

Laying Out Angle Cuts for Bays

Here's how to make angled molding cuts in bays. First, rotate the saw blade to line up with the blade angle of the sliding T-bevel. Assume that this corresponds with a reading on the saw of 43 degrees. To find the actual molding angle, add 90 for a total of 133 degrees.

SAW SETUP FOR BAY WINDOWS

Bay window installations highlight one of the classic questions about molding joints: should you cut odd angles to fit conditions of the house, or cut standard angles and take up any discrepancies along the lengths of molding? On one side of the question, you can painstakingly measure every odd angle down to a single degree and make minute adjustments in the cutting angles. On the other side of the question, you can use standard saw detents that will provide tight joints, and use caulk to fill slight gaps along the wall and ceiling. This second option works in most situations and may be the easiest approach for novice do-it-yourselfers.

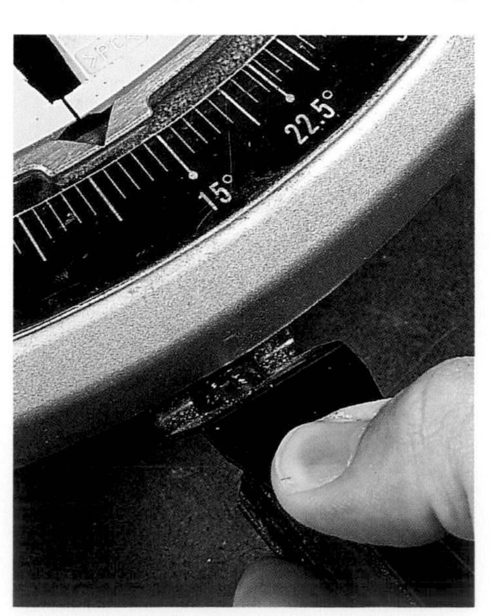

When you release the handle lock *and rotate the saw and table, you'll feel the detents manufactured into the scale.*

Most power miter saws have *detent settings (at 22½ deg.) designed for making miter cuts on bay windows.*

You need a variety of angled joints *to continue crown molding around a bay window.*

Second, divide that angle in half (66½ degrees in this case) to find the cutting angle. To transfer this measurement back to the saw scale and make your cuts, subtract the number from 90 degrees, which in this case is 23½ degrees.

On outside corners, place the crown molding upside down and angled against the fence, set the miter gauge to the left, and cut with the good piece to the right of the blade. Follow the same procedure on the left side of inside corners, and cope the final joint.

Installing the Crown

The safest approach is to use two sets of scrap pieces to check your inside and outside corner joints. Despite all the planning and figuring, you may need to make a few adjustments before duplicating the cuts on your full-length molding stock.

In most cases, you'll be trimming a bay window with two outside corners and four inside corners, but some bays have two inside and two outside corners. If there is a slight variation in the angles on inside corners, you can account for the differences when you shape the coped joints.

If the outside corners are slightly irregular, you have two options. The first is to use the saw detents to cut the joints and then fill any gaps between the molding and the wall or ceiling. The second, which can be time consuming but will probably result in a better-looking job, is to cut and fit pieces for each corner, trimming the back of the miters until you get a tight joint.

***You can extend built-up cornices** to box in windows and conceal drape or blind hardware.*

Built-Up Cornices

Some specialized molding suppliers offer large, complex, and expensive cornice moldings that include details such as dentil blocks and other intricate features. But even if you stick to local sources and more reasonable prices, your molding design does not have to be limited to stock types.

To create larger and more complex trim, or to match an existing pattern, you can combine several different sizes and patterns into one built-up shape.

***The cornice above a doorway,** right, is made by nailing a crown molding on top of an inverted Colonial base molding.*

***The intricate cornice** above combines several moldings, including dentil block and egg-and-dart, for a formal look.*

You install built-ups the same way you install stock cornice. But the job takes longer because you need to repeat the sequences of cutting joints at corners with each layer of different components. For example, you might start with a base panel made of a pine 1×6, trim its bottom edge with cove molding, add a strip of dentil block or egg-and-dart, and continue to build up features in whatever combination you like.

You might experiment with gluing and nailing together built-up lengths on the bench and installing the elements as a group. This may be possible if your built-up molding is simple and made of only a few basic shapes. Generally, though, it creates difficult conditions and unsatisfactory results at the joints.

Here's a recap of some of the most important installation points. First, establish a level reference line on the wall for the bottom edge of the cornice. On all but the most irregular walls and ceilings, keep the trim level, which helps you to make tight joints, and fill small gaps along walls and ceilings with joint compound or caulk.

Nail the bottom of the molding to wall studs and the top to ceiling joists. Studs and joists often fall in the same line, but you should check with a stud finder (or test with a finishing nail) to be sure of their locations. Where joists run parallel with the wall and don't provide nailing support, add nailing blocks or try to reach the wall top plate with 16d finishing nails.

Most cabinet manufacturers *offer crown molding that matches their cabinets as an option, opposite top.*

Combine individual molding profiles, *above, to create a built-up cornice that looks like one piece.*

Polyurethane products, *opposite bottom, can duplicate the look of just about any classic molding profile.*

In traditional homes, *left, crown moldings add a touch of elegance that completes the design.*

A cornice, *right, provides a transition between the wall and the sloping ceiling and ties the gable-end wall to the rest of the room.*

Coping Chair Rails

WHAT YOU'LL NEED

- Clamps and measuring tape
- Utility knife and coping saw
- Flat and round rasps
- Chair rail molding

TRIM TIP: If the teeth of your rasp tend to break out thin edges of the cope, try wrapping the rasp with sandpaper to make fine adjustments.

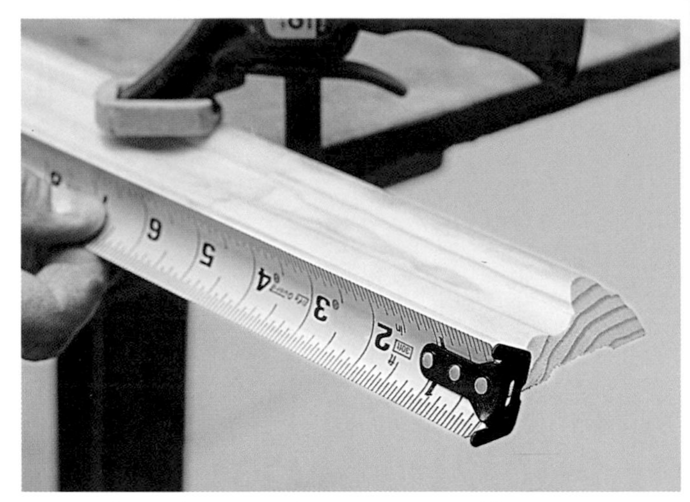

1 Make a miter cut, and measure the molding. Leave an extra inch or two in case you need to trim the cope.

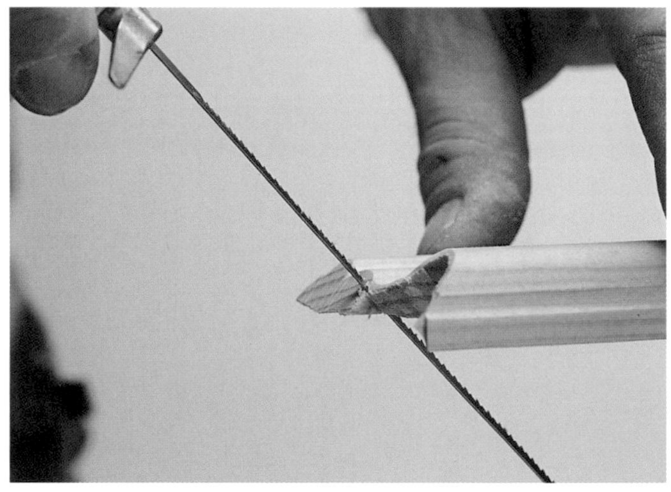

4 Back-cut the molding along the line of the miter. Be careful not to make the edge too thin.

5 Use a tapered, half-round rasp to clean up the edges of the rounded surfaces along the edge of the cut.

Picture Rails, Chair Rails & Friezes

The picture rail was developed to hang framed pictures without damaging plaster walls. Instead of driving a nail for each picture frame, the idea is to hang supporting hooks on the strip of molding.

When installed below cornices, a picture rail also doubles as frieze molding, which creates an upper horizontal band of wall surface. That band is often treated differently from the main wall surface—for example, with wallpaper or a complementary paint color.

The chair rail is another molding component that has more than just a decorative function. The idea is that a chair pushed back from a table will bump the wood molding instead of damaging the wall surface.

These three elements—picture rail, frieze, and chair rail (plus base molding, covered in the next section)—can be used either by themselves or in combination to decorate a wall.

INSTALLING PICTURE RAILS

A picture rail is easy to install compared with complex, angled cornices. If you are installing the feature on one

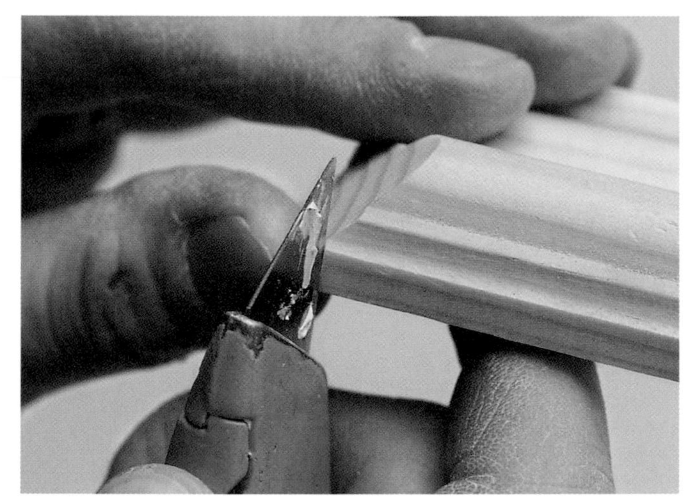

2 Use a utility knife to trim off the feathered edge of the miter cut, which is easily broken during assembly.

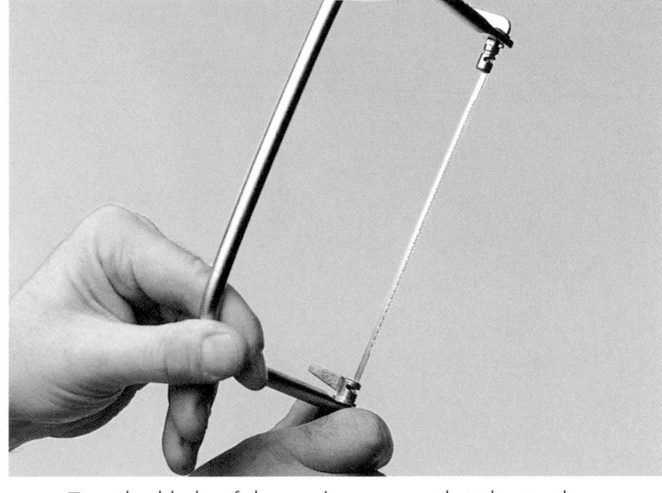

3 Turn the blade of the coping saw so that the teeth are facing at a right angle to the bow of the saw.

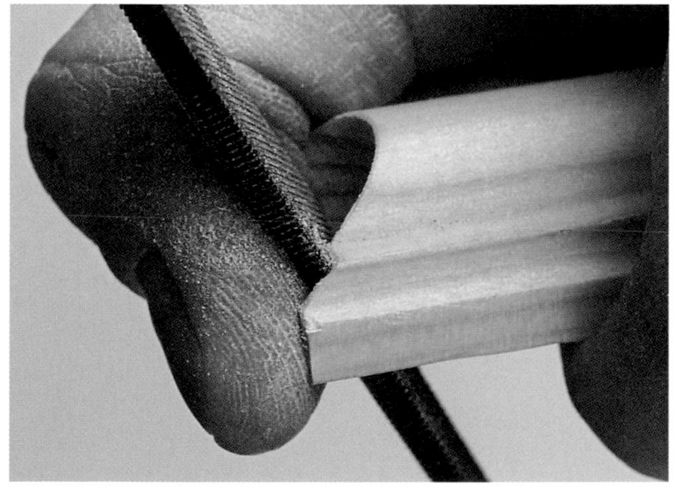

6 Use a flat rasp (or laminate file) to clean up square edges where the profile will fit against the adjoining piece.

7 Test the cut on a piece of molding with the same profile, and make final adjustments as needed before fastening.

wall, simply square-cut the ends and fasten the piece to the wall studs.

In special cases where you plan to hang large frames, consider using larger molding stock and screws (pre-drilled and countersunk into wall studs), which have more holding power than nails. Match the picture rail to the picture framing hooks or other hanging systems to be sure the connections will be secure.

Installing Friezes

To make a frieze in a room with an 8-foot ceiling, consider using 1-inch panel molding instead of picture rail molding. In rooms with high ceilings, larger stock is fine, although it should be considerably smaller than the cornice molding.

You have four main options for finishing a frieze: add wallpaper, add a decorative paint finish, leave the upper band with the same finish as the rest of the wall and use the trim as an accent, or simply add a different color or tone of paint to the frieze.

The proportion of the upper band to the main wall is a matter of taste. But if you're adding wallpaper, you may want to adjust the frieze strip slightly so that the paper pattern will be balanced in the space.

Installing Chair Rails

WHAT YOU'LL NEED

- Chalk-line box and pencil
- Moldings and saws
- Hammer and nails or nail gun
- Wood glue and wood filler
- Sanding block and sandpaper

TRIM TIP: If you use a pneumatic nailer, check the molding surface before finishing to be sure that all nailheads are set below the surface.

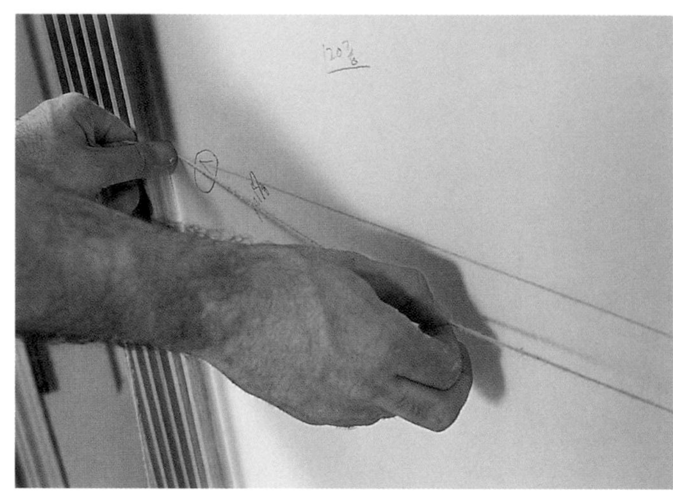

1 After establishing the height of your chair rail, use a chalk line to mark a level line across the wall.

2 Attach a cleat, such as a 1x4 (planed to ½ in.) with ogee, below your line; mark the 45-deg. reveal cut on the cap.

3 Run a liberal bead of glue along the cleat, serving as the main rail, to strengthen the connection to the cap piece.

4 Fasten the cap to the rail using a hammer and finishing nails or a pneumatic finish nailer.

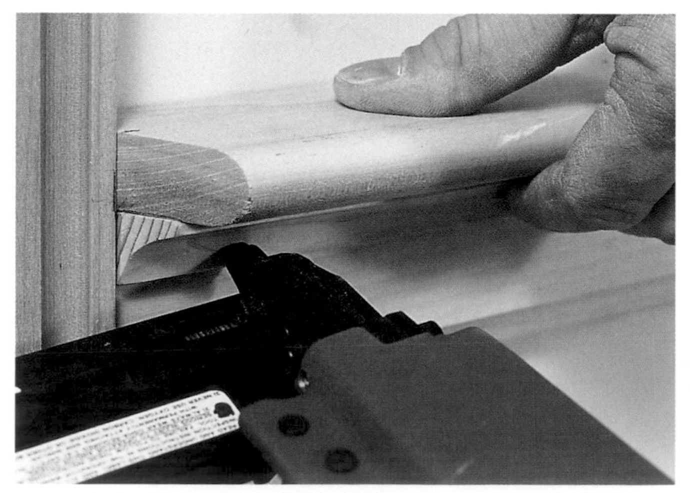

5 Finish the installation by attaching a cove molding below the cap. Then fill nailholes and sand all surfaces.

Installing Chair Rails

You can buy stock chair rail profiles, which tend to be fairly narrow, or build your own custom trim. The choice depends partly on how you will treat the space between the rail and the base molding along the floor—painting, papering, or covering it with paneling or wall frames.

To build up a chair rail, start with a main board of 1×4 poplar or D Select pine, and mill a cove detail into both edges of the board. You can also use different router bits to add beading or groove details. You might want to use the board with milled edges only, or add more depth to the chair rail by building up the center section with a combination of moldings.

To cap off wainscoting, you might want a chair rail that resembles typical trim along a windowsill. A top piece with a rounded edge can serve as a shelf. Below this piece you can install an apron that trims the top of the wainscot paneling.

A chair rail *makes a distinctive dividing line between flat-surfaced and framed sections of walls.*

You can extend a basic chair rail *with a plate rail, typically with a groove that holds plates propped up for display.*

A high-profile chair rail *can be used to cap off a wall-frame treatment and mirror the frame details.*

The base trim *on this Arts and Crafts bottom rail is a simple baseboard with cap and shoe molding.*

When you plan custom bases, *consider the height of obstructions such as baseboard heaters or registers.*

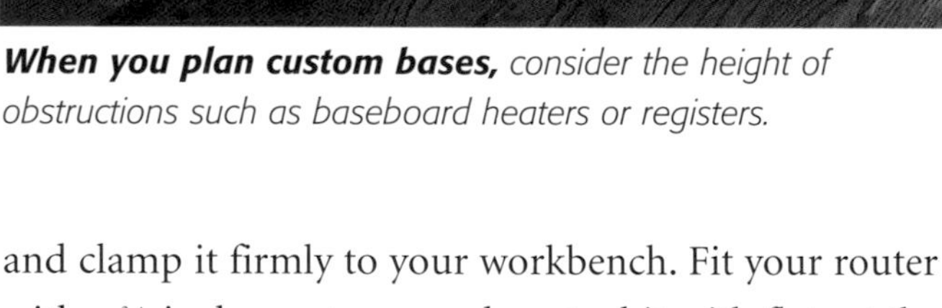

Baseboard Trim

You have many base trim options. For example, you can buy stock Colonial-style bases as tall as $5\frac{1}{2}$ inches, which may be fine in most rooms. But these boards are slightly less than $\frac{1}{2}$ inch thick and often look too thin on their own, although they can serve well as part of a built-up base treatment.

About the smallest built-up base that will look good is a 1×4 board with a base cap molding. In many houses, you'll want the more substantial look of primed pine 1×6 stock that is often finger-jointed and available in 16-foot lengths. These boards come primed on all four sides and are often in better condition than standard pine boards.

Routing Details into Stock

You can build up a base with combinations of different moldings. But you also can rout the details you like into plain-faced stock. To begin, select the better side of the board, which is usually the side that is primed more smoothly. Clean up the face with a light sanding, and clamp it firmly to your workbench. Fit your router with a $\frac{3}{8}$-inch quarter-round router bit with flats at the top and bottom. Then make some test cuts, and set the depth as needed.

Run the router across the top front edge of the board, but don't try to remove all of the wood in a single pass. Instead, use a series of passes, increasing the depth of cut each time, and finish by hand-sanding any chatter marks. A foam sanding block works well for this.

Base Trim Installations

In rooms with level floors and plumb walls, installing base trim is a straightforward job. If the floor has a few ups and downs, it's a little more complicated.

Generally, if a floor is out of level no more than $\frac{1}{2}$ inch, you can install the baseboard level and cover any gaps with base shoe molding. (This isn't a problem in carpeted rooms.) But if the floor is out of level more than $\frac{1}{2}$ inch, you'll need to plane the bottom of the baseboard or rip it at an angle to fit. If you plan to install wall frames for wainscoting, the top of the base trim needs to be level all around the room.

Routing Base Profiles

WHAT YOU'LL NEED

- ◆ Router and bit
- ◆ Clamps
- ◆ Lumber

TRIM TIP: To prevent friction burns as you rout details along the edge of a board, use a bit with a roller guide. It moves slowly along the board while the bit shank spins at high speed inside and away from the wood.

1 Select a profiling bit with a roller guide that rides along the edge of the board.

2 Set the router on the edge of the board to see the depth of the bit. You may want to make a test cut on scrap.

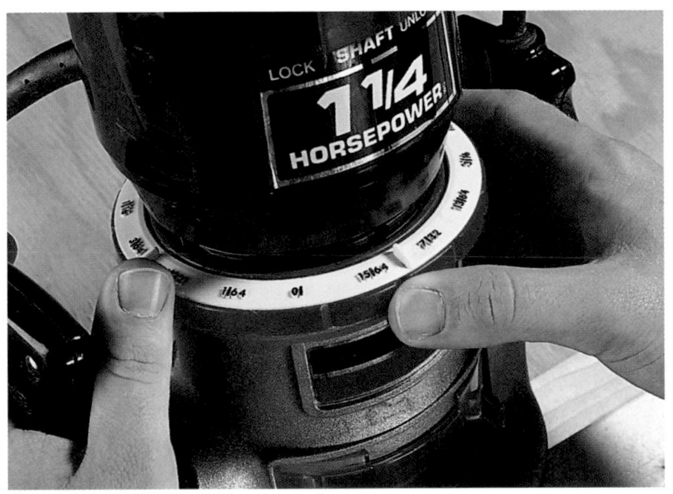

3 Adjust the depth of cut on the router. Some have a collar on the housing; others have a calibrated knob.

4 To work safely, clamp the board securely to a bench, and be sure the clamps are out of the router's path.

5 Always make your cut pushing against the rotation of the bit, and use multiple passes to avoid chatter marks.

Establishing Floor Levels

Working off of a level reference line, determine the distance from the line to the floor on each side of the room and at both sides of all doorways and passageways. The shortest distance between the reference line and the floor indicates the floor's high point. The greatest distance indicates the low point.

If the difference between the low and high points is more than ½ inch, it's best to trim the bottom of the baseboard where it traverses the higher floor areas. Remember that you have some margin to play with because the shoe molding or carpeting will hide gaps. As a general rule, you can raise the base over the lower areas of the floor by about ½ inch, which reduces the amount of trimming.

Installing Base Trim

When you install base trim, it's good practice to cope all inside corners and miter all outside corners. You may want to make some test cuts on coped joints, particularly if the room has irregular surfaces.

You can attach base trim to the wall with panel adhesive and add carpenter's glue to the joints. (Most carpenters also drive finishing nails into the wall's 2×4 soleplate and into studs every 16 inches.) To reduce the number of holes (at least on smaller bases), you can take several steps to conceal most if not all of the nails.

Baseboard Gap Detail

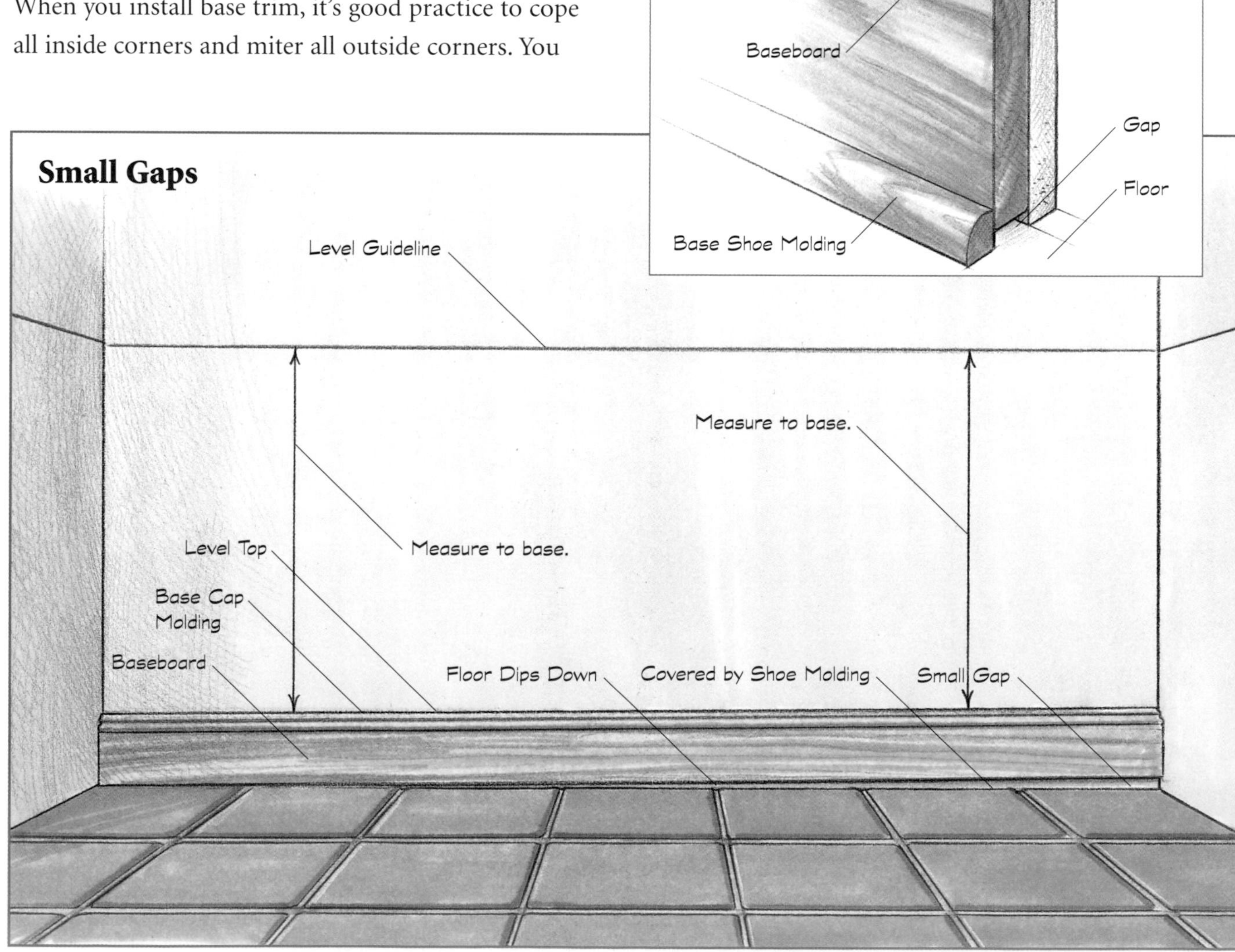

First, apply at least one coat of primer and finish paint to raw baseboard before installation. (If you are using primed, finger-jointed boards, give them a second coat of primer.) Then nail the bottom of the baseboard close enough to the floor so that the shoe molding will cover the nailholes. Follow by toenailing through the top edge of the baseboard into wall studs so that the cap molding will conceal them.

Remember, though, that toenailing can cause splitting along the edges of the base. You will gain fastening power, which is important on larger bases, if you also sink at least one nail through the middle of the board into each stud.

Finish base trim *with shoe molding (often a quarter round) along the floor and base cap molding that matches the surrounding trim style.*

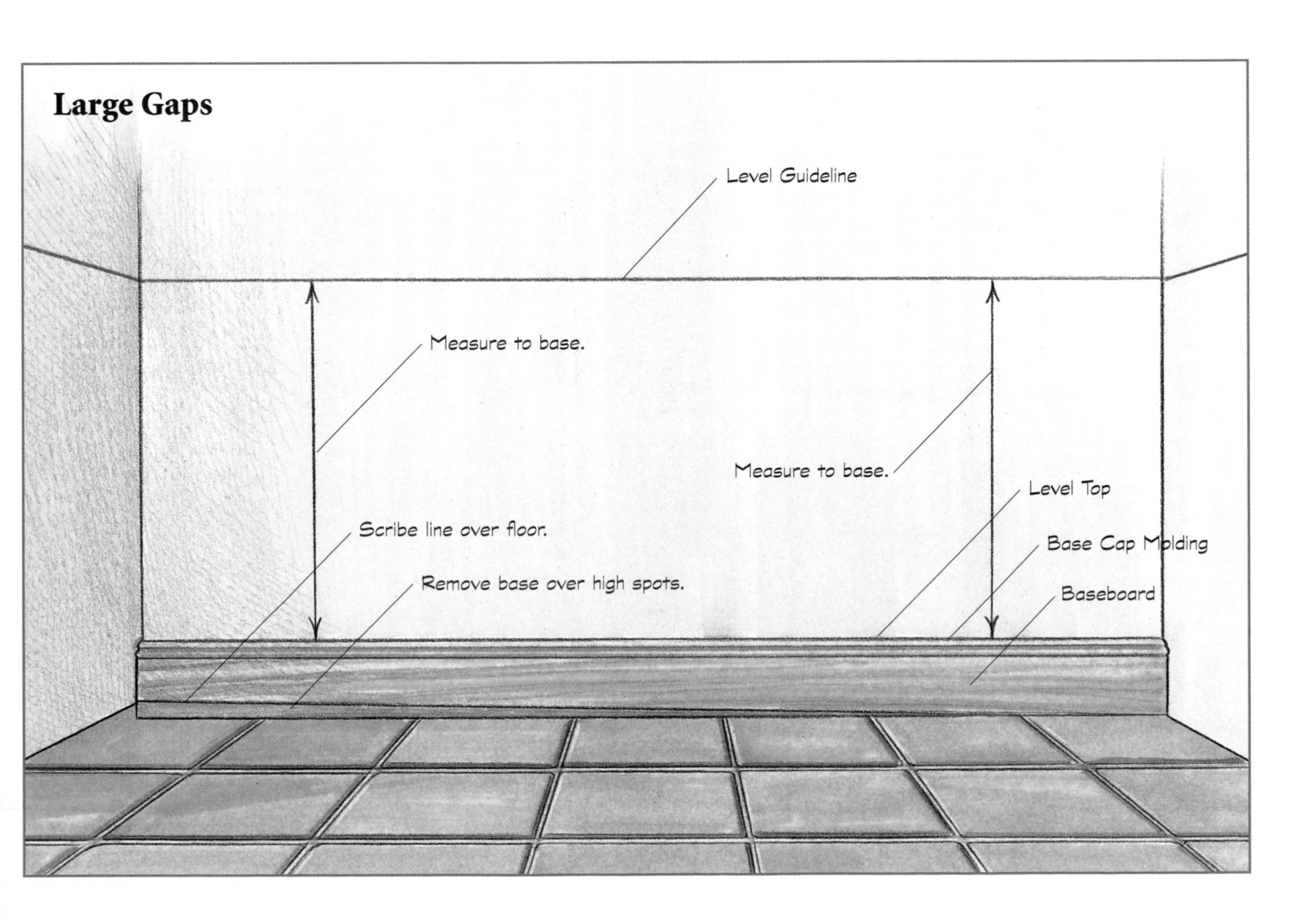

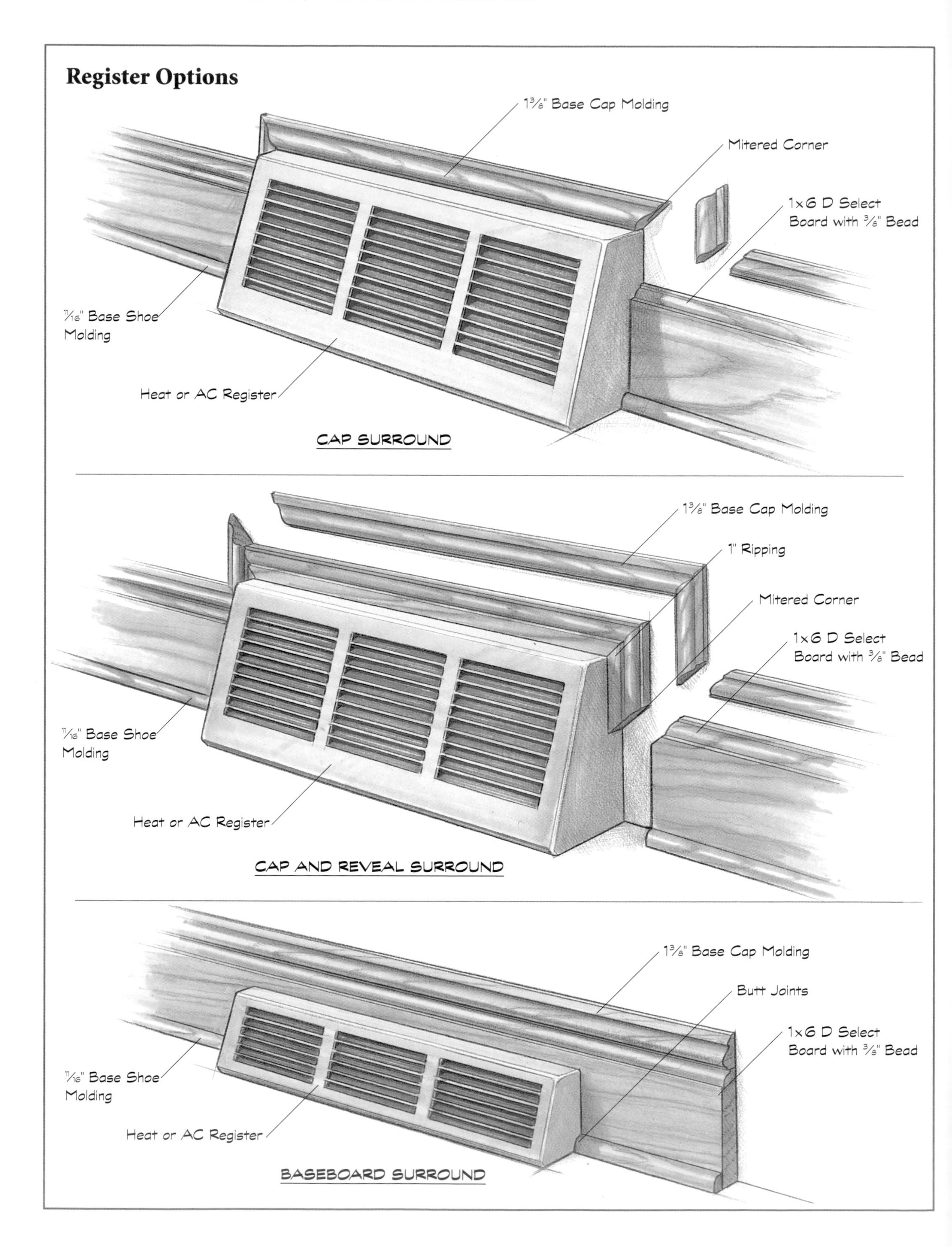
Register Options
1⅜" Base Cap Molding
Mitered Corner
1x6 D Select Board with ⅜" Bead
11/16" Base Shoe Molding
Heat or AC Register
CAP SURROUND
1⅜" Base Cap Molding
1" Ripping
Mitered Corner
1x6 D Select Board with ⅜" Bead
11/16" Base Shoe Molding
Heat or AC Register
CAP AND REVEAL SURROUND
1⅜" Base Cap Molding
Butt Joints
1x6 D Select Board with ⅜" Bead
11/16" Base Shoe Molding
Heat or AC Register
BASEBOARD SURROUND

Installing Base Cap Molding

Cap molding makes a nice finishing detail along the base. But most cap molding has a fairly fragile profile that tends to splinter during cutting. To reduce splintering, place a thin strip of wood not much taller than the base cap between the cap and the saw fence.

You may also need to make some adjustments to the standard installation around heat registers. Some are taller than typical built-up base trim, and some are shorter. You can deal with these situations in either of two ways. Both require planning the entire base layout carefully in advance.

One approach is to butt the sides of the baseboard to the sides of the register and to run the base cap molding over the exposed top, mitering the base cap from corner to corner. Another approach is to set both the base cap molding and the top inch of the baseboard over the register so that it appears to be inset.

Because the register covers are removable, you can simply run the base across the wall in some cases, mark the area of the supply duct, make a corresponding cutout in the base, and install the register cover on top of the molding.

It's important to use glue and nails to fasten molding joints securely around heat registers because the flow of hot air can cause more than standard wood shrinkage. With painted moldings, it helps to prime the backs and edges of the molding.

This register *is neatly framed by carrying the top couple of inches of the baseboard and base cap molding around the top edges.*

A chair rail and picture rail, *above, add dimension to a wall.*

The frieze area, *above right, complements the main wall color.*

Baseboard treatments, *right, tie other molding elements together.*

Painted baseboards, *below, can make receptacles less obtrusive.*

The wall treatment *of the frieze area, above, echoes the color scheme of the stairway in the room beyond.*

CHAPTER 8

CREATING WALL FRAMES

Wall frames can add a custom trimwork touch to any room but tend to work best in formal rooms, such as living and dining rooms. Looking like a series of large picture frames, they can provide an elegant raised-pattern design along a bare stretch of wall. For a more sophisticated approach, paint the interiors of the panels a complementary color, creating a three-dimensional illusion of differing depths and densities. Combine them with a distinctive chair rail and baseboard molding for a truly unique trimwork treatment—one that is appropriate for a variety of house styles and designs. Installing wall frames is easier for the average do-it-yourselfer to accomplish than raised-panel wainscoting, and after you master a few basic techniques, you'll find that the frames go up quickly.

Three-dimensional wall frames, *a picture rail, and an elaborate cornice accentuate the drama of this sitting room.*

Design Basics

Wall framing dates to the mid-1700s, the Georgian period, when plaster began to replace wooden wall panels in the decoration of homes.

Pioneered in the 1750s by British architect John Adam, wall frames provided elegant accents for large expanses of flat plaster and helped popularize contrasting color schemes, enhancing a room's sense of space. Over the next hundred years, wall frames became standard in European interiors. Heavy wooden paneling did not return to vogue until the Victorian era.

Wall-frame trimwork divides walls into large, aesthetically pleasing units. It makes a stronger statement than you can make with paint or wallpaper alone. You can design and install a wall-frame treatment just below a chair rail or both above and below it. The frames above the rail maintain the same width and the same spacing from other elements on the wall as those below. A well-designed wall-frame treatment follows these basic design principles.

Scale and Proportion. In a well-proportioned design, the base molding is taller than the chair rail, and the chair rail looks more substantial than the door and window casings. The molding used in the wall frames is the smallest element on the wall. But all of these elements should be scaled to the size of the room.

Balance. In a symmetrical arrangement, if a wall can hold only three wall frames, you can make the middle one wider. If a wall can hold five frames, make the middle and two end frames narrower. You can even use both approaches in the same room when doors and windows dictate fewer or more frames.

Rhythm. Repetition of an element, such as a wall frame, gives a design a feeling of rhythm and draws the eye along. You can also create rhythm by progressing from small to large elements and by contrasting differing frame sizes.

Emphasis. Wall frames lend dramatic emphasis to the lower wall and serve as a pedestal for the middle portion of the wall. If you choose not to use wall frames below the chair rail, using different wallpapers above and below can have a similar but less effective impact.

Harmony. Architecturally speaking, harmony is a pleasing balance between diversity and unity. Diversity comes from the intersections of various horizontal and vertical moldings on the wall, and the repetition of the wall frames shows a unity of design.

***This wall-frame treatment** exhibits the principles of scale and proportion, balance, rhythm, emphasis, and harmony.*

The paint scheme *in this newly remodeled room emphasizes the uniformity of the vertical and horizontal margins.*

Intervals

An interval is the area within an individual wall frame, defined by the frame's outside dimensions. Unlike margins, for which dimensions must be constant (except for special areas like bays with windows), interval width and height can vary as needed to accommodate placement of doors, passageways, windows, fireplaces, and other elements.

Arriving at the right wall-frame size and shape is largely a matter of intuition. Basic design concepts presented in this chapter will help guide you in the process, but by just holding the margins constant and allowing the dimensions of the intervals to expand and contract (within reason) in response to wall runs, you can maintain an overall sense of proportion, balance, and continuity.

Margins

Margins are the spaces above, below, and in between wall frames. A margin of $2\frac{3}{4}$ to 3 inches usually looks best. You can make all the margins identical in a design, or you might want to vary the margins above and below the frames a little. Try making both the top and bottom margins wider, or make just the top margin narrower. As a general rule, the difference should be $\frac{1}{2}$ inch or less, and no margin should ever be less than $2\frac{1}{2}$ inches.

You can break from uniform margins near windows or in narrow wall sections on one or both sides of a door. You can also reduce horizontal margins under a window. When a space is too narrow to insert a wall frame, just leave it empty.

Under a window, make the wall-frame width line up with the outside edges of the window casing. For a bay window, this usually means that the vertical margins between the frames under the windows will differ greatly from those on the rest of the wall.

The wall frames *in this bay line up with the window casings, and the vertical margins are wider than those in the rest of the room.*

Design Gold

The underlying principle for selecting intervals in a wall-frame treatment is known as the Golden Rectangle, a concept conceived by the architects of ancient Greece. According to this concept, the eye finds the shape of a rectangle more pleasing than that of a square. The principle further holds that the ideal dimensions for a rectangle occur in a ratio of approximately 3 : 2. (See "Golden Rectangle," right.) You can rely on this time-tested principle for interval shapes and dimensions.

When determining dimensions for a series of wall frames, consider the overall look you want to achieve. Do you have standard 8-foot-high walls or custom 9- or 10-footers? Is the room a cavernous great room or a more intimate sitting room? The impact of the look will be determined by the height and orientation of the wall frames and the subsequent rhythm they generate.

Horizontal versus Vertical Orientation

Wall-frame treatments 36 inches or less in height are generally designed using horizontal frames, that is, with their longer sides horizontal. This orientation results in a restrained, moderated look. (In small rooms, narrow, vertical frames may work well.) Install the top edge of the chair rail at 32 or 36 inches for this treatment. You can incorporate a subrail in the design if you place the chair rail at 36 inches but not at 32 inches. At the latter, shorter height, the four elements (chair rail, subrail, wall frames, base molding) would be too crowded for a pleasing appearance.

Wall frames in a vertical orientation are generally more suitable for designs in which the chair rail is at a height of 60 inches. This height is most appropriate for 9-foot or taller walls and may be overwhelming on 8-foot or shorter walls. The tall and narrow shape gives the frames more presence: at these heights, they are especially effective in larger rooms. The main benefits of this orientation are a heightened sense of rhythm and texture as well as an increased emphasis of the frame's vertical properties. Use a tall, substantial base molding to help the design look rooted.

GOLDEN RECTANGLE

One time-honored architectural design principle holds that the ideal size for a rectangle is one in which one side is a little over 1.5 times larger than an adjacent side. (The actual aspect ratio is 1 : 0.635, or 1.575 : 1.) The drawings below illustrate the basis for the principle and a practical application.

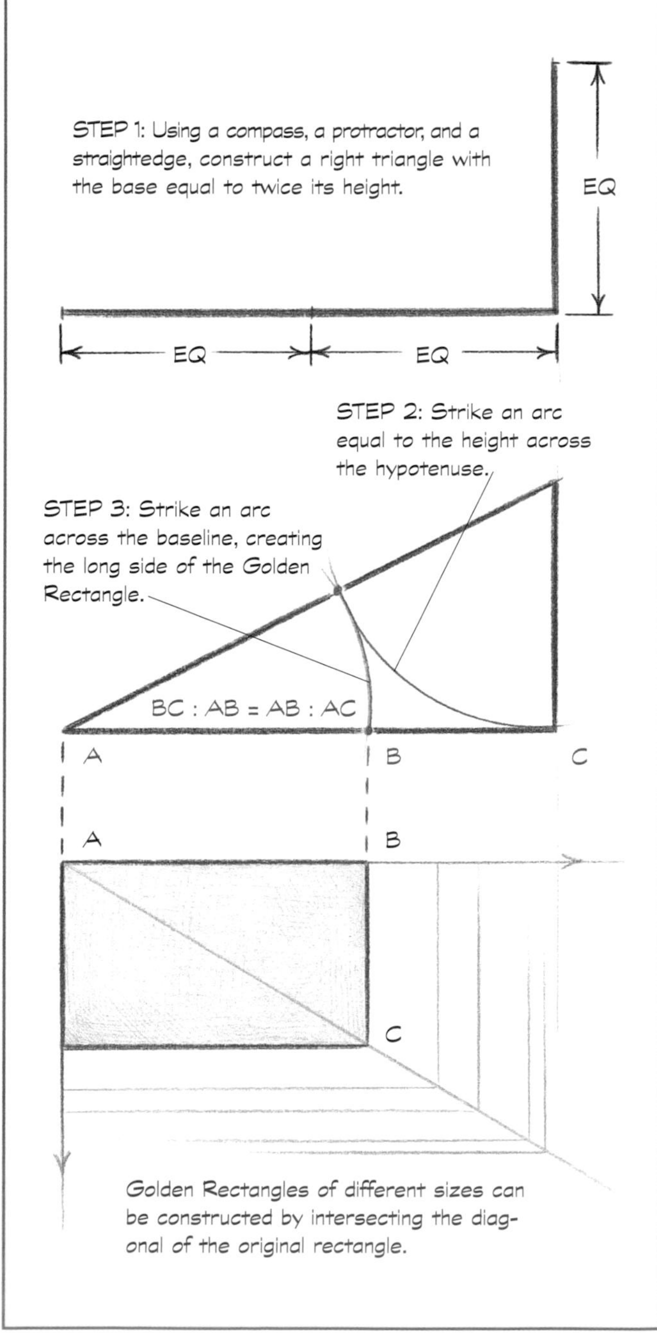

Golden Rectangles of different sizes can be constructed by intersecting the diagonal of the original rectangle.

Exceptions to the rule *abound in real-world applications: these wall frames depart from the Golden Rectangle ideal, but their design suits the situation beautifully.*

Tall wall frames *make a grand statement in the dining room below, and the vertical orientation and bright color treatment impart a feeling of energy.*

Horizontal and vertical orientation of wall frames greatly affects the rhythm of the treatment. The wider the wall-frame intervals are, the more time it takes the eye to make the transition from one interval to the next as its field of vision travels across the wall. Therefore, horizontal wall frames impart the feeling of a slower, more passive pace, whereas vertical frames give the impression of a faster, more active pace. The idea of rhythm and pace can be further enhanced by the color scheme you choose when you paint: brighter colors for vertical treatments; more subdued colors for horizontal frames.

Wall Frame Layouts

Measure each wall run in the room, making allowances for doorways, windows, and other openings. Estimate how many ideally sized wall-frame intervals will fit into each run. With your estimate in hand, fill out the worksheet at left for each wall.

DETERMINING VERTICAL DIMENSIONS

In a room with either an 8- or 9-foot ceiling, the recommended chair-rail height is 32, 36, or 60 inches. Avoid heights between 36 and 60 inches, or the room will appear cut in half horizontally.

To determine the vertical dimension of a wall frame, put your own dimensions into the following steps:

- Width of chair rail **3½"**
- Width of margin between bottom of chair rail and top of subrail **3"**
- Width of subrail **1"**
- Width of upper horizontal margin **3"**
- Width of lower horizontal margin **3"**
- Height of base molding **6⅞"**
- Height of chair rail minus sum of vertical dimensions **(36" – 20⅜") =15⅝"**

The result is a wall-frame height of **15⅝** inches.

DEALING WITH OUTLETS AND SWITCHES

If a vertical side of a wall frame falls on an electrical outlet, either move the outlet or install an outlet box extension and a spacer frame into which you can butt the side of the wall frame. (See the photo opposite.)

Turn off the power to the outlet at the circuit breaker; then remove the outlet cover and the outlet's two mounting screws. Pull the outlet out of its box. Slip it through a ¾-inch box extension, and line up the mounting holes among the outlet, box extension, and box. Using mounting screws ¾ inch longer than the original ones, fasten the outlet through the extension.

To make the frame, rip an 18-inch piece of one-by stock down to a width of ¾ inch. From that, assemble a

Wall Frames Worksheet

Use the information given in this worksheet to determine the width of your wall-frame intervals. First, estimate how many intervals would fit each run of wall yet be equivalent to each other. For example, if you had a 12 × 18-foot room, you might make an estimate based on 36-inch-wide intervals. The 12-foot wall would have four, and the 18-foot wall would have six. (Of course, the actual intervals will end up being smaller, just over 32 inches, because you'll have to account for 3-inch margins. This is merely to arrive at an estimated number of intervals with which to work.) Then make the following calculations for each wall:

Length of wall run **(L of WR)**
Width of vertical margins **(W of VM)**
Number of intervals **(# of I)**
Number of vertical margins **(# of VM)**
(proposed number of intervals plus one)

1. (W of VM × # of VM)

2. (L of WR - Step 1)

3. (Step 2 ÷ # of I)

4. Total from Step 3 = average interval width

Continue modifying estimates for each wall run until you are able to determine the closest possible sets of interval widths for all the walls in a room.

TRIM TIP: Depending on the room, widths of wall frames usually vary from wall to wall. This is okay as long as you keep variations as small as possible while trying to maintain dimensions close to the ideal 1:0.635 ratio of the Golden Rectangle. Of course, doors and windows will dictate exceptions to this rule.

The Dynamics of Height

32" Wall-Frame Treatment with Horizontal Frame

36" Wall-Frame Treatment with Horizontal Frame

36" Wall-Frame Treatment with Vertical Frames

60" Wall-Frame Treatment with Vertical Frames

four-sided frame with mitered corners, just long and wide enough to accommodate the box extension. The exterior dimensions of the frame will be slightly larger than those of the outlet cover. Ease the outside edges of the frame with sandpaper. Apply dots of panel adhesive to the back of the frame, and slip the frame over the extended outlet. The outlet's "ears" may extend just a bit past the extension, so you may have to cut shallow grooves in the inside top and bottom of the frame to clear them. Replace the outlet cover.

Then, when it comes time for installation, you'll hold the wall frame in position, mark where it intersects the outlet, cut that section out, and install the frame as usual. Switches present an obstacle only if the chair rail is at 60 inches. In this case, consider moving the switch. Call an electrician if you're not familiar with moving switch boxes and other electrical work.

Electrical outlets *may interrupt wall frames. In these cases, install an electrical box extension, make a wooden box to enclose the extension, and allow the side segments to butt the frame.*

A single motif unit, *which comprises a wide interval flanked by narrow intervals, is seen clearly on this wall.*

Repeating Wall Frames

As you think about the design of your wall-frame treatment, you might want to make use of a motif (a repeated design) of different frame sizes. A motif in which a wide wall frame is flanked by narrow ones establishes a rhythm of narrow-wide-narrow—an example of bilateral symmetry.

Each section of a wall-frame motif (narrow-wide-narrow) is called a unit. Typically, a short run of wall will contain a single unit, and a longer run of wall might contain two. You'd need an unusually long wall to accommodate three or more units.

The total number of narrow intervals must always exceed the total number of wide intervals by one. In addition, when you use more than one unit on a wall, a narrow interval must always serve as a narrow flank between the unit just ended and the unit just beginning. Therefore, two units of a motif will look like this: narrow-wide-narrow-wide-narrow.

Motifs enhance the dynamics of a wall. To determine the width of both narrow and wide intervals in such a design, see "Motifs Worksheet," right.

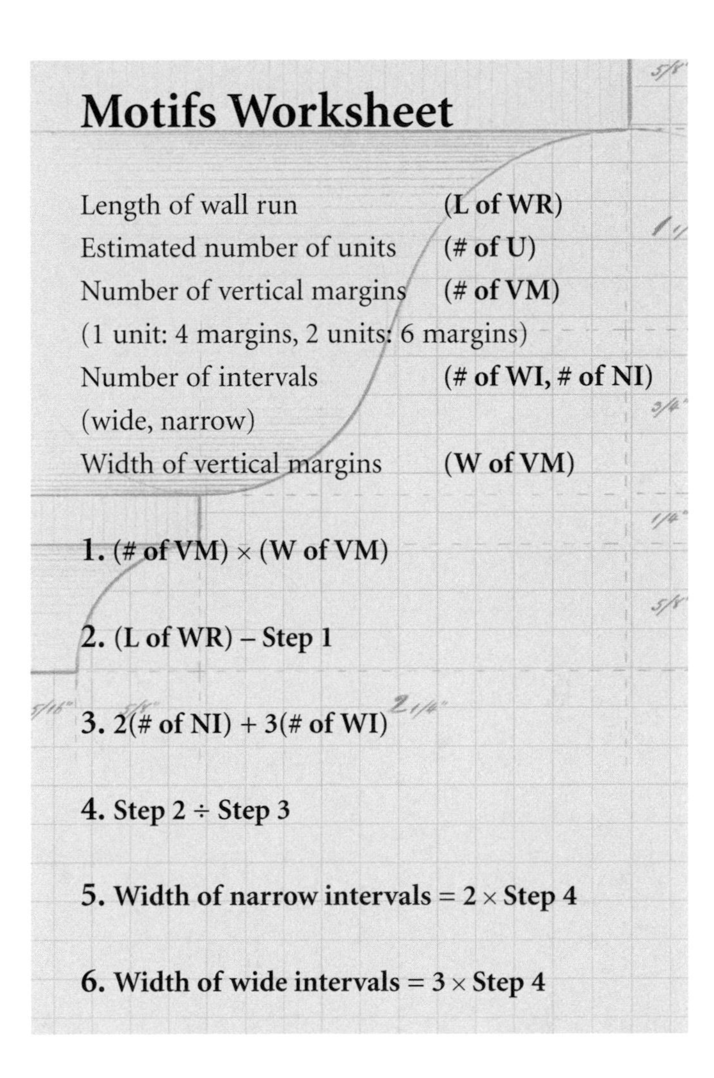

Motifs Worksheet

Length of wall run	(L of WR)
Estimated number of units	(# of U)
Number of vertical margins (1 unit: 4 margins, 2 units: 6 margins)	(# of VM)
Number of intervals (wide, narrow)	(# of WI, # of NI)
Width of vertical margins	(W of VM)

1. **(# of VM) × (W of VM)**

2. **(L of WR) – Step 1**

3. **2(# of NI) + 3(# of WI)**

4. **Step 2 ÷ Step 3**

5. **Width of narrow intervals = 2 × Step 4**

6. **Width of wide intervals = 3 × Step 4**

DRAMA FOR YOUR WALLS

Wall frames create an illusion of depth and density because 1) they are three-dimensional and 2) they divide the wall area into smaller, denser segments. The three-dimensional quality of wall frames is fundamentally different from that of the alternative treatment: raised panels. Despite the name, raised panels actually produce a concave-like, or receding, effect whereas wall frames are more convex, protruding outward. In terms of sculpture, concave units create negative space while convex units create positive space. Raised panels, therefore, deliver a uniform sense of volume, mass, and density, while wall frames create a higher level of tension and dramatic interest.

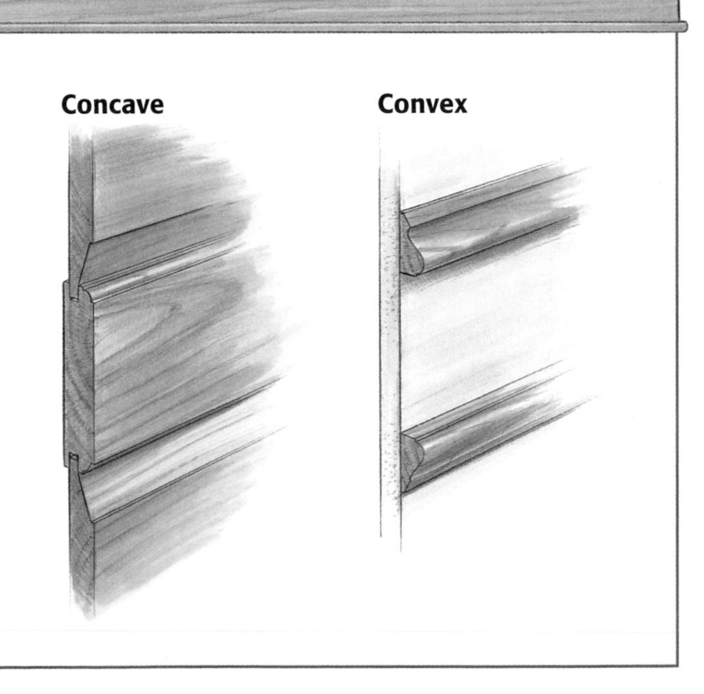

Installing Wall Frames

What You'll Need

- Power drill with screwdriver bit and 3/4" drywall screws
- Pneumatic nailer or hammer and nails
- Power saw (to cut plywood, etc.)
- Measuring tape, pencil, and level
- Scrap plywood and one-by lumber
- Base cap molding for wall frames

TRIM TIP: The quickest, most accurate way to attach each wall frame to the wall is to use a spacer block below the rail rather than trying to align the frame with a guideline.

1 Attach a small piece of plywood (with two adjacent factory edges) to a 2 x 2-ft. sheet. Leave a margin of 1⅜ in.

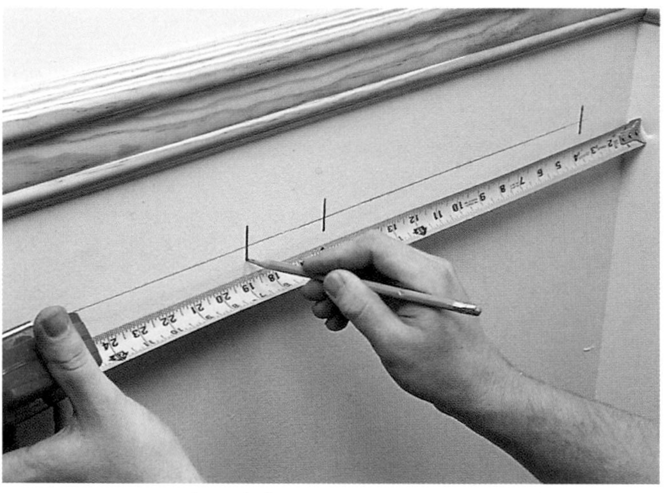

4 Measure and mark the top corners of each wall frame along the guideline. Then apply adhesive to the first frame.

5 Using the spacer block from Step 3, align the wall frame with the corner marks, and fasten it in place using 6d nails.

Assembling Wall Frames

The most frequently used molding for making wall frames is base cap molding, also called panel molding. Its dimensions are usually 11/16 × 1⅜ inches.

Do not install wall frames piece by piece on the wall. It's quicker and more accurate to assemble wall frames on a table using a jig prior to installation.

Wall-Frame Assembly Jig

To make an assembly jig, screw a square corner of a piece of scrap plywood onto a larger piece of plywood (at least 2 × 2 feet), leaving the equivalent width of the molding on two adjacent sides of the larger piece. (See "Installing Wall Frames,"above.)

This will allow you to press glued edges of mitered molding tightly together on the jig and sink brads into each side of the joint using a hammer or a pneumatic brad nailer. Begin by joining long sides and short sides. Then join pairs of the two-sided units.

Try to make each wall frame using the same molding stock from the same source (and the same bundle if possible). Otherwise, there is high probability that the profiles of the molding won't line up exactly.

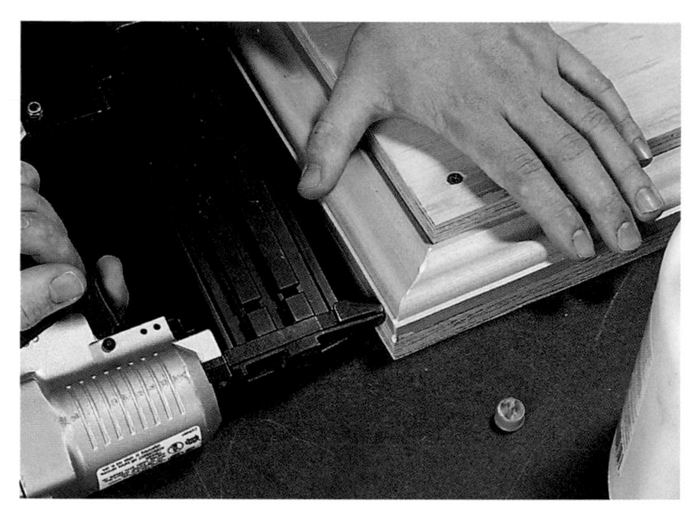

2 Apply glue to the mitered ends, and fasten them using an air nailer or hammer and brads. Keep your fingers clear.

3 Cut a block the same width as the top margin, place it against the chair rail, and scribe a guideline on the wall.

6 With the top edge fastened, plumb the vertical sides of the frame using a level, and attach them using 6d finishing nails.

7 Double-check that the bottom of the frame is level, and then fasten it. Fill all holes, and caulk all around the frame.

Installing Wall Frames

Cut a small block the size of the top margin, and use it to scribe a line below the chair rail (or subrail, if you're using one) to represent the top edge of the wall frames. Hold the block against the bottom of the rail; hold a pencil at the bottom edge of the block; and slide the block across the rail along all the wall runs. Measure and mark the top corners of each frame on this line.

If you intend to nail the wall frames into place by hand rather than using an air nailer, predrill the wall frame for 6d finishing nails, and insert the nails before positioning the frame on the wall. Because you'll be nailing between studs over most of the wall (so you won't have solid nailing surfaces), you'll need to use panel adhesive to stick the frames to the wall. Using a caulking gun, apply dots (not lines) of adhesive to the back of each frame.

Hold the block you used to draw the reference line up against the chair rail or subrail; butt the frame against it; and nail the top edge. Use a level to plumb the sides; then nail the sides and the bottom edge. Once you've installed all the units in a room, caulk the perimeter of each wall frame, both inside and out.

Case Study: Dining Room with Bay Window

The floor plan on the opposite page shows the room at right, with a bay window and two doors. Here's how to prepare an area like this for a wall-frame treatment:

Measure the lengths of all wall runs. On the walls with windows, measure only the distance between the outside edges of the side casings of each window. Use the worksheet on page 168 for calculating the widths of wall frames to arrive at a suggested width for the frames on each run of wall surface.

Frame Widths

On any given wall, try to make all frames the same width. An exception occurs on a wall with one or more windows. Remember: a wall frame under a window should align with the outside edges of the window's casings.

Make the widths of the wall frames on all the walls as similar as possible. To do this, you may need to adjust the number of frames on each wall.

In this example, you have only three runs of wall, **A**, **E**, and **H**, on which you can make the frame widths similar to within 3 inches. The lengths of all of the other runs are so short that each can accommodate only a single wall frame.

Wall frames *and cornices transform this large dining area from a cavernous space, right, to a warm, inviting room, even without furniture, top.*

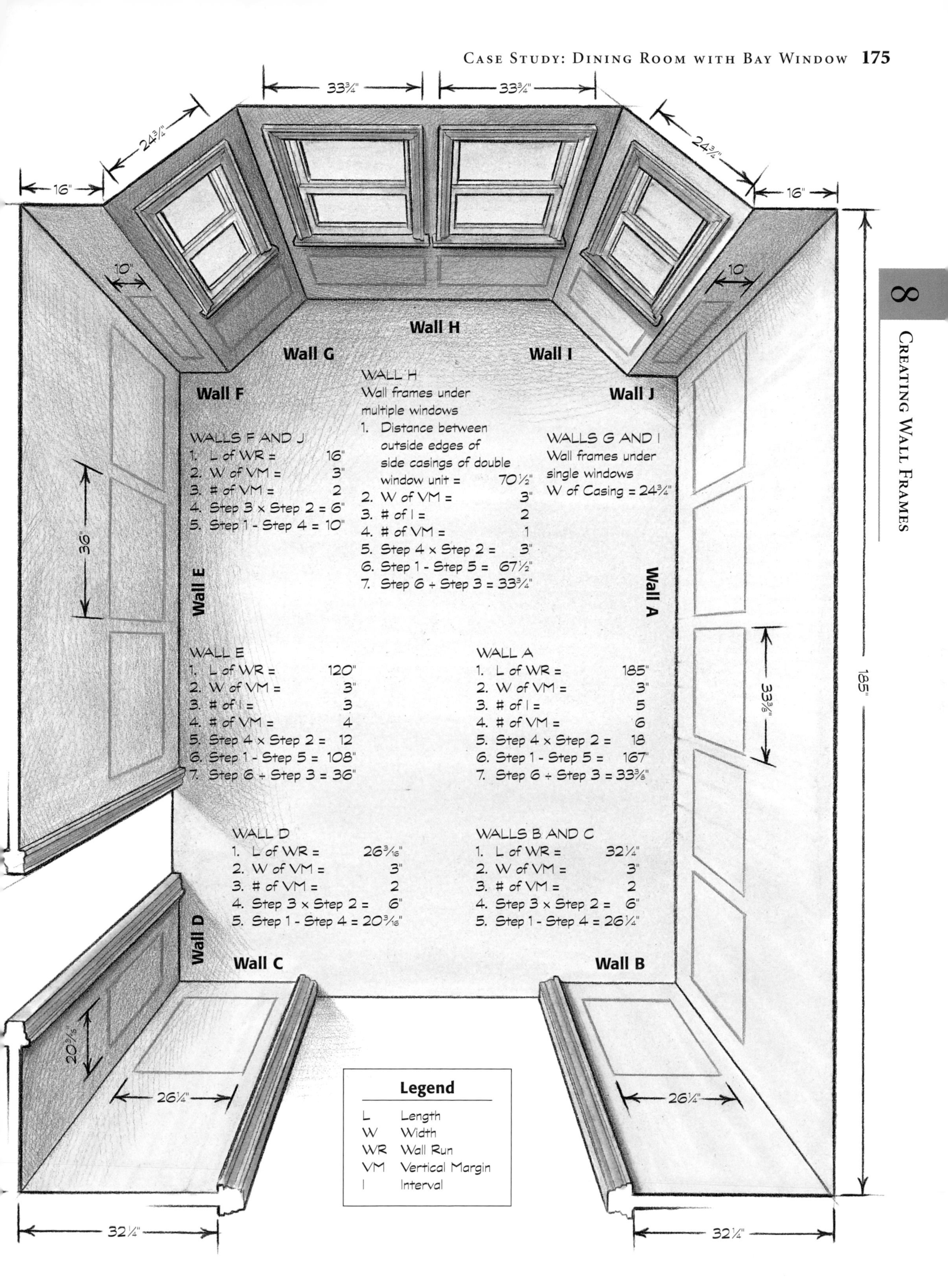
33¾"
33¾"
24¾"
24¾"
16"
16"
10"
10"
Wall H
Wall G
Wall I
Wall F
Wall J
WALL H
Wall frames under multiple windows
1. Distance between outside edges of side casings of double window unit = 70½"
2. W of VM = 3"
3. # of I = 2
4. # of VM = 1
5. Step 4 × Step 2 = 3"
6. Step 1 - Step 5 = 67½"
7. Step 6 ÷ Step 3 = 33¾"
WALLS F AND J
1. L of WR = 16"
2. W of VM = 3"
3. # of VM = 2
4. Step 3 × Step 2 = 6"
5. Step 1 - Step 4 = 10"
WALLS G AND I
Wall frames under single windows
W of Casing = 24¾"
36"
Wall E
Wall A
185"
33⅜"
WALL E
1. L of WR = 120"
2. W of VM = 3"
3. # of I = 3
4. # of VM = 4
5. Step 4 × Step 2 = 12
6. Step 1 - Step 5 = 108"
7. Step 6 ÷ Step 3 = 36"
WALL A
1. L of WR = 185"
2. W of VM = 3"
3. # of I = 5
4. # of VM = 6
5. Step 4 × Step 2 = 18
6. Step 1 - Step 5 = 167"
7. Step 6 ÷ Step 3 = 33⅜"
WALL D
1. L of WR = 26³⁄₁₆"
2. W of VM = 3"
3. # of VM = 2
4. Step 3 × Step 2 = 6"
5. Step 1 - Step 4 = 20³⁄₁₆"
WALLS B AND C
1. L of WR = 32¼"
2. W of VM = 3"
3. # of VM = 2
4. Step 3 × Step 2 = 6"
5. Step 1 - Step 4 = 26¼"
Wall D
Wall C
Wall B
20³⁄₁₆"
26¼"
26¼"
32¼"
32¼"
Legend
L Length
W Width
WR Wall Run
VM Vertical Margin
I Interval

This tone-on-tone color scheme *is more subdued than the one on the opposite page, but the 3-D illusion is just as successful.*

Painting Wall Frames

The right paint job will enhance your wall-frame treatment tremendously. While you'll find more information about paint colors in Chapter 3, "Combining Color, Pattern & Trim," page 44, it seems appropriate to mention two strategies here. You can either paint the entire wall treatment with a single color of low-luster paint, or use a tone-on-tone approach to enhance its depth.

Single-Tone Scheme. Using a single color of semigloss or eggshell paint gives your walls a Neoclassical, sculpture-like look. Visually, the area inside the wall frames recedes, or seems farthest away, while the moldings seem closer to you, and the rest of the wall floats in between.

Tone-on-Tone Approach. With this approach, you again use one color, but in three different shades. This creates subtle differences in the perceived depth of the different elements. The darker the shade of paint on a section of wall, the more it recedes visually, while lighter shades appear to lift elements off the wall's surface. Normally the deepest shade is used for the area inside the wall frames, a slightly lighter color for the surface outside the frames, and white paint with just a hint of the color for the moldings.

Painting the wall frames *with a multi-tone color scheme, bottom left, accentuates the three-dimensional nature of the treatment. Darker areas recede while lighter areas appear to come toward you. Using a single-tone color scheme, top left, makes the 3-D effect more subtle.*

Thin strips of wood, *above left, form a simplified version of wall frames between large chair rail and baseboard trimwork.*

The wall-frame-type treatment, *left, is used to embellish the skirting enclosing a bathtub.*

Wall frames *work well with a variety of design styles, such as the traditional dining room shown above.*

Long walls, *right, benefit from the addition of wall frames. Note how the last interval follows the incline of the stairs.*

CHAPTER 9

Staircase Wall Frames

Installing wall frames is a sophisticated technique for enhancing any room. The next step is to continue the frame treatment up the stairs to complete the trimwork theme you've established. The process becomes a little more complicated on the stairs because you must deal with angles that vary from 90 degrees. The sides of the frames in a stairwell stay plumb, but the top and bottom pieces follow the slope of the stairs and the chair-rail treatment, resulting in frames shaped like parallelograms and giving the trim assembly a highly unified, sloped look. Installation of the treatment is extremely challenging but not beyond the ability of a careful, handy do-it-yourselfer. This chapter covers wall-frame layout, as well as measuring and cutting the angles necessary for the project.

Wall-Frame Angles

WALL-FRAME ACUTE ANGLES

Wall frames above a stringer are parallelograms, which have the following characteristics:

- Opposite angles are always equal.
- One pair of opposing angles is always acute, or less than 90 degrees; the other pair is always obtuse, or more than 90 degrees.
- All four angles always add up to 360 degrees.

The vertical sides of the wall frames must be plumb; the horizontal sides run parallel with the stringer.

The first step in building staircase wall frames is to find their acute angle. You can determine the angle by cutting an identical one and measuring it. (See "Measuring the Angle," below.) You can also use a protractor to read the angle that you'll copy off the stringer, or skirtboard. (The stringer is the board that runs up the wall beside the steps. The staircase treads and risers are either mortised into the stringer or butted against it.)

Using a Protractor. You probably remember using a protractor in your high school geometry class. It's a transparent plastic circle or half circle with degree marks etched around the perimeter. You simply place the tool over an angle and read its measurement. Protractors come in handy when working with trim, especially when you're dealing with angles other than 90 and 45 degrees. Determining various angles may seem intimidating, but it's really quite straightforward.

To use a protractor to find your angle, place a straight board lengthwise on the staircase stringer, and strike a line on the wall along the board's upper edge, parallel with the stringer. Drop a plumb line on the wall intersecting the line you just struck, and mark the resulting angle, shown as angle **A** at right. Place the center of a protractor on the intersection of the plumb line and the line you struck, making the plumb line the baseline for the protractor. (The sloped line will point toward the right.) Determine the acute angle between the sloped line and the plumb line. That's all there is to it.

WALL-FRAME OBTUSE ANGLES

Using the acute angle you've just found, you can determine the obtuse angles for the wall frames. (See the instructions in the illustration at right.) Once you know the measurements of the two acute angles and the two obtuse angles, divide each by 2 to determine the angles you'll cut into the sides of the miter joint.

Measuring the Angle

WHAT YOU'LL NEED

- ◆ Pry bar
- ◆ Spirit level and pencil
- ◆ Sliding T-bevel
- ◆ Table saw or power miter saw
- ◆ Scrap one-by lumber

TRIM TIP: A sure-fire way to accurately measure the wall-frame acute angle is to cut a piece of scrap lumber to emulate the angle, and then measure it.

1 Remove all trim from the stringer skirtboard so that you have a flat area from which to work. Then, using a 2-ft. level and pencil, draw a plumb line down to the top of the skirtboard.

Calculating Wall-Frame Angles

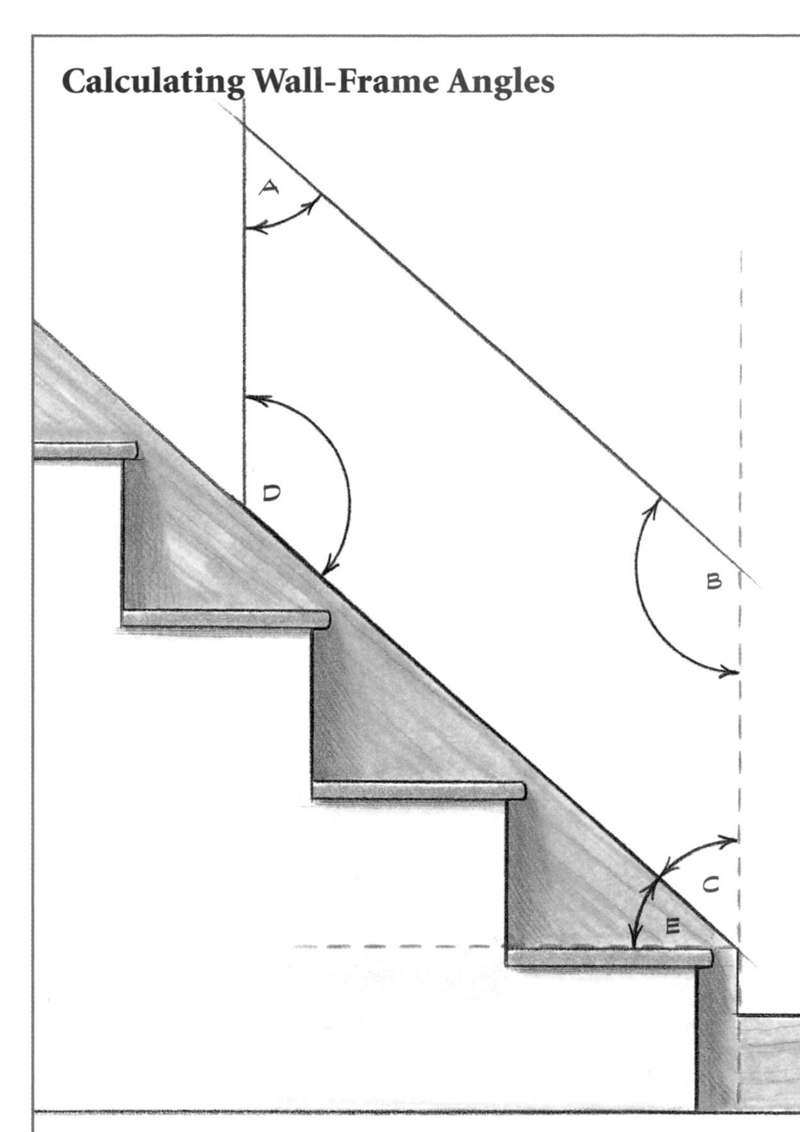

Remember: the sum of the angles of a parallelogram equals 360°, and the opposite angles are equivalent.

Once you know one of the wall-frame acute angles (text at left), you can determine the obtuse angles in two steps, as follows:

1. Subtract the sum of the acute angles from 360°.

   360 - (Sum of acute angles) = (Sum of obtuse angles)

   360 - (A + C) = (B + D)

2. Divide the result from Step 1 by 2 to get the obtuse angle

   (Step 1) ÷ 2 = (Obtuse angle)

   (B + D) ÷ 2 = B (or D)

To determine the stringer angle **(E)**, subtract from 90° the wall-frame acute angle **(A)** you measured previously (text at left).

90 - (A) = (E)

2 Align the handle of a sliding T-bevel with the plumb line, and adjust the blade to sit flat on the skirtboard. Lock the blade to capture the angle, and use it to mark a scrap piece of one-by lumber.

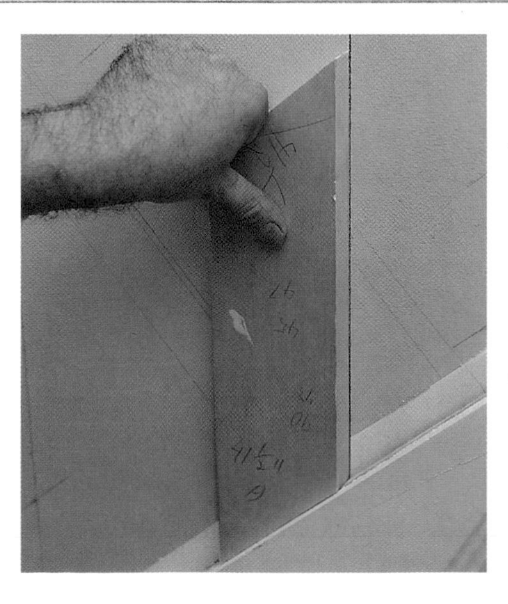

3 Cut the marked one-by using a table saw or power miter saw, and lay it on the skirtboard as shown. If the long edge aligns with the plumb line, the angle is accurate. Measure it using any method you prefer.

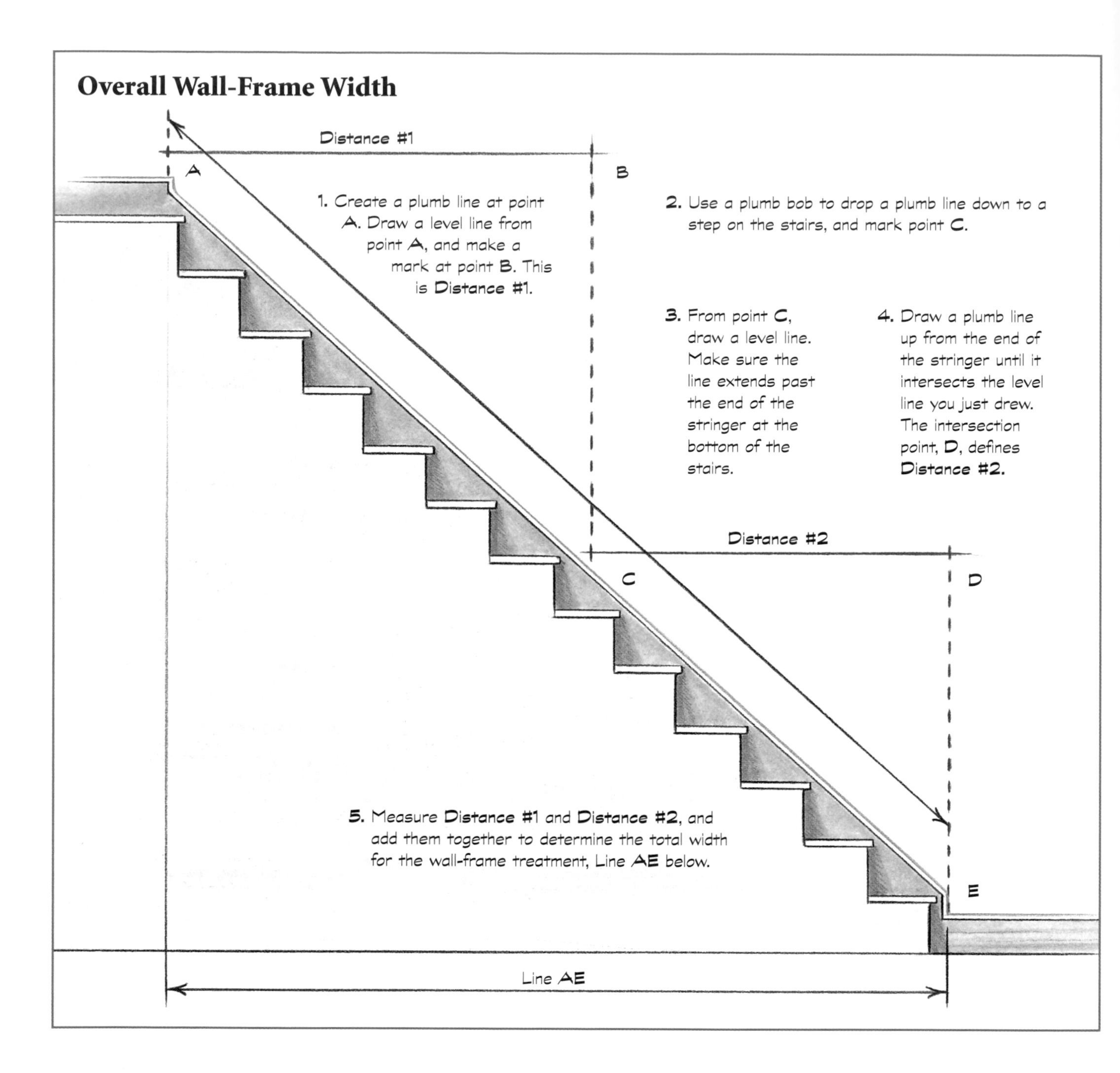

Sizing Wall Frames

Before you can lay out the wall frames on the staircase wall, you need to determine the overall width of the wall-frame treatment in the stairway, represented by line **AE** in the drawing above. The easiest way to do this is to measure the horizontal distance across the stairway wall from a plumb line at the beginning of the stairs to a plumb line at the end. After you know the exact space to fill, you can go on to determine the size of the individual wall frames.

Determining Overall Width for Wall Frames

Measure the overall width of a wall-frame treatment in one or two "giant steps." (See the drawing above.) Mark plumb lines where the stringer meets the baseboard at the top and bottom landings. From the top, mark a level line as far out as you can safely reach. Then mark Distance #1 by dropping a plumb line to a stair. Repeat the above procedure to determine Distance #2, and so on, until you reach the end of the stringer. Add your total distances.

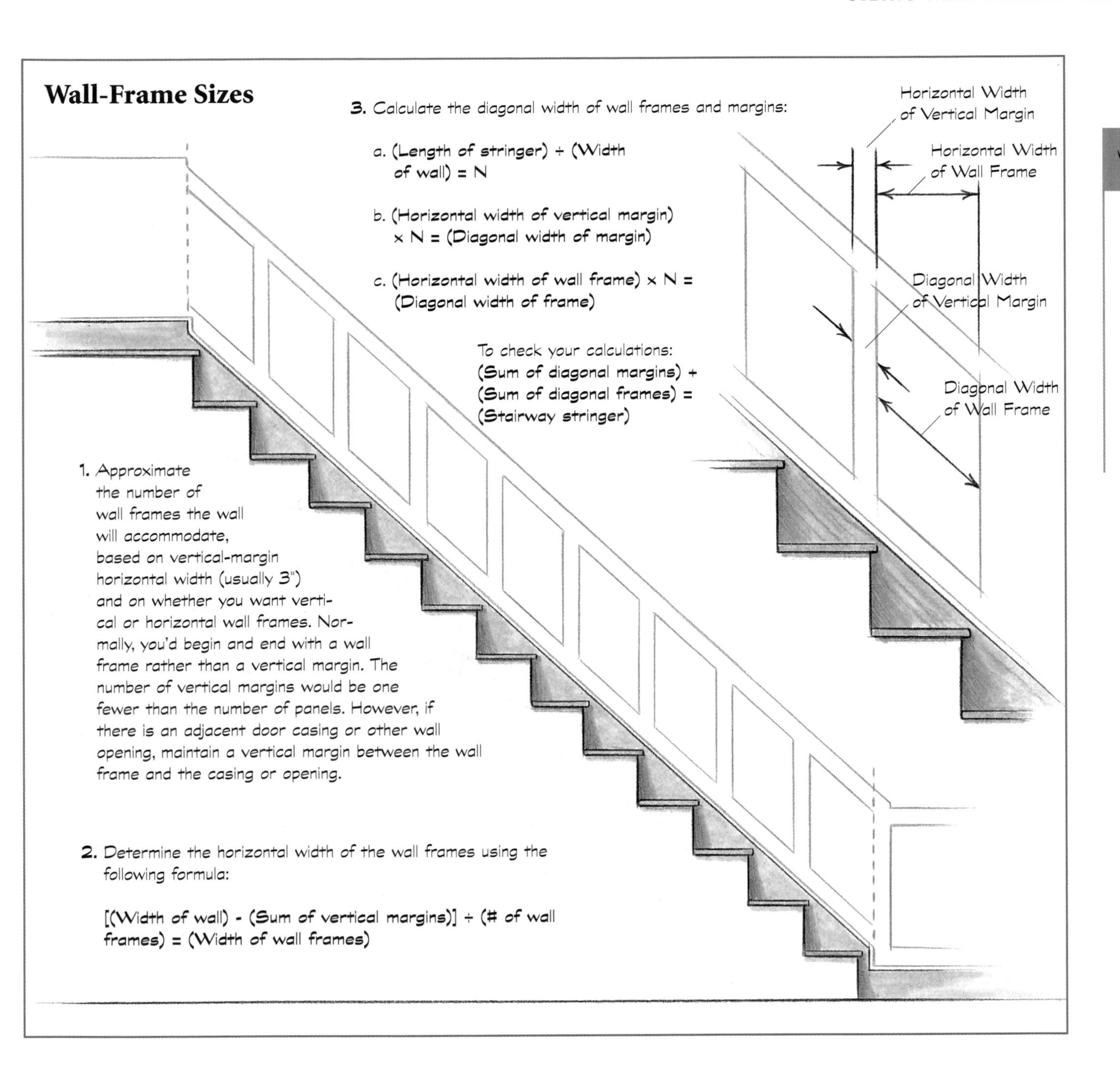

Determining Individual Widths

Once you know the overall width available for wall frames in the stairway, you must calculate the individual wall-frame widths. The process requires three steps.

1. Decide whether you want vertical or horizontal frames, and approximate the number of wall frames you'll need. (See the photos on page 191 and the drawing above.) Try to match existing wall frames if you have any. If not, use a configuration that will work in nearby parts of the house.

2. Determine the individual horizontal wall-frame widths, following the instructions in the drawing below. If you're trying to match other wall frames, adjust your frame total, if necessary, and repeat the calculations until you end up with a width close to that of the existing frames.

3. Using the horizontal width you just determined, calculate the diagonal width of the wall frames. This is the dimension you need in order to lay out the frames along the length of the stringer.

Chair Rail Location

The next step in installing the stairway wall frames is to lay out the chair rail location on the wall. Once you've laid out and installed the chair rail, you work down toward the floor, installing the wall frames and base cap molding.

CHAIR RAIL AND BASE MOLDING ALIGNMENTS

After you've determined the various angle measurements and wall-frame dimensions required (pages 182 to 185), you need to find the exact point on the wall at which you want the chair rails (and, if applicable, subrails and base cap moldings) to meet. It's usually best to align their joints with that of the stringer and base trim. Exceptions may be dictated by differing heights of components on the landings. Here are some suggestions, based on possible situations.

Situation 1. The base is the same height as the staircase stringer. (See the top illustration opposite.) Make the transition of the base cap on the plumb line of the transition between the base trim and stringer.

Join the two lengths of chair rail so that the bottom

Alternative to Chalk Lines

WHAT YOU'LL NEED

- Power miter saw
- 48" T-square and pencil
- Spirit level
- Scrap one-by lumber

TRIM TIP: Many times, especially in older houses, the walls are wavy, making it difficult to snap chalk lines. You may end up with double lines when you snap a line over a hollow in the wall, for example. Using a straightedge and T-square to strike lines is often more accurate.

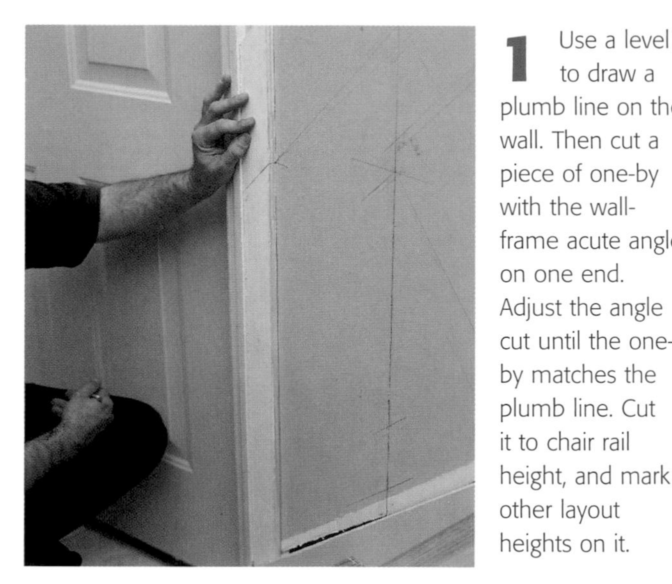

1 Use a level to draw a plumb line on the wall. Then cut a piece of one-by with the wall-frame acute angle on one end. Adjust the angle cut until the one-by matches the plumb line. Cut it to chair rail height, and mark other layout heights on it.

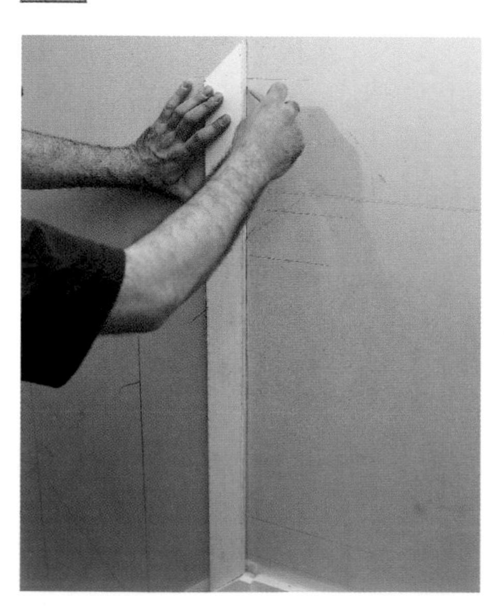

2 With the straightedge angles precisely adjusted, you can use the board to strike plumb lines anywhere on the stairs and to make other layout marks for the wall-frame design.

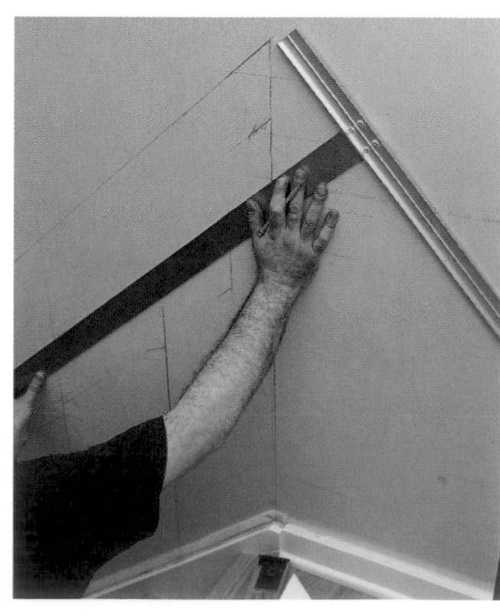

3 Use a 48-in. T-square to connect layout marks, and strike long horizontal guidelines exactly parallel with the stairway.

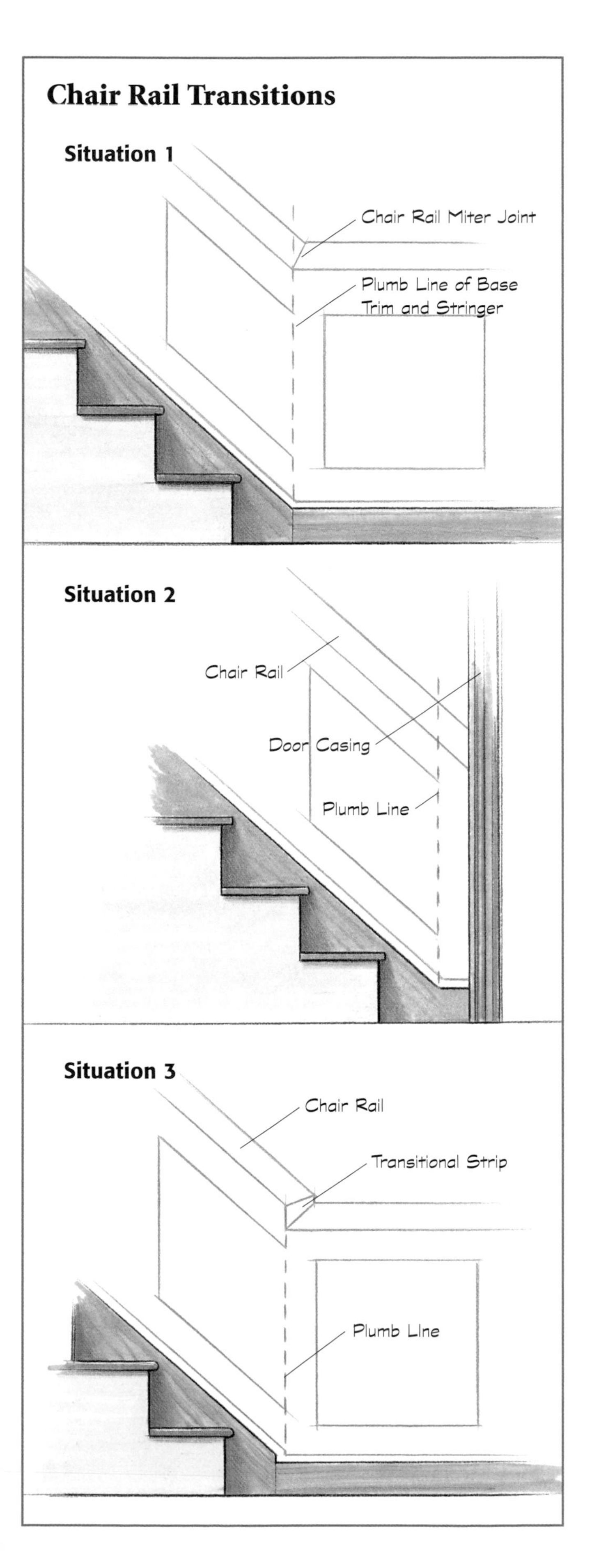

of the joint falls on the same plumb line as that of the stringer. When you also have a subrail, make its joints align with the chair rail's.

To find the angle between the stairway and landing chair rails, add 90 degrees to the wall-frame acute angle you found earlier. For example, if the acute angle is 48 degrees:

90° + 48° = 138°

Divide this angle in half to determine the miter cut:

138° ÷ 2 = 69°

Situation 2. The door casing of an adjacent passageway is close to the beginning of the stringer. Here, you'll have the chair rail run directly into the side of the casing that is closer to the stairs and that runs parallel to the plumb cut of the stringer. (See the drawing at left.) The angle you cut into the end of this chair rail is the same as the wall-frame acute angle.

Situation 3. You plan to install the same wall-frame treatment on both landings, and the stringer is higher than the base. In this case, you have two options:

Option 1. Miter the stairway chair rail directly into the chair rails on the upper and lower landings. The difference in height between the base and the stringer will make the stairway wall frames shorter than the frames on the landings. (See photo on page 189.)

Option 2. Raise the chair rail over the stringers by inserting a transitional 90-degree strip piece between the landing and stairway chair rails, as in the drawing at left. This lets you make the height of the wall frames over the stringer the same as those at both landings. Miter the bottom of the transitional piece into the chair rail with a 45-degree cut. The intersection of the chair rail over the stringer with the top of the transitional piece forms the same angle as the wall-frame obtuse angles. To determine the dimensions of the transitional piece of chair rail, do your layout on paper or directly on the wall where the trim will go.

Laying Out a Chair Rail Transitional Piece

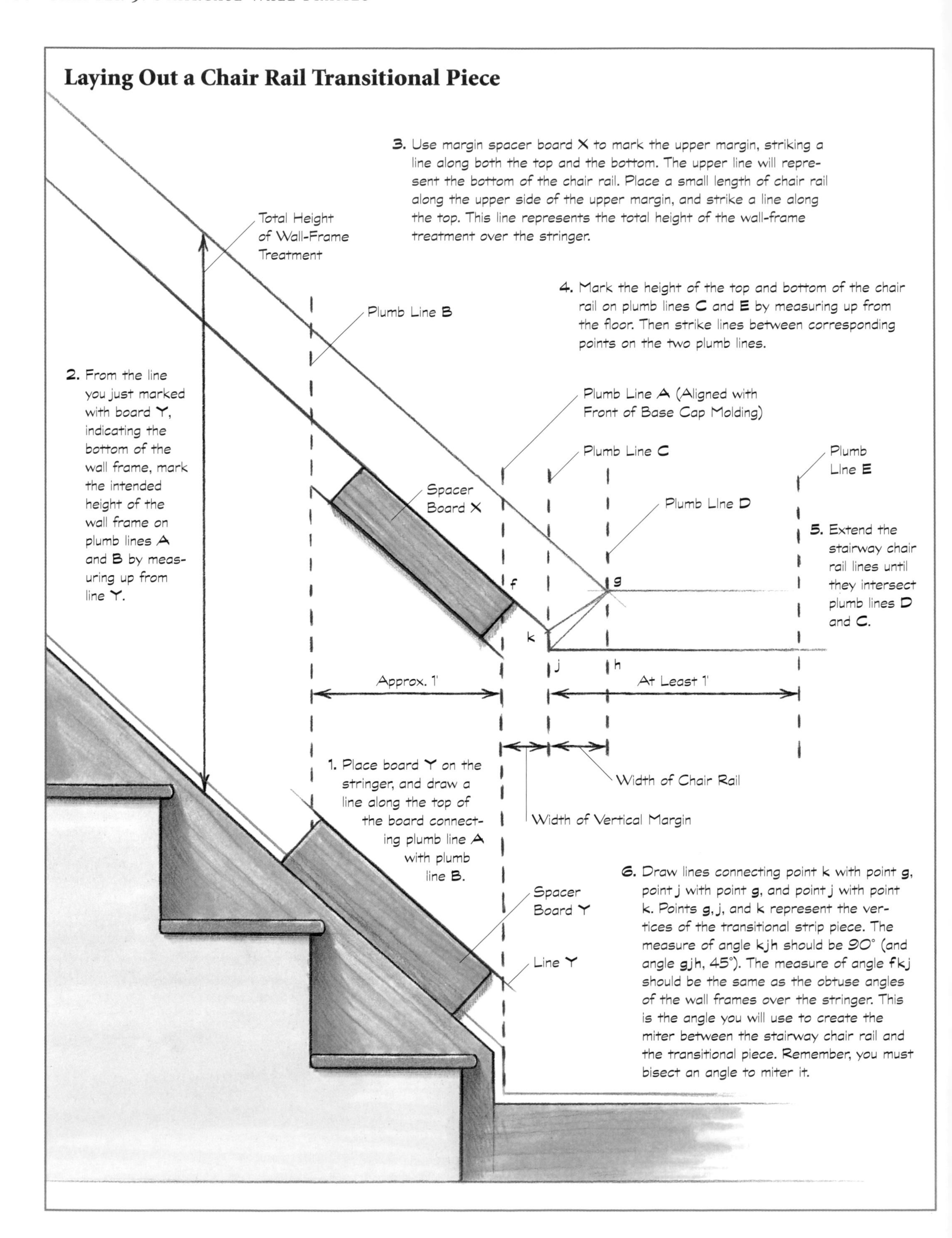

Laying Out Stairway Chair Rails

To pinpoint the location of the chair rail and its transitions, estimate the height of the chair rails and decide how wide you want the horizontal margins. (The top horizontal margin should match the vertical margins; the bottom margin can be smaller.)

After estimating the height of the chair rail over the stringer and the lower landing, drop plumb lines that will be taller than these estimated heights. One example of this process is shown in "Laying Out a Chair Rail Transitional Piece," opposite.

Using Spacer Boards to Locate Chair Rail Placement. With all the plumb lines marked on the wall, rip two boards about 18 inches long to serve as margin spacer boards. (See the illustrations on page 190 for similar boards.) One spacer board should equal the planned width of the vertical margins and the top horizontal margin, assuming that the vertical and the top margins are the same. Use the other spacer board to lay out the bottoms of the wall frames. Rip it to a width equal to the planned width of the lower margin plus the width of the base cap molding. (See the drawing opposite for how to use the spacer boards for chair rail layout.)

Laying Out Landing Chair Rails

Moving to the landing, mark the height of the top and the bottom of the chair rail by measuring up from the floor. Follow the instructions in the illustration opposite for determining the transitional strip piece between the landing chair rail and the stairway chair rail, if it's necessary in your case.

Door casings *are sometimes a little too far for the chair rail to butt them; in these cases, the molding has to make a short jog.*

The smooth chair rail transition *is possible because the stairway wall frames are smaller than those on the landing.*

SMART TIP *Using Spacer Boards for Vertical Spacing Layout*

Here's an easy way to simultaneously lay out both the vertical margins and the location of each diagonally shaped wall frame. Again, always start and end with a wall frame and not a margin. The only exception occurs when a stringer butts at one or both ends to a door casing. In this situation, you need to insert a vertical margin to separate the wall frame from the door casing.

To lay out the wall frames and mark the vertical spacing, you will use two template spacer boards.

First Spacer Board. Cut the wall-frame acute angle into both ends of a narrow board that has a length equal to the combined width of one wall frame and one vertical margin. You'll use this to double-check your calculations and simultaneously mark wall-frame widths and margin spacing. Place the spacer lengthwise on the stringer so that its lower end falls precisely on the plumb line marking the start of the first wall frame.

Draw a line along the upper edge of the spacer, and mark the point where the board ends. Move the board up the stringer, as shown, repeating the marking process until the upper end of the board reaches the point at which the last wall frame will fall at the top end of the stringer. This should be precisely where the stringer abuts the baseboard, so the spacer should overshoot the baseboard by the width of the vertical margin. (If the frame mark doesn't fall as shown, you'll need to remeasure or recalculate your spacing to determine why.)

Second Spacer Board. Cut the wall-frame acute angle into the end of another board ripped to the width of the vertical margins. Cut this board about 1 inch shorter than the distance between the chair rail and the stringer. Place the board vertically on the stringer at the lower side of each point you marked with the other spacer board. Holding a spirit level on the spacer board to be sure it is perfectly plumb, strike a line along each side of the board with a pencil, and repeat up the stairs as shown.

Marking Wall Frames

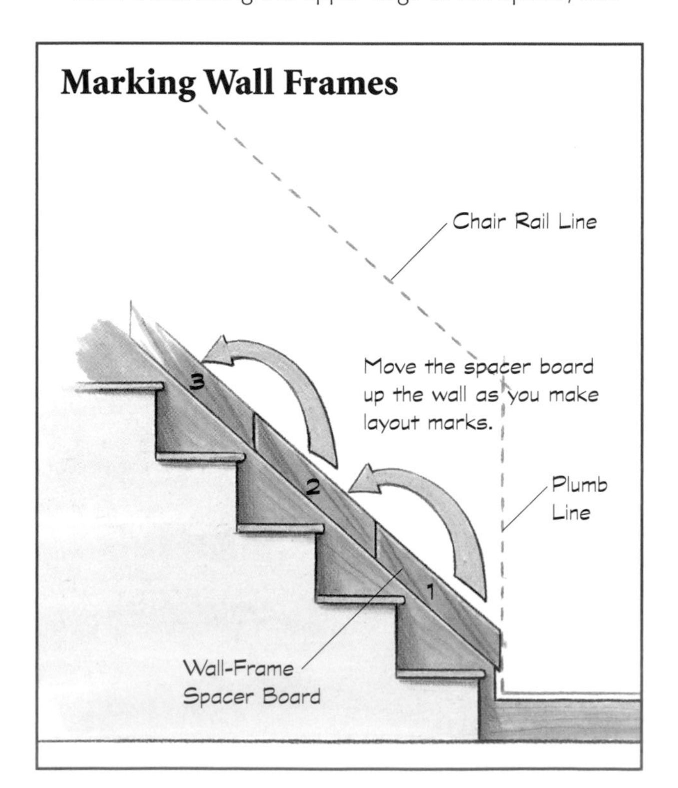

Marking Vertical Margins

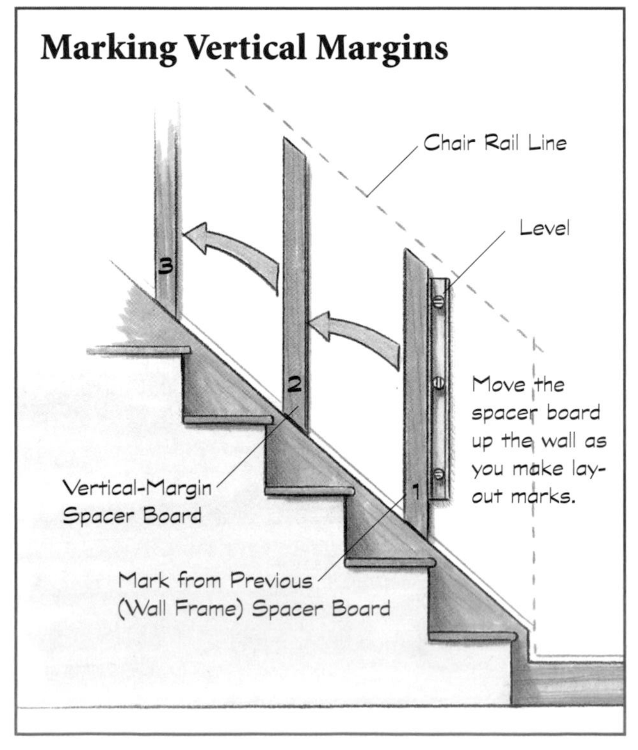

Installing the Frames

You should have already removed the stringer's existing cap molding in your preparation and layout procedures. If you haven't, remove it now because you'll be replacing it with new base cap molding.

Lay out on the wall the transition of the chair rail at the lower landing, as described previously. Then lay out the transition at the upper landing. A number of different situations may exist at the top of the stairs. Deal with them by applying the general design principles of wall-frame treatments and trying to be as consistent as possible. Draw guidelines representing the top of the chair rail on the stairs and on the two landings. Make sure that the stairway's chair rail height is the same at both ends of the stringer. Install the chair rail. (See "Installing Chair Rails," pages 150 to 151.)

Now mark the upper and the lower horizontal margins. To do this, place the upper-margin spacer board against the underside of the chair rail. Holding a pencil at the bottom of the spacer board, slide it the full length of the chair rail to strike a pencil guideline. Next, while sliding the lower-margin spacer board along the top of the stringer, run a pencil line to mark the top of the lower margin.

If you're installing a subrail, rip a spacer board to the desired width, and strike a line on the wall. This is the easiest and most accurate way to determine exactly where the subrail should fall. If the transition points for the subrail don't coincide precisely with those for the chair rail, adjust them as necessary. (See the bottom right photo on page 189.)

Next, lay out the vertical margins for the wall frames. The best way to do this is using spacer, or layout, boards. (See "Using Spacer Boards for Vertical Spacing Layout," opposite.)

The installation process *for wall-frame treatments in staircases is the same whether the frames are horizontally oriented, left, or vertically oriented, right. You will have chosen the configuration that most closely matches the wall frames in the upper and lower landings or an adjoining room.*

Jig for Cutting Acute Angles

WHAT YOU'LL NEED

- Screwdriver (and/or drill), 1¼" screws
- Sliding T-bevel and pencil
- Hold-down clamp
- Plywood
- Scrap one-by lumber

TRIM TIP: Using a bench-top table saw and a simple plywood jig is a safe, efficient, and foolproof way to cut many trim members at angles of less than 45 degrees.

1 Cut a piece of plywood about 12 to 14 in. square, and screw a 1x2 to one edge.

3 Set a sliding T-bevel to the angle you want to cut, and transfer the angle to the saw side of the jig.

4 Screw a scrap piece of flat trim or one-by lumber to the jig, aligned with the angle guideline.

After you've laid out the wall frames on the wall, you must cut the frame members. For angles that fall between 45 and 90 degrees, you can just dial in the appropriate angle on the power miter saw and make the cut. Remember to subtract the angle you want from 90 degrees to find the setting, as explained on page 126 in Chapter 7.

For angles less than 45 degrees, you need another approach. The safest method is to build the table saw jig described above. The jig attaches to your saw's miter gauge and uses special hold-down clamps to keep the molding in place during the cut. You'll have to reassemble the jig and move it to one side or another of the table-saw blade for each different type of cut, so make every cut you'll need before adjusting the jig.

Labeling Molding Cuts. Cutting and storing trim pieces of many different sizes and angles for use at a later date can result in a confusing array of material when it comes time for final assembly. A good way to prevent this problem is to label the trim pieces as you cut them with the size and direction of the angle cuts, as shown in the illustration opposite. That way, you'll know at a glance how the pieces should go together:

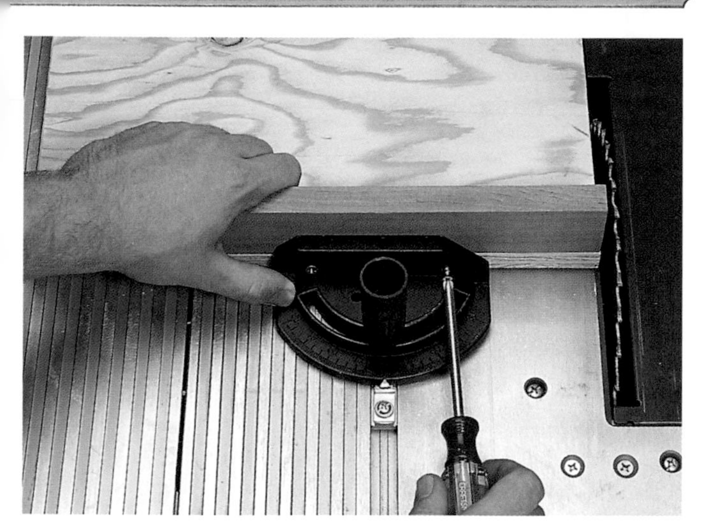

2 Screw the jig to the table saw's miter gauge, aligned flush with the blade. (The blade guard is removed for clarity.)

5 Screw hold-down clamps to the angled member of the jig to hold trim pieces firmly in place as you cut them.

that, for example, 24 degrees L goes with 24 degrees R and 66 degrees L goes with 66 degrees R, and so on.

It's best to cut all vertical sides at one time and then all diagonal sides. The quickest way to do this is to total up the pieces you'll need (for example, 18 vertical sides and 18 diagonal sides), and crosscut them a few inches longer than the final required height. That way, they'll all be ready for final cutting. Cut and label the angle that is less than 45 degrees on the vertical pieces; then cut and label the angle on the other end of the molding pieces. Repeat the procedure for the diagonal pieces. Now you're ready to assemble the wall frames.

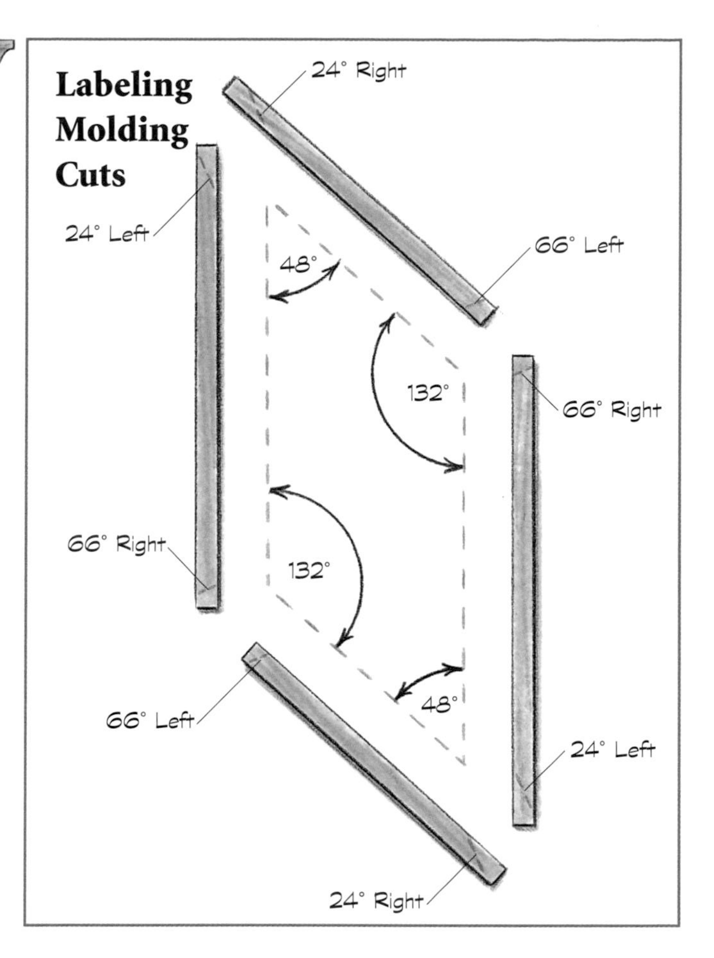

The narrow upper and lower margins *used in this staircase's wall-frame treatment make for tall vertical intervals.*

Smart Tip — How to Make Wall-Frame Assembly Jigs

This type of jig helps you hold the glued, mitered ends of two pieces of molding firmly together while you fasten them. You'll need two such jigs: one for acute angles, as shown, and one for obtuse angles.

Cut two short, narrow wood strips so that they form the acute angle of the wall frames. Cut and join them as precisely as you would the actual moldings; otherwise any error will be carried to all the frames. To form the acute angle, cut the right half of the angle into the end of one strip and the left half of the angle into the other strip.

Position the two strips so that they form a point near the corner of a work surface, such as a sheet of plywood or particleboard that measures about 2 x 2 feet.

Back the point of the strips away from the corner, as shown. This gives you room to drive fasteners into the joints of the wall frames. Join the jig strips by screwing or nailing them to the work surface.

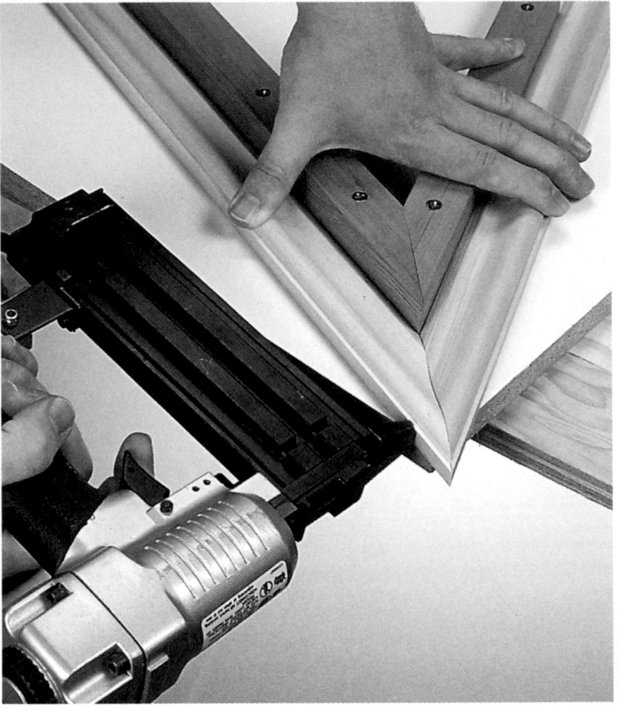

A jig like this, *secured to a work surface, allows you to hold the frame pieces for a tight fit and secure nailing.*

Assembling the Wall Frames

Carpenter's glue and a pneumatic brad nailer are a good means of assembly, although a pneumatic nailer is by no means required. Glue and nail each corner, first joining each of the vertical lengths to one of the diagonal lengths and then fastening the pairs of sides together. (See "How to Make Wall-Frame Assembly Jigs," above.) Allow the glue to set for about 15 minutes between procedures.

With the frames constructed and the glue set, use the spacer boards shown on page 188 to position the frames, sticking them to the wall with dots of panel adhesive. Then nail them in place with 6d nails.

Base Cap Molding. Now that you've installed the frames, the last procedure is to apply a base cap molding to the top of the stringer and the base trim on the landings. In most cases, the landing base trim ties directly into the front of the vertical edge of the stringer. In this situation, two possibilities may occur:

Base Trim without Cap. If the base trim on the lower landing is shorter than the stringer and does not have a cap or you don't want one, apply base cap molding to the stringer only. Bevel the end of the molding to match the acute angle of the wall frames, and end it at the plumb line of the stringer.

Base Trim with Cap. If the lower-landing base trim has a cap or you're installing one, apply the molding to the taller front vertical edge of the stringer and on up the stairway. (Note: The angle between the landing base cap and the cap on the front edge of the stringer is 90 degrees. The angle formed as the base cap molding makes the transition from the front vertical edge of the stringer onto the diagonal portion of the stringer is identical to the obtuse angle of the wall frame.)

Fully assembled, *installed, and painted, a wall-frame treatment in a staircase makes an elegant traditional statement.*

The wainscot *above complements the casing trimwork around a window located on a stair landing.*

Trimwork on stairs, *below, allows you to continue the molding design up to the second floor.*

An open design *for railings and balusters, left, allows the stair wall-panel system to show through.*

Stair panels, *above, follow the incline of the stairs, resulting in parallelograms rather than rectangles.*

Stair landings, *below, provide the opportunity to install elaborate chair-rail and base moldings.*

CHAPTER 10

Wainscoting, Pillars & Pilasters

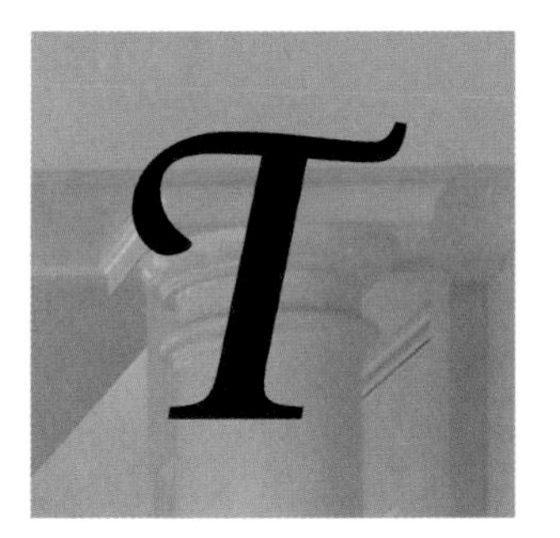

The term wainscoting covers a wide range of materials and moldings that you can combine in frames and panels to create a decorative treatment for the lower portion of a wall. This practical trimwork technique not only protects the wall, it also adds a distinctive design touch that works well in many house styles. You can run wainscots up to chair rail height or higher and cap them with a thin strip of trim or a wide shelf. Pillars and pilasters also provide a classic touch to any room. Most pillars used today are strictly ornamental rather than structural. Pilasters are a favorite way to enhance the appearance of a fireplace mantel. You can also combine the three treatments with short walls as a distinctive way to define main entrances and passageways.

Panel-style wainscoting *can unify elements in a small room.*

Installing Bead-Board Wainscoting

Bead-board, tongue-and-groove wainscoting was widely used from 1800 up to the early 1900s. Today it is mainly associated with capturing the look of country-style kitchens and bathrooms.

Bead-board is available in several forms, including milled lumber, prepackaged wainscot kits, and 4 × 8-foot sheets of ¼-inch plywood. Milled lumber is the most authentic but the most costly and time-consuming to install. Also, individual boards can develop gaps as moisture levels fall and the wood shrinks. Despite these drawbacks, nothing quite substitutes for the real thing.

Wainscoting kits generally consist of sheets of paneling that you glue to the wall with panel adhesive. The cap and the base molding provided in kits may be undersized and not very decorative.

For many do-it-yourselfers, 4 × 8-foot sheets of plywood work best. The cost is reasonable, and the sheets generally won't open up and show gaps.

Basic Components

You can run bead-board wainscoting between a baseboard and a top nosing or shelf without any other elements. At the other end of the spectrum is the kind of complete wainscoting system shown at right.

The uppermost component, a cap, typically consists of a nosing and a supporting strip of apron. Below that is a top rail with vertical stiles on each end, panels enclosed by rails and stiles and separated from one another by the muntins, and finally a bottom rail. These components can form a frame around the boards or plywood panels.

A stile is a vertical member at the end of a run of wainscoting that extends from the top of the top rail down to the bottom of the bottom rail. Other vertical sides of frames are formed by muntins, which run between the rails.

There are many other ways to treat wainscoting using just some of these components. But in most cases there is at least a transition between the cap on top and the base trim at the bottom.

Bead-Board Wainscoting

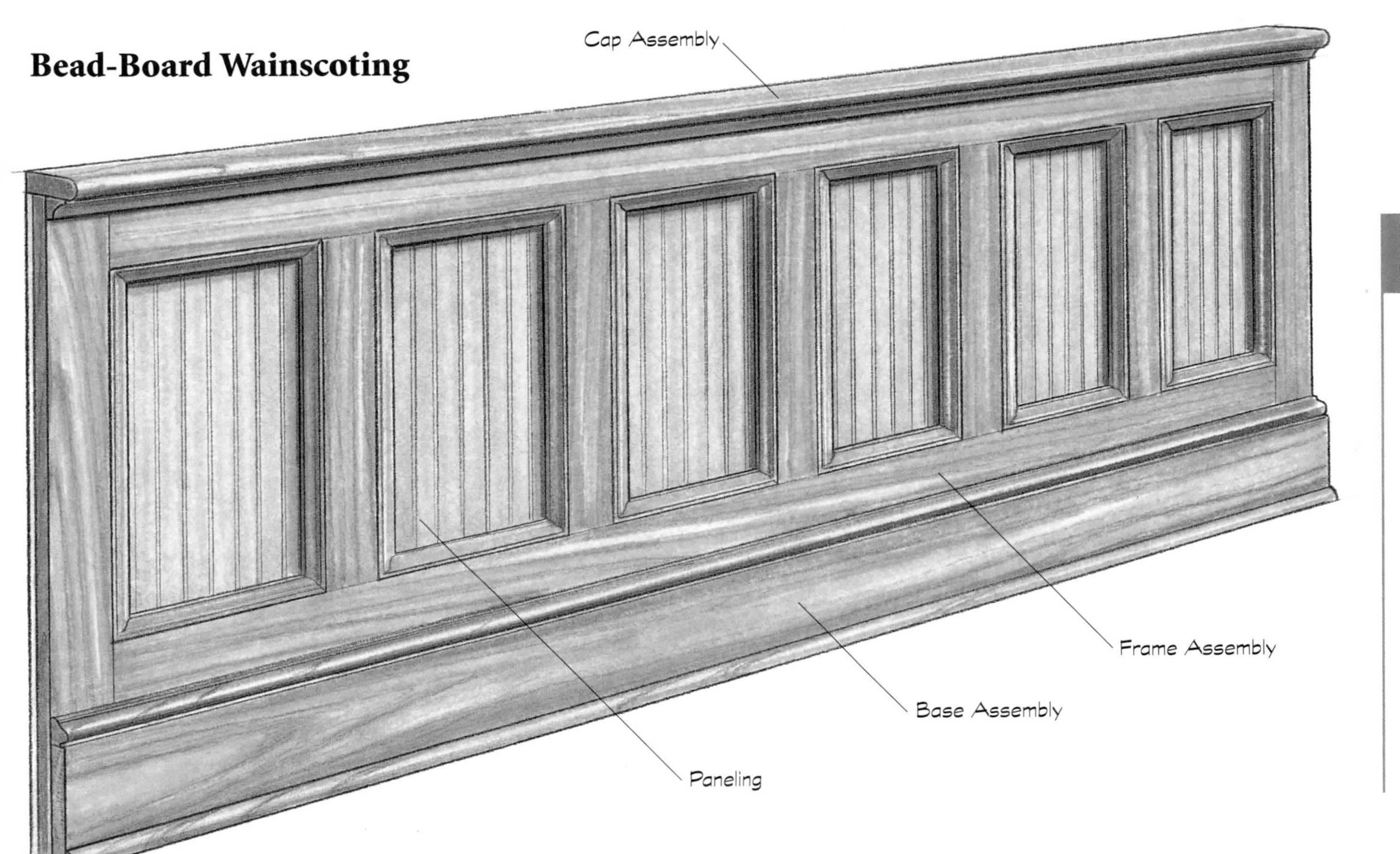

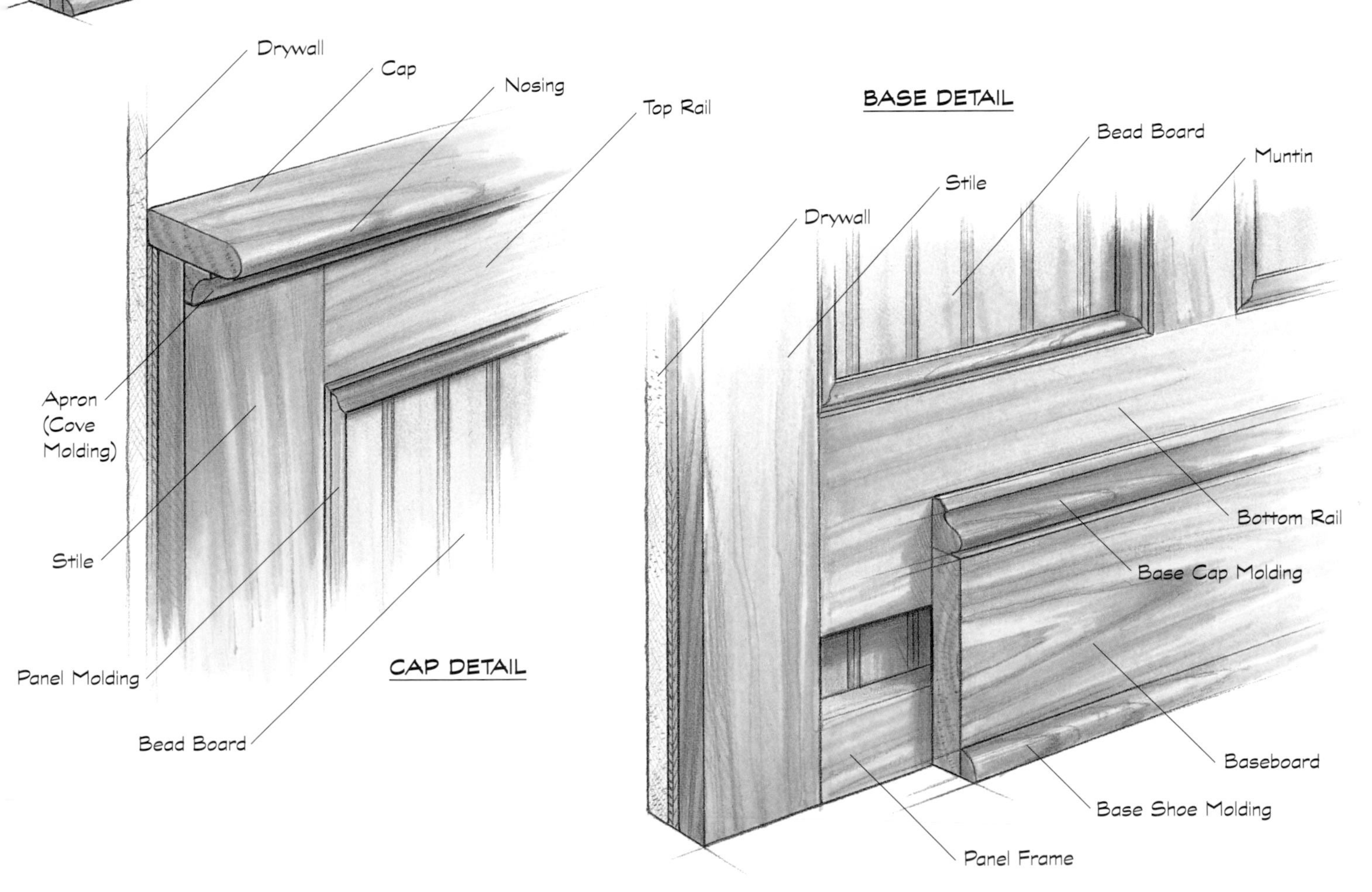

Wainscot Materials

You can use many different materials both for the main wainscot sections and for the framing components. Your choice depends on several factors, including the style and treatment of other moldings in the house and whether the materials are available locally and at a reasonable price.

Oak is a traditional choice, but buying wide ¾-inch-thick boards for framing components can be costly. You can use pine or other softwoods—or composite materials if you plan to paint the walls.

Many professionals now use medium-density fiberboard for trimwork that will be painted. Some varieties come with a smooth surface that takes paint well. The material has other advantages, too. For example, composite material has no grain, which means it won't warp and twist the way some wood can. And the material is dimensionally stable, which means it won't shrink or swell noticeably with seasonal changes.

Wainscot Stiles

You can use several types of stiles for different situations—for example, to soften the transition from the wainscoting to a door or window casing or to make stile-to-stile transitions. Of course, conditions on site can mean that you have to alter typical joinery details, particularly in older homes with irregular walls.

Adjacent to Door and Window Casings. Because a stile is slightly thicker than a standard 11⁄16-inch-thick casing, it should have a decorative detail to accomplish the transition from the stile to the casing. If the width of the stiles is 3 inches, for example, the detail could be a ⅜-inch bead, making all stiles adjacent to a casing a total of 3⅜ inches.

On walls with windows, the best approach is to install separate bench-built units on each side of the window and under the window. The stiles that require beaded edges will be butted up against the side casings of the window. These stiles belong only to the units that will be installed on each side of the window. The unit under the window poses the one exception to the rule that all units begin and end with a stile because this unit begins and ends with a muntin.

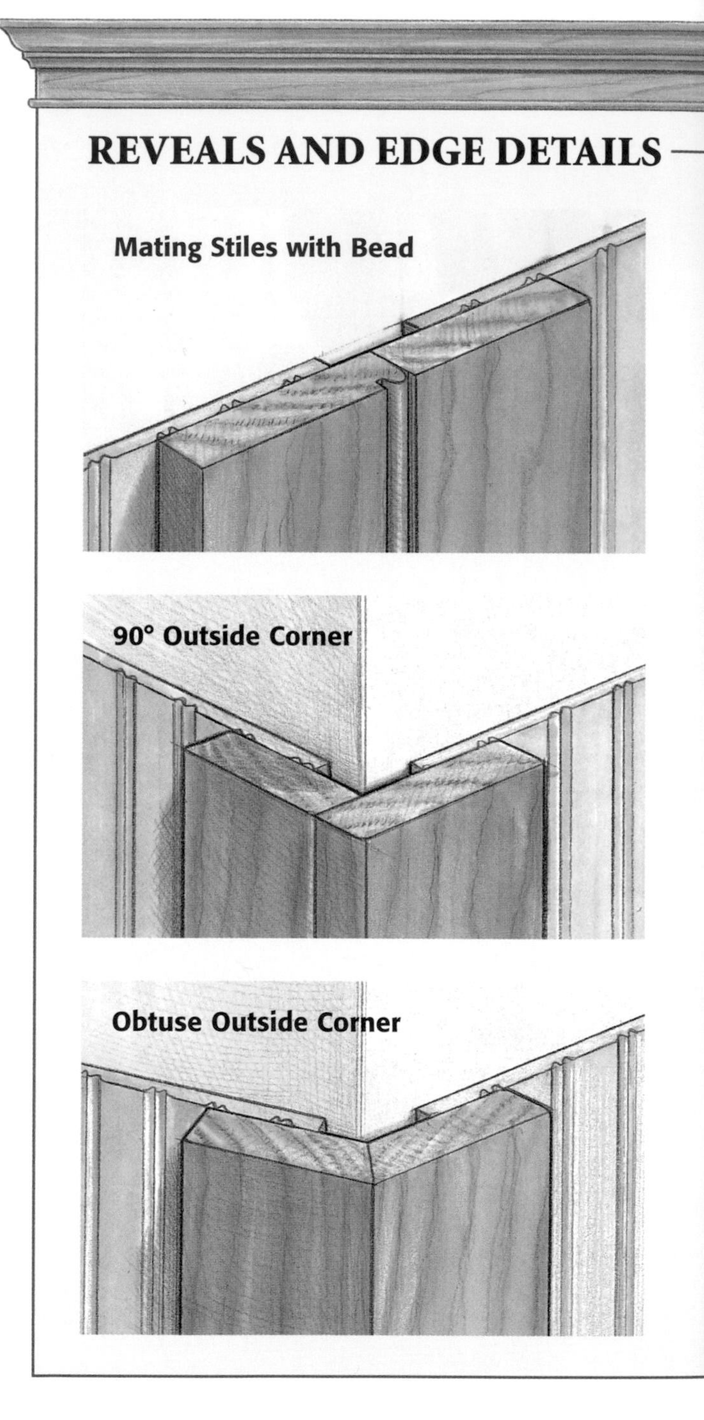

Adjacent to a Prebuilt Unit of Wainscoting. In order to use two or more separate prebuilt units of wainscoting on a single wall, you need to create an appropriate visual transition from one unit to another. You can accomplish this transition by routing a decorative detail onto the outer edge of one of the two stiles that

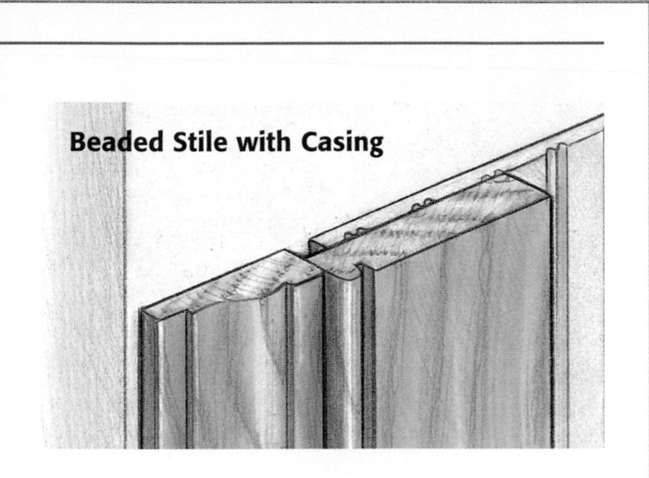

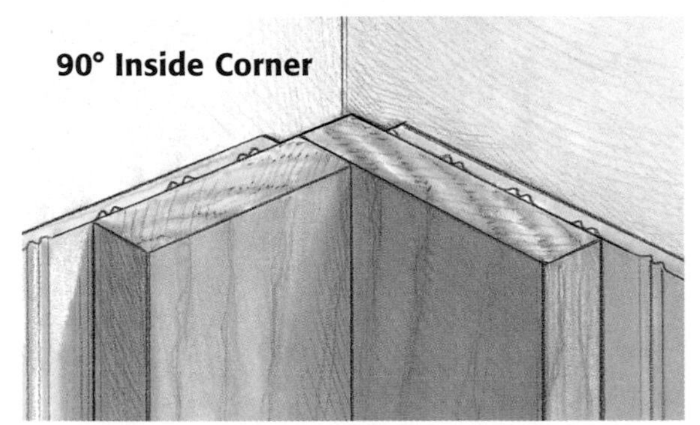

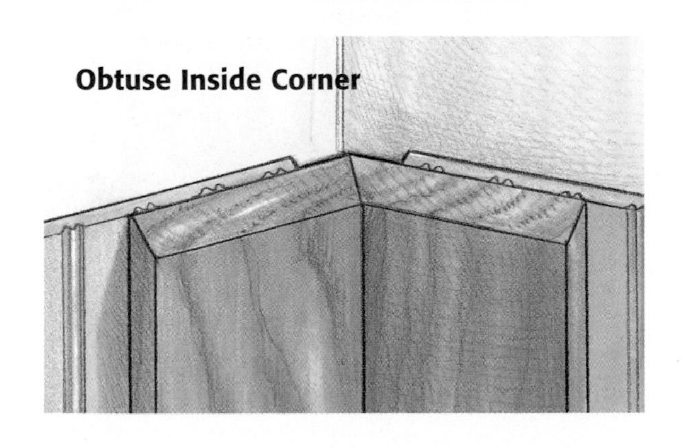

will contact each other when the units are joined. Typically, you can use a ⅜-inch bead detail. In the interest of symmetry, the detail should be centered between the two units.

Wainscot Muntins

Muntins are positioned between the top and the bottom rails and between the stiles. All of the muntins should be the same width.

The only place where you would use muntins instead of stiles at the ends of a unit of wainscoting is under a window trimmed out in the picture-frame style. This is because the top edge of the unit gets a decorative detail milled into it, and it's easier to mill a single rail than a rail plus the end grain of the stiles.

Wainscot Rails

Wainscoting made with a complete set of components needs a top and a bottom rail, but you could make up panels on a tall installation using one or more subrails as well. Subrails can form a pleasing box pattern with the muntins.

Wainscot Top Rail and Cap

Wainscoting is usually topped off with a cap made of a nosing and an apron. The nosing is typically a ¾-inch-thick board with a rounded-over front edge. The nosing is designed to rest squarely on the top edge of the top rail. The apron underneath is usually a ¾-inch cove molding.

Here's how to plan the overall width of the cap section: you add the radius of the rounded-over front edge to the combined thickness of the panel and the apron. Then you increase the total dimension by the dimension selected for the spacing between the front top edge of the apron and the point at which the rounded-over front edge commences. The larger this distance becomes, the more the apron will be obscured by the nosing.

The apron is designed to overlap the upper face of the top rail as it is positioned against the bottom edge of the nosing.

The width of the top rail should equal the width selected for the visible portion of the rail plus the height of the cap's apron.

In a typical design with a 3-inch visible rail, you might use a ¾-inch cove molding for the apron and make the top rail 3¾ inches. After the apron is applied, the remaining rail segment will be the 3 inches you want.

Assembling Wall Frames

What You'll Need

- Combination square and pencil
- Clamps
- Plate joiner and biscuits
- Carpenter's glue
- Mallet or hammer and tapping block

TRIM TIP: It's important to square up the pieces to start with. Then, even a tick mark across the joint will serve as an accurate registration mark for the plate joiner.

1 Once the boards are set squarely in place, draw a line across the joint to guide your plate joiner cuts.

3 Follow the same procedure on the end of the adjoining board, and the two recess cuts will line up.

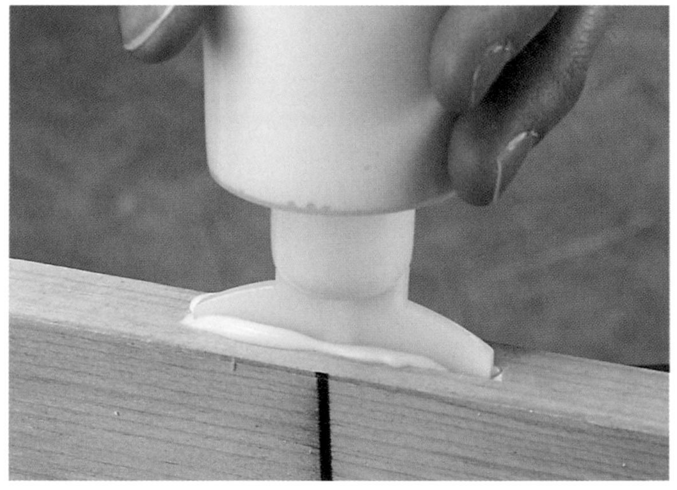

4 Insert carpenter's glue in the cuts. You can do this with a brush or a special applicator shown above.

Wainscot Bottom Rail and Base Trim

Paneled wainscoting has an inherently solid and weighty look that calls for a base treatment on the tall and thick side. So in many installations with paneled wainscoting, you may want to use base trim consisting of a 1×6 board and an 11/16 × 1⅜-inch base cap molding.

The baseboard is overlapped onto the bottom rail by at least ½ inch, and the 1⅜-inch base cap sits on top of it. This means that the bottom rail of the wainscot should be at least 4⅞ inches wide to maintain a 3-inch reveal.

Joinery Systems

The traditional method for building paneled wainscoting used tongue-and-groove joints between all the pieces. While this is still the best way to build raised-panel wainscoting, it's much easier to build flat-panel wainscoting using a plate joiner.

A plate joiner, sometimes called a biscuit joiner, is a power tool that cuts a curved groove in a piece of wood. After cutting matching grooves into two pieces of wood, you insert a football-shaped wafer of compressed wood—the "biscuit"—and some glue. The wafer aligns the two pieces of wood and joins them

2 Set the depth of cut of the plate joiner; then line up the notch on the shoe with your mark and pull the trigger.

5 Set compressed wood wafers into one side of the joint; tap the other board into place; and clamp overnight.

together. The glue causes the wafer to swell, creating a strong and stable joint.

Every joint must be squared up and securely clamped. That means you'll need clamps that exceed the height of the frame to draw the rails and the muntins together, and clamps that exceed the length of the unit to draw the stiles and the rails together. On long assemblies, you may need to string together several clamps.

When joining the muntins to the rails, strike lines at the center points on both ends of the muntins. On the rails, mark off the points where the center of each of the muntins should fall. When joining the stiles to the rails, strike lines at the center points on both ends of the rails. Place the stiles up against the rails, and extend these centerlines onto the stiles. Join the vertical and horizontal members of the frame by first joining the muntins to the rails and then joining the stiles to the rails.

Once you have constructed the frame, assemble the panel by attaching ¼-inch birch or pine bead-board paneling to the backside of the frame. Then install an $^{11}/_{16}$ × 1$^{1}/_{16}$-inch cove molding along each of the four inside edges of each frame to create a finished transition from the face of the frame to the panel.

Laying Out the Room

To begin, strike a level reference line all around the room. Use it to establish the height you want for the wainscoting, which usually is 36 inches off the floor. If you plan to case out passageways that are wrapped with drywall, start with that work. (See "Creating Jambs" and "Installing Jambs," pages 102 to 107.)

Plumb up the corners of the room if necessary by installing shims with panel adhesive at the floor or at the 36-inch mark, depending on whether a wall leans in or out.

Because some of the units of prebuilt wainscoting will not extend all the way into a corner, make sure that the shims are at least an inch wider than the combined thickness of the frame and panel so that the wainscoting is sure to catch them.

Measure the lengths of all of the individual runs of wall along the 36-inch height line. Whenever there is a shim in a corner at the 36-inch height line, always measure off the face of the shim.

On most projects, and particularly where there are complications such as windows, passageways, and other interruptions in the wainscoting, it's wise to draw a diagram of the room on a sheet of graph paper and indicate the length of each run of wall. You also may want to take the time to sketch out some of the joinery details. Of course, it's always a good idea to try a few test pieces with scrap wood.

Mission-Style Wainscoting

In place of the panel assembly found in typical wainscoting, Mission wainscoting simply allows the surface of the wall to fill the area that would otherwise be filled by a panel. The alternating pattern of narrow stiles separated by expanses of wall surface creates the effect of a colonnade. The choice of wood is important in this style because it often reaches higher on the wall than standard wainscoting. You can use lesser grades of wood and paint the assembly, but Mission wainscot is normally intended to be stained and clear-sealed.

Basic Components

Paneled and Mission wainscoting culminate with a decorative top. In both treatments the top also consists of two components, a shelf-like surface and an apron supporting it. However, unlike paneled wainscoting capped off with a short nosing and an apron, Mission wainscoting is generally topped off with a plate rail approximately 60 inches off the floor.

The most typical style these days has three horizontal members: a plate rail, a bottom rail, and base trim. Another approach, presented opposite, features the use of a fourth horizontal member: a subrail below the plate rail. Such subrails were frequently used in the more ambitious versions of the original Mission wainscoting treatments. They are optional, of course, but can significantly increase the overall level of detail and texture.

End-Wall Treatments

When both ends of this type of wall treatment terminate at right-angled inside corners, keep things simple by eliminating the end stile. (See the photo on page 208.) You can, however, use a stile with a decorative detail to accomplish the transition from a shop-built unit of wainscoting to a door casing.

Plate Rail Details

You can top Mission wainscoting with either a narrow or a wide shelf. Generally, this component is left square-edged, as opposed to the rounded-over nosing used in some other styles. You don't have to use the shelf to display plates, but it is a pleasing option you can build in to the top of the shelf simply by routing a groove to catch the bottom edge of plates.

***Sometimes Mission-style wainscoting** uses wood panels. The style can follow through on furniture as well.*

Mission-Style Wainscoting

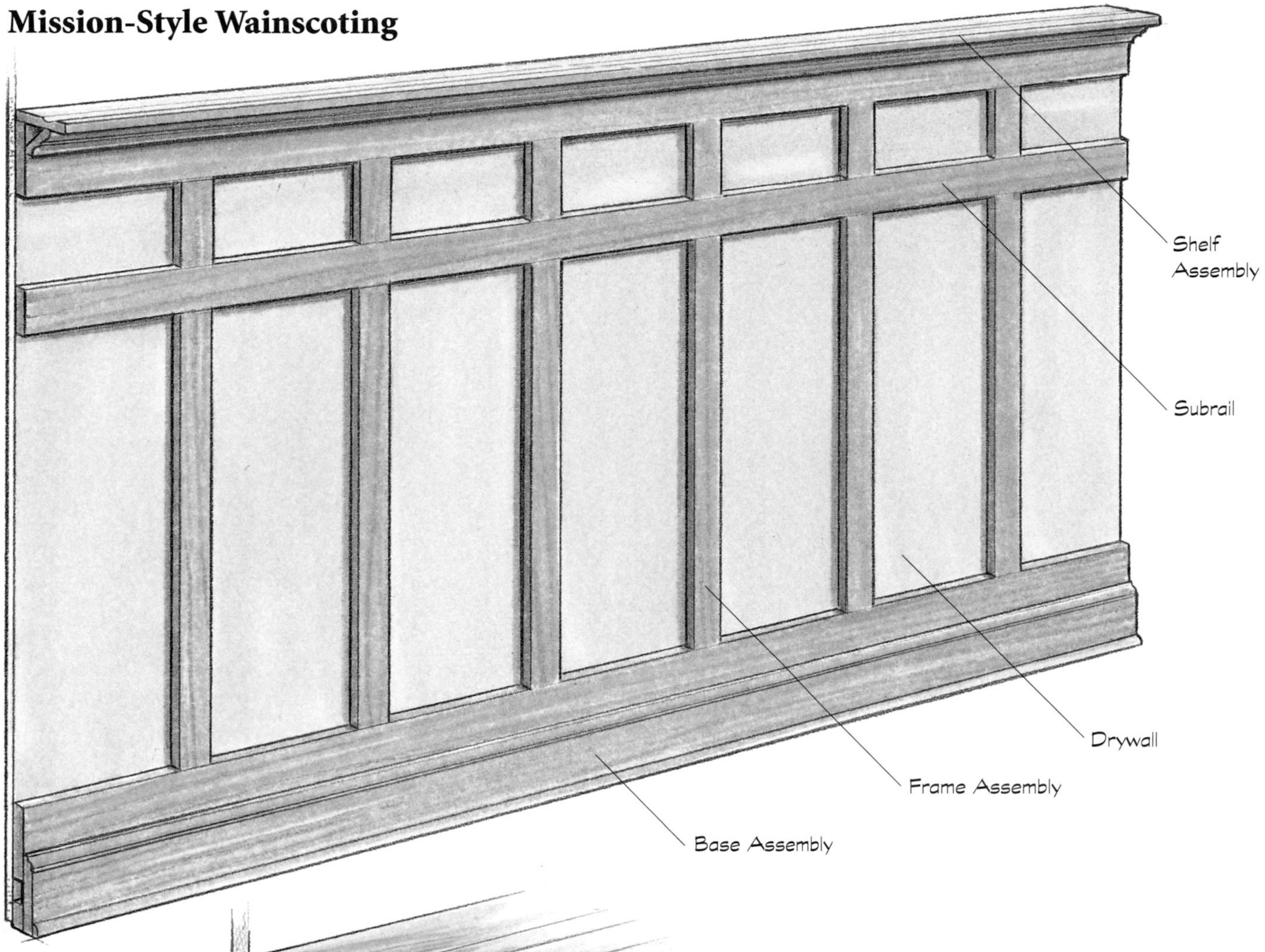

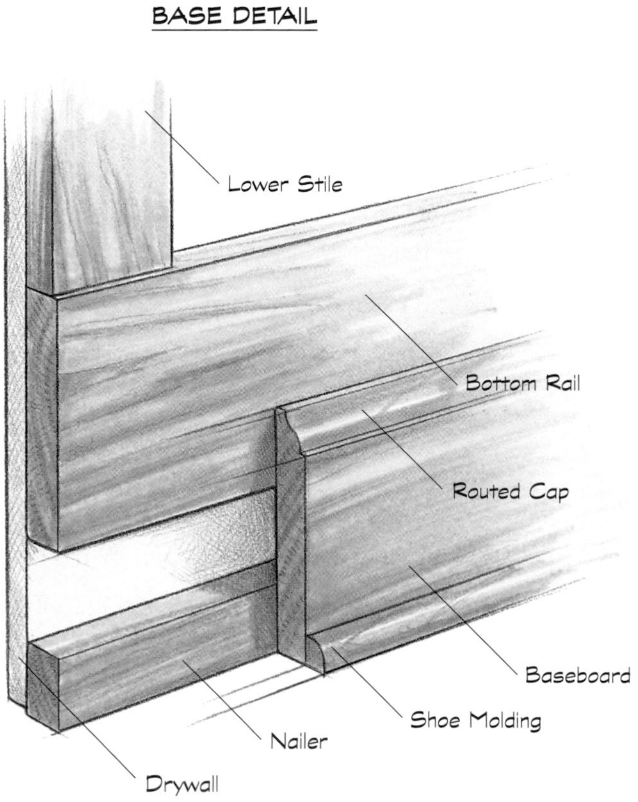

Shelf Assembly
Subrail
Drywall
Frame Assembly
Base Assembly

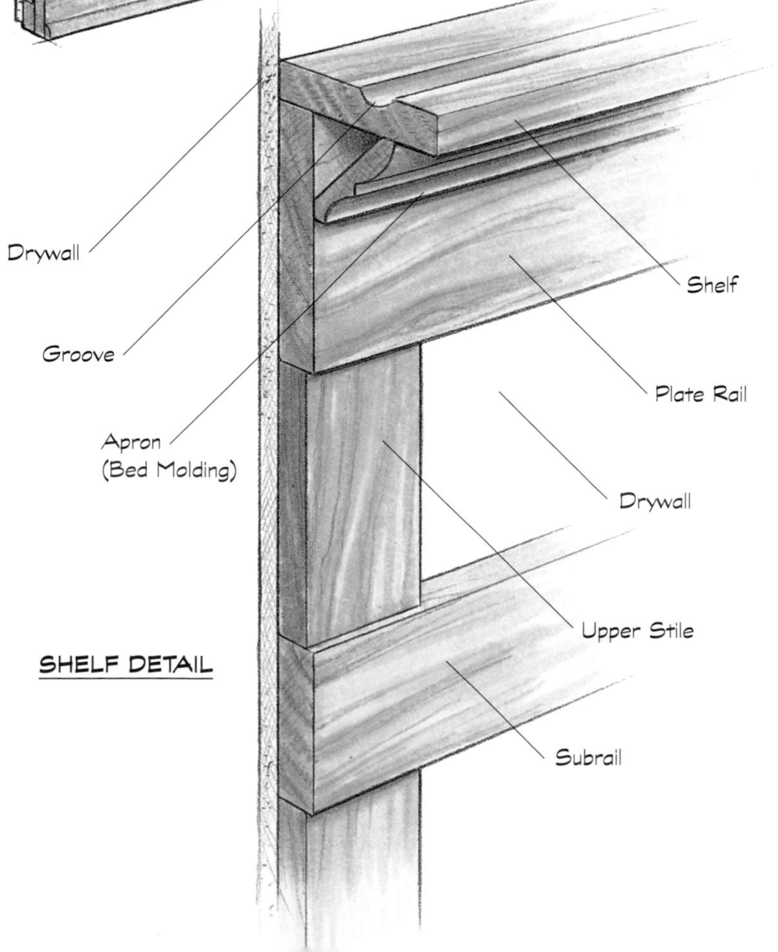

SHELF DETAIL

Drywall
Groove
Apron (Bed Molding)
Shelf
Plate Rail
Drywall
Upper Stile
Subrail

BASE DETAIL

Lower Stile
Bottom Rail
Routed Cap
Baseboard
Shoe Molding
Nailer
Drywall

This wall treatment *includes a subrail and upper midpoint vertical strips to create a decorative top section.*

Planning the Installation

You should install the horizontal components of the wall treatment first. Start by establishing a level reference line, and work off it to strike level lines representing the bottom edge of the plate rail and the top edge of the bottom rail.

You can use butt joints to form all inside right-angled corners and miter joints to form all outside corners. Install the plate rail first. Then install the subrail (if you choose to use this option) about 9 or 10 inches below the bottom edge of the plate rail. Establish a level line at this height by running a pencil along the bottom edge of a spacer board while pushing it along the bottom edge of the top rail. You can use this technique in several areas, provided that you have carefully leveled the first horizontal component. But check the subrail for level in any case.

Installing the Apron

After all three rails have been installed, you can fasten the apron molding that will soften the transition from the underside of the plate shelf to the vertical face of the top rail. Fit a scrap piece of the apron in place, and establish a guideline where the bottom edge of the apron falls.

Install the apron molding along the guideline, coping all inside corners and mitering all outside corners.

Use outside corners to terminate the apron when it intersects door and window casings. Run the bottom edge of the apron all the way to the points at which the vertical side edges of the top rail meet the outside vertical side edges of the casings. This way, when the return is assembled, it will overlap onto the face of the adjacent casing, forming a highly attractive transition.

Planning the Plate Rail Shelf

After you have installed the apron all the way around the room, you can install the shelf of the plate rail. There are two operations you need to take care of before you fasten this component in place: milling the plate groove and notching the shelf ends where the board laps onto adjoining casing.

The milling operation is optional, of course. You may prefer to have a plain-surfaced shelf where you can set picture frames and other items. But if you would like the upper side of the shelf to have a holding groove for plate display, mill this detail into the shelf boards before you install them. It is always easier to work on a board when it's firmly clamped to a workbench, where you can use power tools in a safe and comfortable position.

Milling and Cutting the Shelf

Start by setting up your router with a ¾-inch roundnose bit designed to cut grooves. Then adjust the depth of cut so that the bit will cut about ⅜ inch into the wood. (You may want a deeper groove to hold larger plates or platters.) You can set this margin initially by dialing down the depth setting on your router. But it's wise to set the router with the bit along the board edge and double-check with a ruler.

Next, adjust the router guide so that the groove is about 1 inch from the outer edge of the shelf. Then make the rout, working against the bit rotation so that the router doesn't tend to race ahead out of control. In hardwood (and with some deep routs) you'll get better results milling the groove in two stages, using one pass to remove most of the wood and a final pass with a slightly deeper setting to leave a smooth surface.

To notch an end of the shelf where it overlaps onto the face of an adjacent door or window casing, hold or temporarily tack the shelf into position over the apron, and mark the point where it meets the adjoining trim. That establishes the length of the shelf that will rest against the wall.

Allowing for a uniform overhang over the apron and the apron return, make another mark for the overall length of the shelf. Then use a scrap piece of stock the same thickness as the adjoining trim to mark the depth of the notch. Cut the notch with a trim handsaw or a saber saw, working carefully into the corner of the notch so that you don't overcut and leave a gap.

Where plate rails *join door or window trim, ease the support molding onto the adjacent trim with a return.*

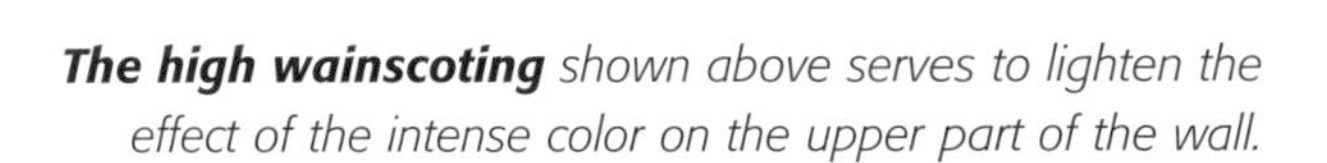

The high wainscoting *shown above serves to lighten the effect of the intense color on the upper part of the wall.*

A plate rail, *below, provides a design touch and needed shelf space in this bathroom.*

Wainscoting treatments *that extend 60 in. above the floor, above, work best in rooms with high ceilings.*

A chair rail and wainscoting, *below, provide protection and an attractive backdrop for furnishings and accessories.*

Classic bead-board wainscoting, *above, adds a decorative touch to a traditional bath.*

Passageway Treatments with Pillars

The following type of installation requires a comprehensive understanding of woodworking tools and skills—and takes a lot of time to install and finish. But the design provides delineation between rooms laid out in an open plan while retaining an open feeling, and it creates a striking passageway.

You also can build pillars on podiums to stand alone in a passageway. In fact, many of the details you'll find on the next few pages can be scaled back if, for example, the adjacent walls do not have wainscoting. But the most complete installation includes many trim components. The ideal treatment extends the wainscoting in a room around into the passageway, but only at the height of the paneling.

The extension forms a knee wall, sometimes called a podium because it supports a decorative column. You can use many styles of columns. Typically, you don't need the column to provide structural support. That job is handled by a header that's usually dropped below the ceiling.

But a column on a podium on each side of a passageway provides the classical appearance of a supported opening. It defines a passageway and adds decorative detail while allowing you to see past the columns into the next room.

Pillars and podiums *create an elegant passageway.*

Typical Podium Plan View

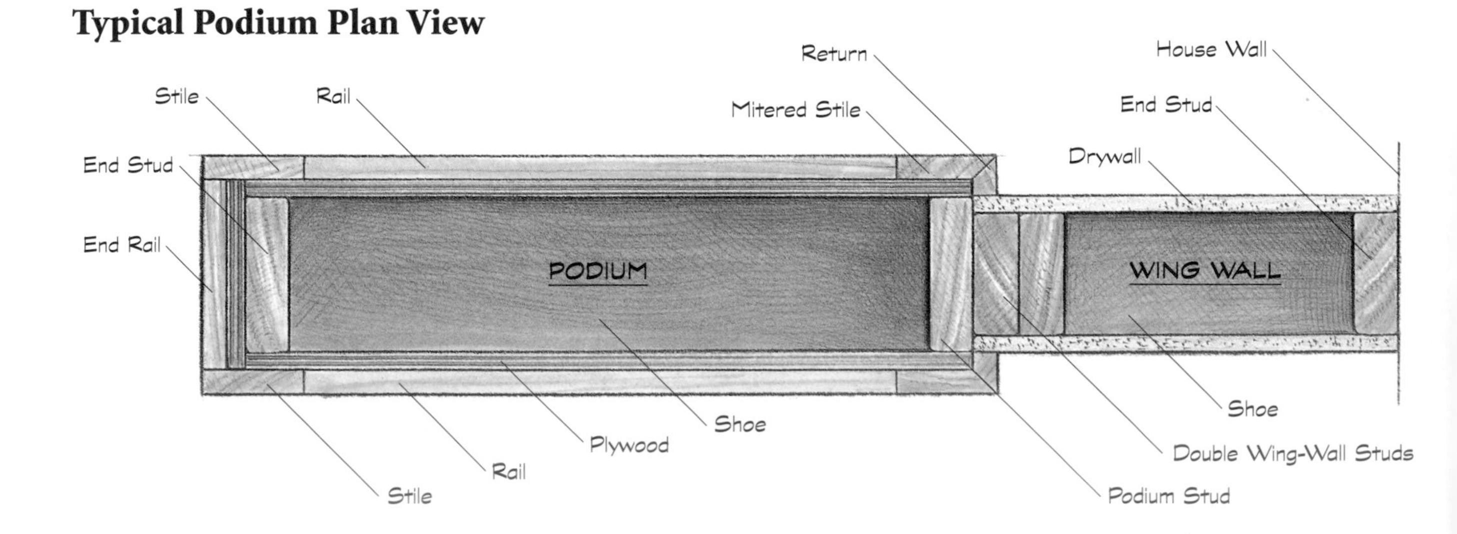

Typical Podium Assembly

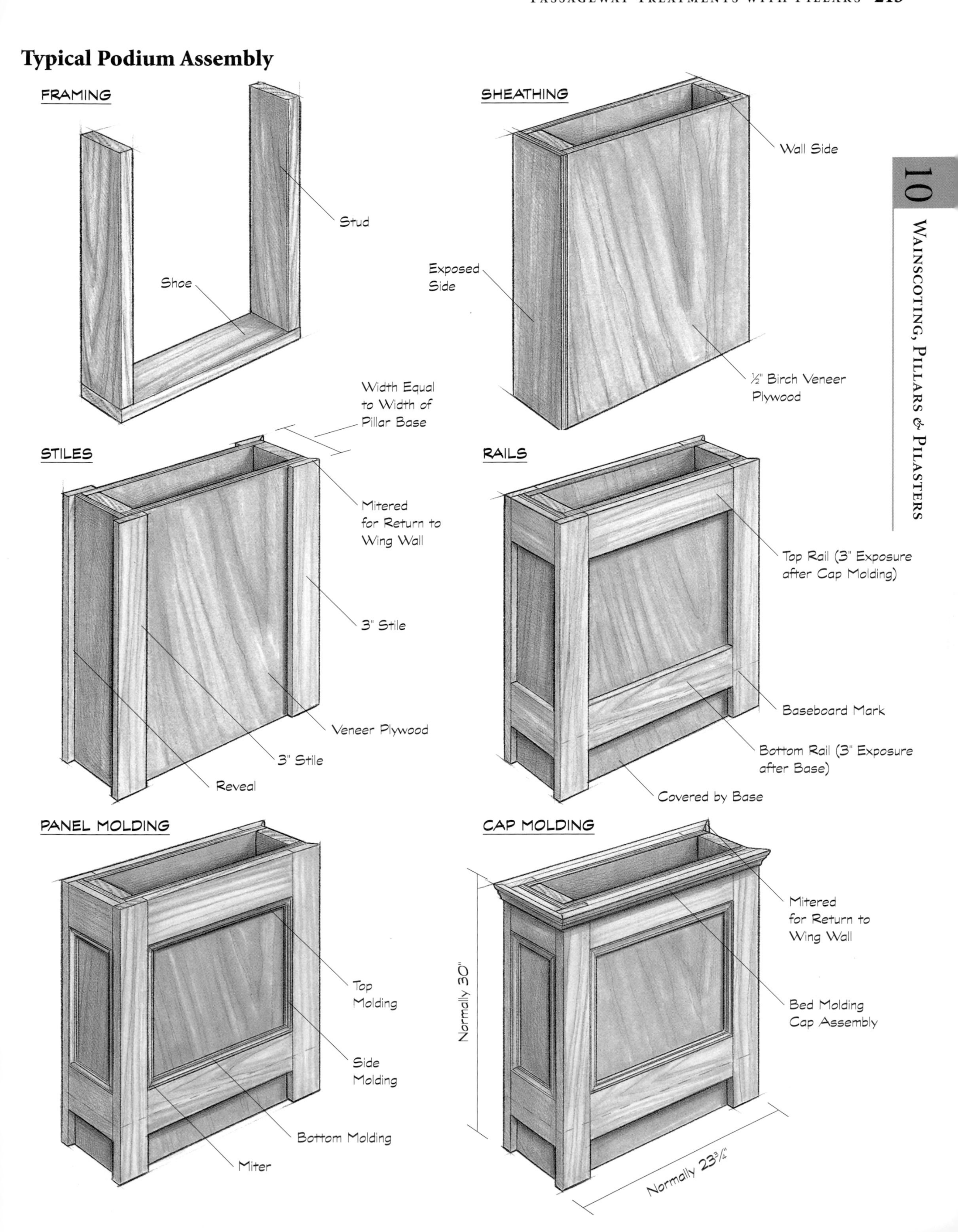

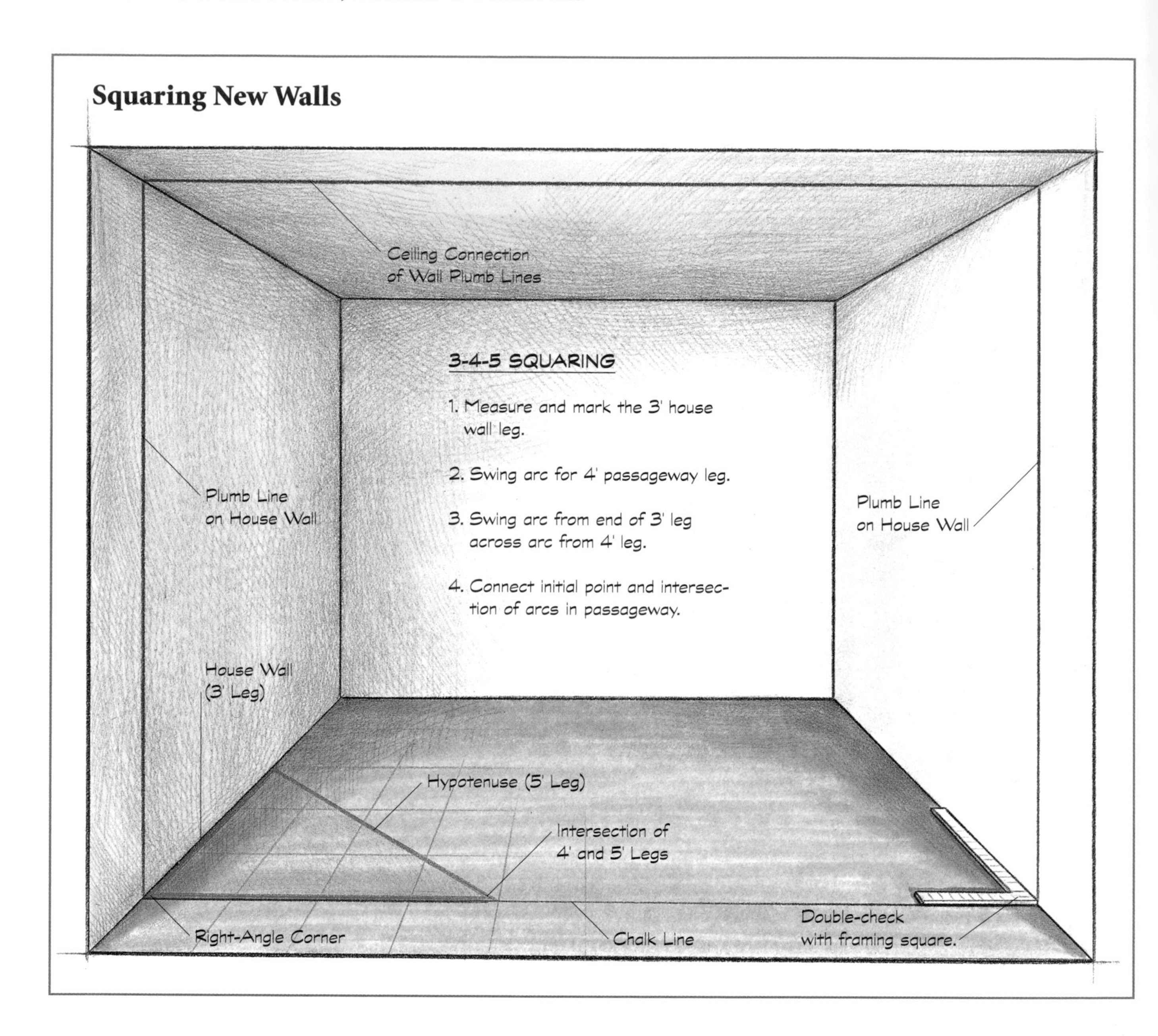

SQUARING UP PASSAGEWAY WALLS

One of the most accurate ways to square up walls relies on a simple bit of mathematics you may remember from school. The idea is to use the proportions of a 3-4-5 triangle. Here's how it works: when the three sides of a triangle are in the proportion of 3 : 4 : 5, one of the corners has to be exactly 90 degrees, no matter what unit of measurement you use, inches or feet, or how long the measurements are.

Start from an initial point where you want the passageway wall to join the existing house wall at a right angle. (See the illustration "Squaring New Walls," above.) Measure a 3-foot leg along the wall and mark that point. Then measure a 4-foot leg extending into the passageway using a string and a pencil to swing a short arc along the 4-foot distance. You can also do this holding a pencil at the end of a ruler, or cut a board to the 4-foot length and use it to control the measurement mark.

Then move to the end of your 3-foot leg, and swing a 5-foot arc back into the passageway. This is the long leg, or hypotenuse, of the triangle. The point where the arcs intersect will be square with your initial point where the passageway wall joins the house wall. Connect the starting point with the intersecting arcs, and your passageway wall will be square.

Podiums with pillars *separate an entryway, even without wainscoting in the adjacent room.*

CREATING A FAUX HEADER

Some passageways have walls on each side that go all the way to the ceiling. Others have a header across the top that's dropped down from the ceiling. (See the photo above.) If a header is already installed, you can make the standard checks for square and level and start trimming. There will be studs to support the molding along the sides and a large built-up timber such as two 2×10s to support the molding across the top.

If you need to fill in the space between the side walls, you can box in the space using a long rectangular frame reinforced with short studs. Set horizontally at the top of the opening, the frame creates a faux header.

Build the box frame on the floor using 2×4s for the perimeter frame and short (say, 6¼-inch) 2×4 studs nailed at least every 16 inches. This will imitate a 2×10 header. You might want to use screws to make the box frame even stronger and to fasten it to the ceiling joists and wall studs before you cover it with drywall.

If you want to enlarge a passageway or build a new one altogether, you should probably hire a contractor to handle the structural alterations. That's because load-bearing headers (unlike a nonload-bearing box frame) carry the weight of ceiling joists and other loads, and you can seriously damage your house's structure if you don't install the header properly.

Fluted Pilasters

A fluted pilaster is one of the most elegant forms of trim. Its shallow vertical grooves add detail and emphasize height. A fluted pilaster smoothly integrated into a room's trimwork is a testimony to the installer's woodworking skills and sense of style.

You can use fluted pilasters to remedy a common interior design problem: a lack of vertical separation between two areas or rooms of a home. This feature is most obvious when two rooms share one continuous wall without either a wing or a cased-out opening where the two rooms meet. This can make a passageway look oddly one-sided with a continuous wall along one end of the opening.

This problem of a passageway that doesn't really look like a passageway occurs most often in newer center-hall Colonials. The front door of these homes usually opens into a hallway with the dining room to one side and the living room to the other. Using pilasters on the wall can help solve these design problems.

Basic Flute Patterns

There are basically two styles of fluting used today: Neoclassical and Victorian. The Neoclassical style is characterized by flutes that are numerous, spaced closely together, and the same length. The Victorian style is characterized by fewer flutes (often only three), with the center flute extending beyond the other two flutes at both the top and the bottom of the pilaster. With this style the flutes often are deeper and spaced farther apart.

Making Flutes

There are several ways to make flutes using either a fixed-base or plunge router. With a fixed-base machine, you can use guides and a jig to run shallow flutes along the entire length of a board. This milling pattern looks fine if the ends of the fluted pilasters (generally cut in ¾-inch-thick boards) butt into thicker material, such as 5/4 plinth blocks.

A plunge router provides more flexibility. This type allows you to lower a rotating bit to a preset depth in a

Pilasters mounted on the wall *of an entry can help to define the space and make a graceful transition between rooms and areas that share a common wall.*

NEOCLASSICAL FLUTED PATTERN

The hallmark of this style is a pilaster surface that is more fluted than flat. It is highly decorative, bordering on ornate, and requires a lot of setup time for the router work. Each time you cut another flute you need to reset your guides.

VICTORIAN FLUTED PATTERN

This style is much easier to make. You need to set up to rout the center flute, of course. But after that one is done, you need to make only one more setup because the margin in from the edge is the same on both of the other flutes.

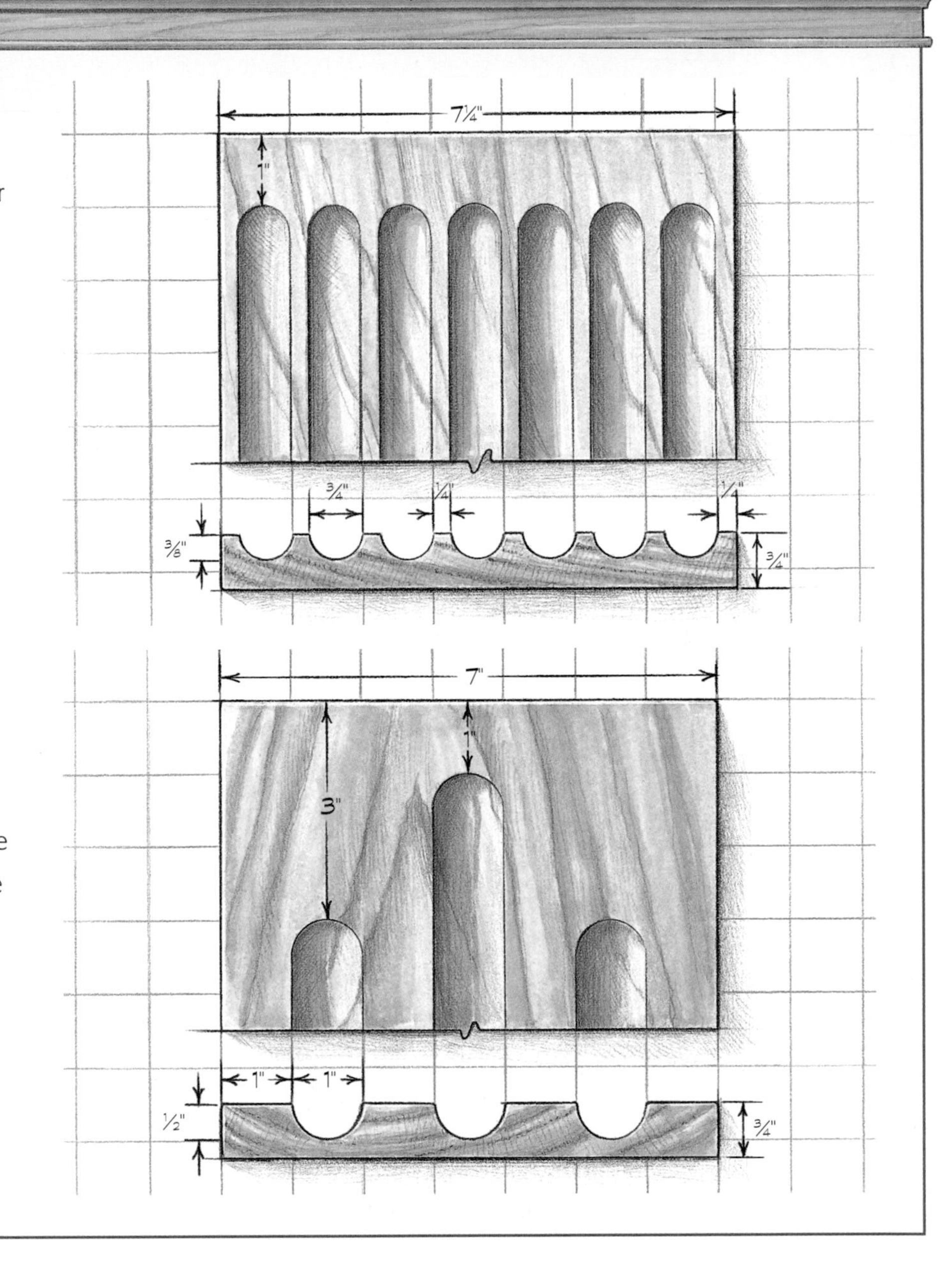

stable and accurate manner. With this feature you can mill flutes of a pilaster that do not run the full length of the board but stop short of the end of the board, or start and stop at various intervals.

A round-nose core-box bit with the following characteristics is an excellent choice for cutting a Neoclassical flute pattern in boards that are ¾ inch thick. The bit should have a ¾-inch cutting diameter, a ⅜-inch cutting radius, and a 1¼-inch cutting length. A ⅜-inch preset cutting depth will produce good-looking boards.

A router bit with a ½-inch shank diameter is preferable to one with a ¼-inch shank diameter because it will produce less chatter and make a cleaner cut. But you don't need to race out and buy new router bits to beat the chatter problem.

Instead, make sure that the board is clamped securely to a solid table that won't shift as you work. Then use multiple passes to take away material in stages. Use a shallow setting on the first cut, deeper settings to remove more material, and a final shallow cut to leave clean surfaces in the flutes.

Routing Flutes

WHAT YOU'LL NEED

- Combination square and pencil
- Plunge router and bit
- Clamps
- Knot-free boards
- Safety glasses

TRIM TIP: Before starting to rout, securely set the depth stop that limits the plunge travel of the router.

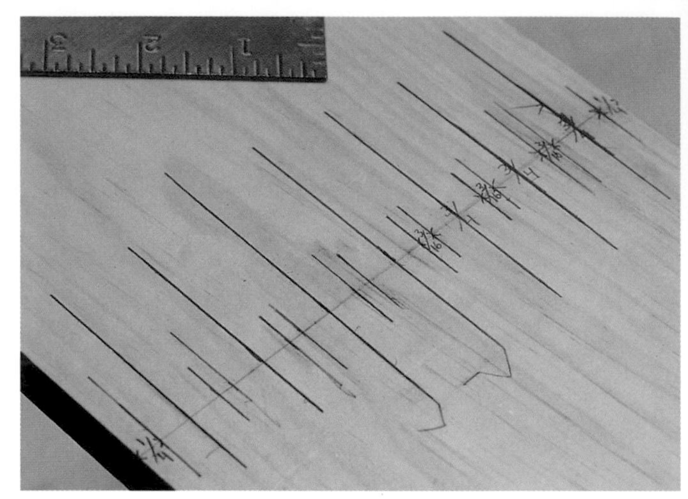

1 Once you mark the locations of the flutes, split each one with a centerline to guide your router alignment.

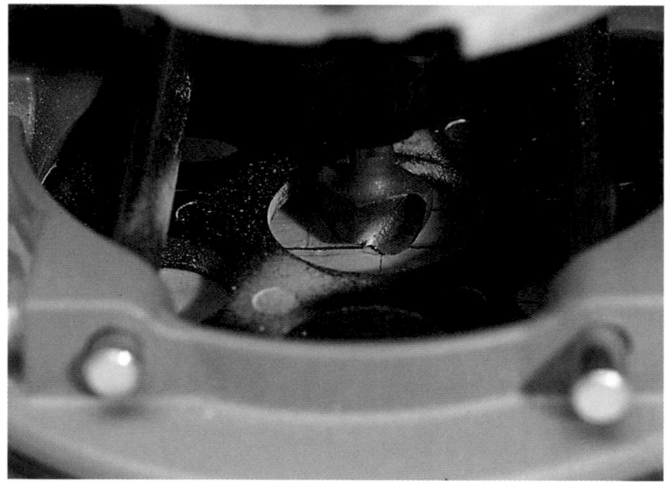

3 With a firm grasp on the router, plunge the bit just enough to make contact and leave a mark on the line.

4 Screw a stop block at each end of the board to limit the travel of the router and the length of the flutes.

SELECTING PILASTER BOARDS

For fluted pilasters you should use boards that are free of knots. If a router bit plows through a portion of a knot, the entire knot may fracture and fall out.

You'll probably need lumber such as 1×8 D Select pine. But be prepared for some variation in grades. At some lumberyards, for example, you can find knot-free boards among the stock of D Select lumber. In other yards, a third grade of lumber, called clear, is offered at an additional premium. However, some of these yards may stick some of the better D Select stock in the pile and call it clear.

It's also important for the board to be as straight as possible. Cabinetmakers and advanced woodworkers can easily deal with irregular lumber if they have large jointers for planing a straight edge onto a board. Unfortunately, a large jointer is an expensive power tool that do-it-yourselfers and even most trim carpenters don't own.

The two edges of the board also must be parallel. This is not often a problem, and it's easy enough to fix on a table saw if a jointer isn't available. Always rip the edge that is not as straight as the other, so that the two edges will at least be parallel.

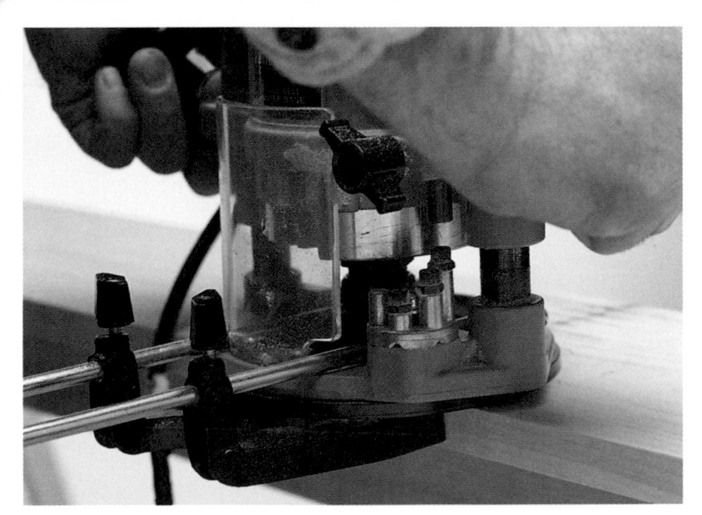

2 Adjust the guide, which travels on a pair of small rails, so that the bit point lines up with the flute centerline.

5 With practice you can get the knack of gradually plunging the router to create a tapered end to the flutes.

Laying Out Flutes

Using a combination square, draw lines across the width of the board indicating the actual location of the cap, base, and mid section (if there is going to be a mid section), and their various components. A spacing of 1 inch between these sections and the flutes looks good, but you can adjust this margin either way.

With a combination square, strike a line across the board in the vicinity of the vertical midpoint of a section that has been designated for fluting. Along this line, indicate the horizontal spacing of each of the flutes. You may want to plan out the spacing on a piece of tracing paper first. Then you can transfer the flute locations to the board. Also take the time to mark a centerline that represents the point at which the center of the fluting bit must fall.

Setting Up Routers

Next, place the router onto the board, and adjust the router guide so that the center of the fluting bit is positioned over the line representing the midpoint of the outermost flute.

Confirm the accuracy of the location by turning on the router and slowly lowering the bit just enough to put a small dimple in the surface of the board. If the dimple is not centered on the midpoint line of the flute, make the necessary adjustment to the router guide before milling.

The spacing of the flutes on both sides of the center flute is designed to be symmetrical. This means that after you rout on one side you can rout the corresponding channel on the other side of the center flute.

If you plan to end the flutes—for example, just before and after a mid-rail block—you need to fasten a stop at both ends of a run of flutes so that each run will begin and end at the same point. Generally, you should work from the outermost edges to the center of the board.

Routing the Flutes

After laying out the pilaster board, clamping it securely, and adjusting the depth of cut on a plunge router, rout the flute in at least two passes. Always work into the wood so the rotation of the bit doesn't tend to pull the router out of your hands. Keep firm control without moving the router too quickly. Maintain steady progress at the fastest pace so that the router can cut cleanly without stressing the motor or causing chattering, which makes ragged cuts.

After the outermost flutes on both sides of the board have been cut, adjust the router guide to cut the next pair of flutes. Before you make any new cuts that require a repositioning of the router guide, be sure that you've made a final cleaning cut to smooth the surfaces of the flutes.

Base, Mid & Cap Sections

All pilasters have a base and cap, and some have a decorative detail in the middle as well that's located 32 to 36 inches above the floor. Each of these sections is composed of two or more subcomponents to provide depth and decoration. (See page 223 for an illustration of these sections.)

You can build up these features one board and piece of molding at a time, attaching each one to the surface below. Another approach is to preassemble the feature and install it as one unit. This may be the best method on large projects with many repeating features that you can make up on a jig.

Attaching the Pilaster

Pilasters should be screwed and glued into place. But odds are that at least one of the sides will not fall on a stud, which means you'll have to use anchors to prevent warping and buckling. One type that works well is a screwlike anchor with large threads and a hollow head into which you can turn a screw. To use this type of anchor, put the pilaster in place and drill pilot holes all the way through. Then remove the pilaster, and screw the anchors into the holes in the wall. Countersink the pilaster holes so that their screws can be filled or plugged. (See "Using Wall Anchors," pages 92 to 93.) Apply dots of panel adhesive to the back of the pilaster to gain additional adhesion to the wall.

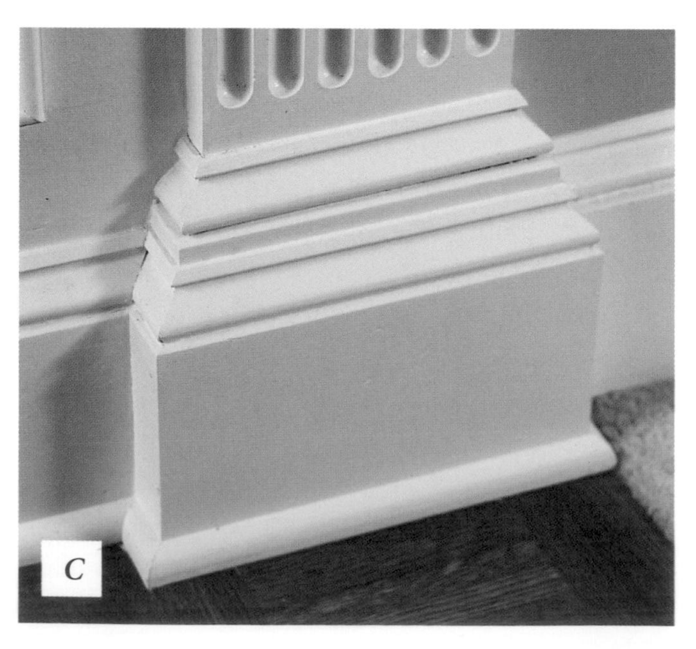

Fluted pilasters *have at least two and sometimes three other components: the top cap (A), the mid feature (B), which may mimic the details of a chair rail, and the base (C).*

Window Cornice Boxes

A typical cornice sits at the the top of the wall and well above most windows that are trimmed separately. But with a few extra joints you can unify a room by altering the straight runs of cornice to create housings for drapes, blinds, and other window treatments.

Designing the Box

There are many ways to add window boxes to walls and trim them with cornice. The first consideration is how much room you need for the rods or other drapery hardware. You need to build the box large enough to accommodate the hardware and the tops of the drapes or blinds even when they are bunched up. Of course, you can make the box somewhat larger in any direction or build one long box over two adjacent windows if you like the look.

If the boxes extend down from the ceiling well past the hardware and are shallow, you probably will need to mount the hardware ahead of time.

Building the Box

You can assemble a three-sided frame with mitered corners on a workbench, and screw the top edges to a nailer mounted on the ceiling. On larger assemblies, it's wise to add additional nailers to support the short side pieces.

Assemble the miter joints with glue and nails, and clamp the assembly in a square position until the glue sets. You could also assemble the pieces around the mounting block (a piece of 5/4 stock or a 2×4, for example) and securely mount the block to the ceiling with the box attached.

Part of the panels that make up the box sides will be exposed, and the upper part will be covered with cornice. Depending on the lumber you use for the project, you may want to mill details into the exposed bottom edges of the box, add additional strips of molding, and prime the assembly before mounting it.

Wrap the window boxes with cornice first. When working with a multipiece cornice treatment, complete each layer around the room before going on to the next.

WINDOW CORNICES

You can transform plain rooms by making jogs in cornice molding that will hold shades, blinds, and other window treatments. You can create individual pockets over each window or continue the molding past narrow wall sections between windows to form a more expansive detail. Housings below the cornice can be painted or papered.

Passageway Surrounds

Passageway surround systems combine many aspects of trimwork, including fluted pilasters with base, mid, and cap features, cornice trim, and paneled molding treatments. The overall concept is to extend the idea of using pilasters in an assembly where they appear to support a large decorative crosshead. You will need to borrow from several other sections of the book for a project of this scope. And, as always, there is no one correct way to design and install the assembly.

But you can use the overall sketch below as a guide, making proportional adjustments to fit your work area. You can also refer to the details at right that show how different types of molding are joined together to form the most crucial components of a surround.

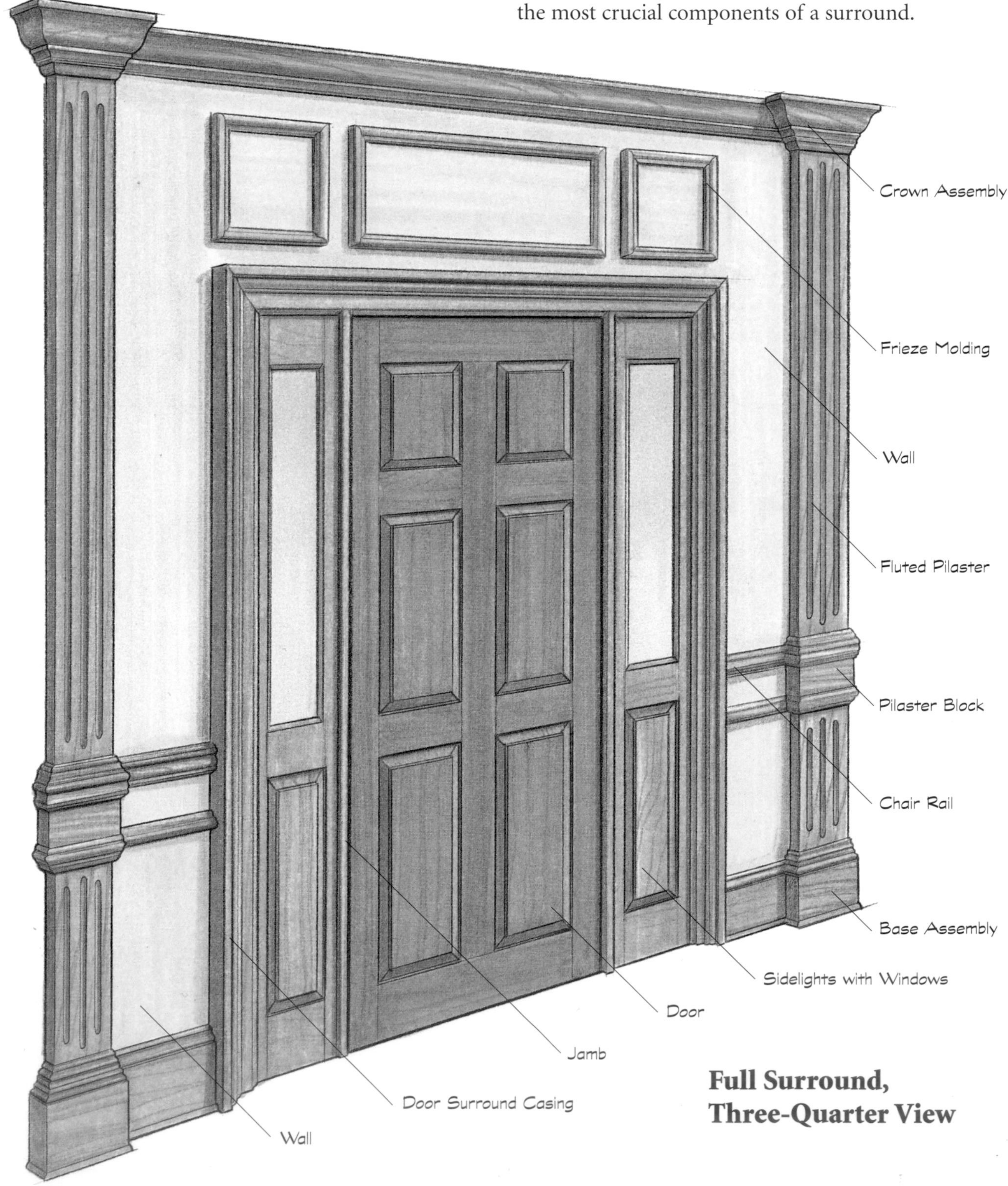

Full Surround, Three-Quarter View

CROWN DETAIL

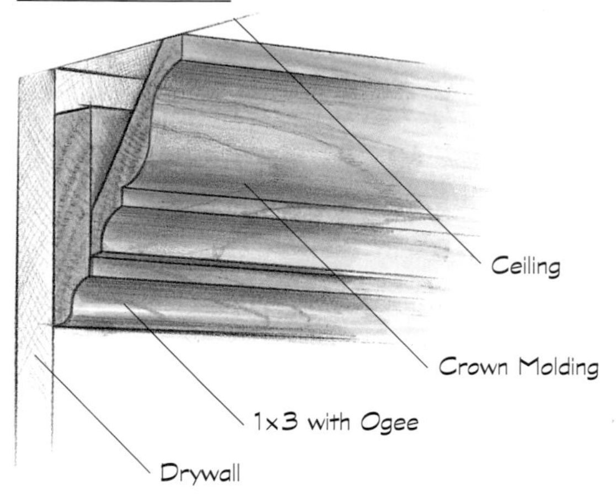

PILASTER BLOCK DETAIL

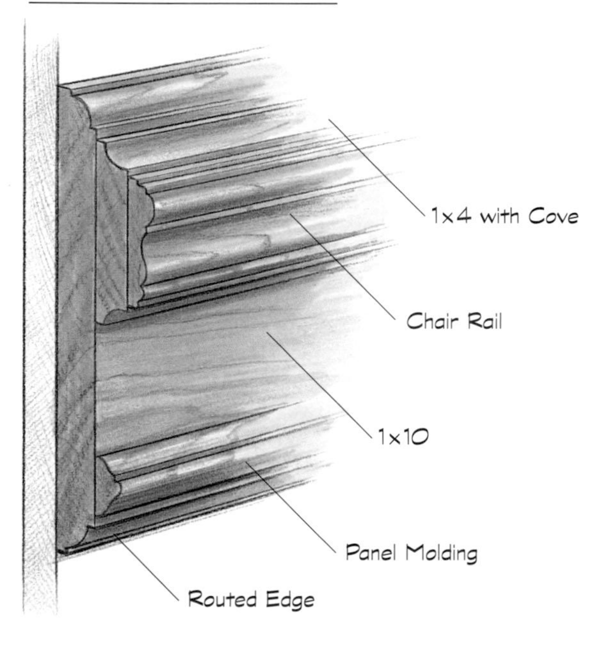

BASE DETAIL

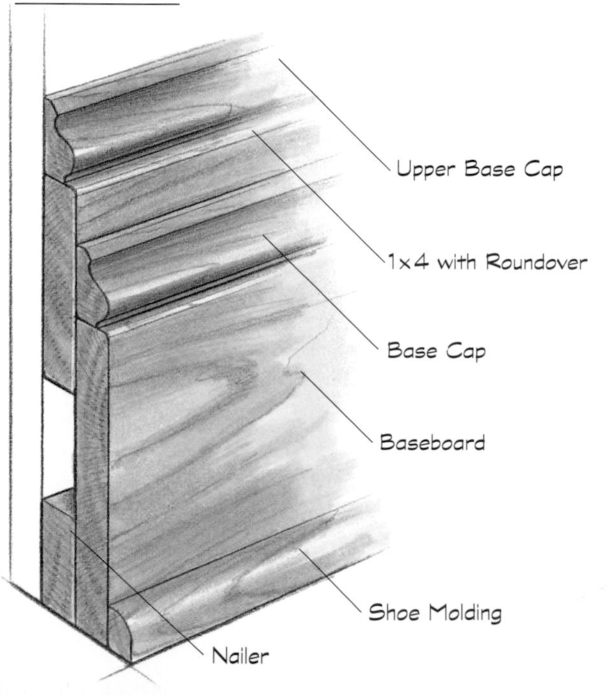

Alternative Pilaster and Cap

ALTERNATIVE HEAD DETAIL

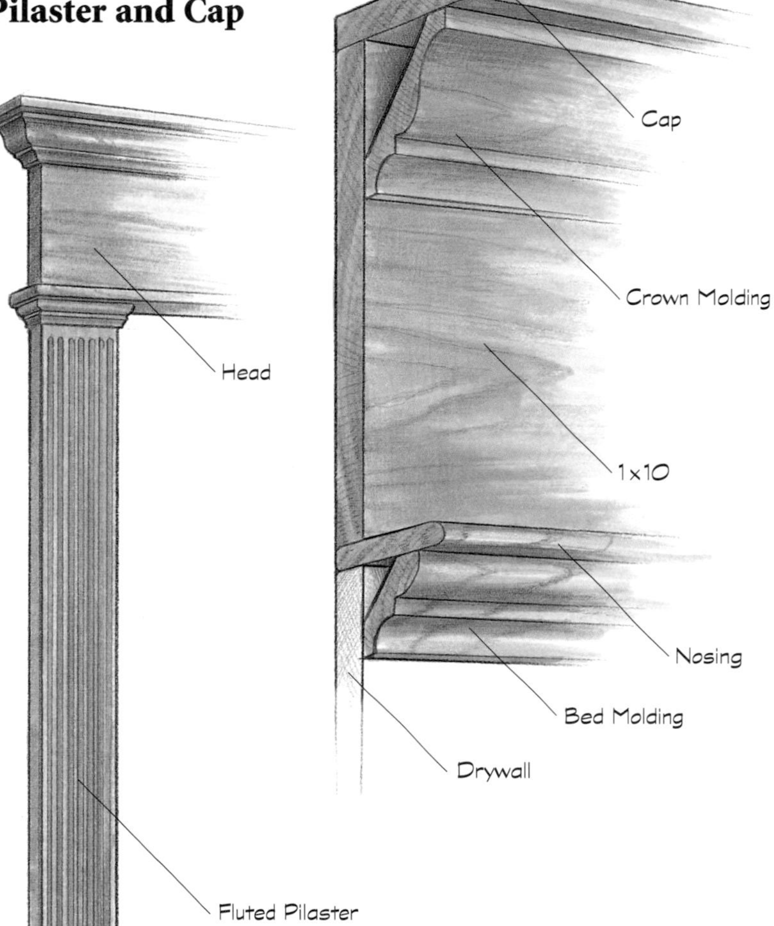

ALTERNATIVE PILASTER BLOCK DETAIL

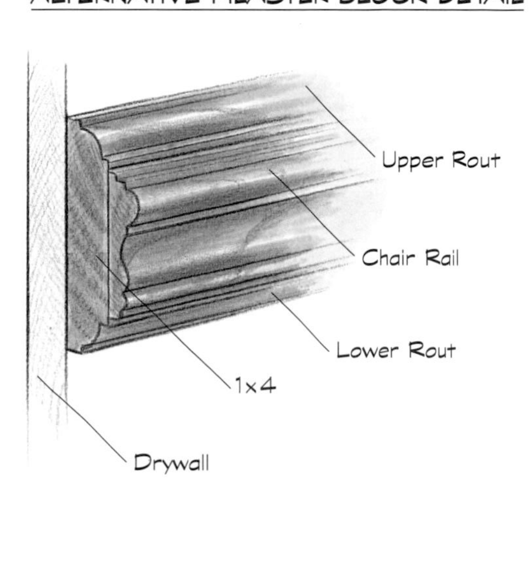

Decorative pilasters, *top left, provide a distinctive way to frame display shelving.*

A classic arrangement, *top right, includes a column that appears to support an entablature.*

In modern homes, *columns are often placed on top of pedestals or half-walls as shown in the room at bottom left.*

A fluted pilaster, *bottom right, can case a door and provide design support for an ornate cornice.*

Decorative columns, *above, are a good way to delineate activity areas in an open floorplan.*

Fluted columns, *above, serve as a distinctive way to flank the entry of formal rooms.*

The variation *on a classic column design shown above left supports an ornamental archway leading to a small sitting area.*

The pilasters *on the fireplace mantel above right appear to support the ornate mantel shelf.*

Narrow columns, *right, work well in small rooms that do not have excessively high ceilings.*

Resource Guide

The following list of manufacturers and associations is meant to be a general guide to additional industry and product-related sources. It is not intended as a listing of products and manufacturers represented by the photographs in this book.

ABI Mouldings
5050 Skyline Way NE
Calgary, Alberta
T2E 6V1 Canada
1-866-730-1850
www.abimouldings.com
Manufactures medium-density fiberboard and wood moldings. The Web site offers product information and architect information.

Architectural Ornament, Inc.
55 Bradwick Dr.
Concord, Ontario
L4K 1K5 Canada
1-800-567-3554
www.architectural-ornament.com
Produces moldings made of polyurethane foam.

Bailey Hardwoods, Inc.
628 Kimble Ct.
Springfield, IL 62703
1-800-800-1913
www.baileyhardwoods.com
Manufactures custom moldings to match existing decorative moldings in older homes.

Balmer Studios, Inc.
271 Yorkland BLVD
Toronto, Ontario
M2J 1S5 Canada
1-800-665-3454
www.balmer.com
Manufactures lightweight foam trim and accent pieces.

Benjamin Moore and Co.
51 Chestnut Ridge Rd.
Montvale, NJ 07645
1-800-344-0400
www.benjaminmoore.com
Manufactures paints, stains, and related finishing products.

Blue Mountain Wall Coverings, Inc.
15 Akron Rd.
Toronto, Ontario
M8W 1T3 Canada
1-866-741-2083
www.imp-wall.com
Manufactures residential wallcoverings and other decorating products.

Brewster Wallcoverings
67 Pacella Park Drive
Randolph, MA 02368

1-800-366-1700
www.ewallpaper.com
Produces and distributes wallpapers, borders, fabrics, and finishing accessories.

Classic Studios, Inc.
37 Boyd St.
Winter Garden, FL 34787-2803
www.clasplas.com
Offers unique designs in molding.

Cumberland Woodcraft Co., Inc.
P.O. Drawer 609
Carlisle, PA 17013-0609
1-800-367-1884
www.cumberlandwoodcraft.com
Manufactures hand-crafted millwork in the form of wall niches, moldings, ornaments, and wallcoverings.

Custom Specialties
www.synmold.com
Manufactures architectural details in four different varieties of millwork.

Do It Yourself Network
www.diynet.com
Offers message boards, articles, and project ideas pertaining to home building and home improvement.

Driwood Moulding Co.
P.O. Box 1729
Florence, SC 29503-1729
(843) 669-2478
www.driwood.com
Produces hardwood architectural millwork.

Flextrim Mouldings, Inc.
210 Citrus, P.O. Box 2260
Redlands, CA 92373
1-800-356-9060
www.flextrim.com
Makes flexible moldings for use on rounded surfaces.

Fypon Molded Woodwork
3846 Green Valley Rd.
Seven Valleys, PA 17360
1-800-955-5748
www.fypon.com
Manufactures a variety of molded polyurethane trimwork.

Jiffy-Trim
P.O. Box 1789
Loomis, CA 95650
1-800-642-8457
www.jiffy-trim.com
Offers a miterless molding system that the company says is equally beneficial to the do-it-yourselfer and seasoned professional.

Melton Classics, Inc.
P.O. Box 465020
Lawrenceville, GA 30042
1-800-963-3060
www.meltonclassics.com
Offers a line of moldings, and architectural columns and details.

Motif Designs
20 Jones St.
New Rochelle, NY 10802
1-800-431-2424
Makes wallpaper, borders, and fabrics for use in many decorating applications.

National Association of Home Builders
www.nahb.org
Offers educational material and resources for home builders, as well as a local builders' association finder.

National Paint and Coatings Association
1500 Rhode Island Ave., NW
Washington, DC 20005
(202) 462-6272
www.paint.org
Represents, as a nonprofit trade association, the paint and coatings industry of the United States.

Oakwood Woodworks
160 Commerce Dr.
Rochester, NY 14623
(585) 334-9220
www.oakwoodww.com
Manufactures solid wood doors and moldings, including matches for existing moldings.

Old House Interiors
Subscriptions: 1-800-462-0211
www.oldhouseinteriors.com
Good resource for finding and researching vendors.

Old House Journal and Old House Journal Restoration Directory
Subscriptions: 1-800-234-3797
www.oldhousejournal.com
Good information and advice offered both on-line and in print.

Old World Mouldings, Inc.
821 Lincoln Ave.
Bohemia, NY 11716
(631) 563-8660
www.oldworldmouldings.com
Offers an online catalog of decorative hardwood moldings.

Ornamental Mouldings
3804 Comanche Rd.
P.O. Box 4068
Archdale, NC 27263
1-800-779-1135
www.ornamentalmouldings.com
Produces a variety of hardwood moldings for residential and commercial installations.

Sherwin-Williams
101 Prospect Ave. NW
Cleveland, OH 44115
1-800-474-3794
www.sherwin-williams.com
Manufactures a variety of paint and related products.

White River Hardwoods/Woodworks, Inc.
1197 Happy Hollow Rd.
Fayetteville, AR 72701
1-800-5558-0119
www.mouldings.com
Offers hardwood moldings in many varieties.

Winsor and Newton, Inc.
11 Constitution Ave.
Piscataway, NJ 08855
(732) 562-0770
www.winsornewton.com
Provides a wide range of artists' paints and brushes for finishing and decorating work.

Outwater Architectural Products
4 Passaic St.
P.O. Drawer 403
Wood Ridge, NJ 07075
1-800-631-8375
www.outwater.com
Supplies extruded plastic and hardwood moldings.

Woodcrafters Lumber Sales, Inc.
212 Northeast Sixth Ave.
Portland, OR 97232
1-800-777-3709
Offers paint strippers, varnishes, shellacs, specialty moldings, and architectural elements.

Pearl Paint
308 Canal St.
New York, NY 10013
1-800-221-6845
www.pearlpaint.com
Offers a wide range of specialty paint and finishing products, including artist's brushes and color-mixing charts.

Royal Mouldings Limited
135 Bear Creek Rd.
P.O. Box 610
Marion, VA 24354
1-800-368-3117
www.royalmouldings.com
Manufactures polymer-based home improvement and construction products for interiors and exteriors.

Special Thanks for Tools & Materials

Hitachi Tools *www.hitachi.com*
Makita Tools *www.makita.com*
Porter Cable Tools *www.portercablepowertools.com*
Ryobi Tools *www.ryobitools.com*
Skil-Bosch Tools *www.boschtools.com*
Zircon *www.zircon.com*

Glossary

Alkyd-based A paint containing synthetic resins. Cleans up with paint thinner or other toxic solvents. Often referred to as oil-based.

Analogous colors Adjacent colors on the color wheel that share an underlying hue.

Backsaw A straight fine-toothed saw often used with a miter box to create clean-edged miter cuts for trim and picture frames.

Baseboard A trim board attached as part of a base treatment to the bottom of a wall where it meets the floor.

Bead A general term referring to a convex, semicircular profile on a molding.

Bench plane A large tool (compared with a block plane) designed to shave wood off the surface of a board.

Bevel An angle other than 90 degrees cut into the thickness of a piece of lumber or other material.

Blocking Small pieces of lumber used to fill a gap in framing or provide a nailing surface. For example, triangular blocking might be used to bridge the gap between the wall and the ceiling and provide a nailing surface for angled crown molding.

Block plane A small single-handled tool that shaves wood from boards.

Casing The general term for any trim that surrounds a door or window.

Caulk A variety of flexible materials used to fill seams and seal connections. The caulk used to fill seams around trim is usually made of siliconized acrylic.

Chair rail A horizontal band of trim installed on a wall between the floor and the ceiling. Usually placed 30 to 36 inches above the floor.

Chalk-line box A string wound inside a container filled with colored chalk that you can use to mark long straight lines.

Chamfer A bevel resulting from cutting the corner off of a board.

Color wheel A graphic representation of the full color spectrum used to describe and compare the relationship among different paint colors.

Combing A decorative paint technique in which you remove a certain amount of paint by dragging a comb or similar object across the wet surface.

Compound miter saw A power saw mounted on a pivoting arm and a swiveling base that allows you to make both bevel and miter cuts.

Cope To cut the end of a molding so that its profile will match that of an abutting piece of similar molding.

Coping saw A small handsaw with a thin, flexible blade used for cutting tight curves.

Cornice Any molding or group of moldings used in the corner between a wall and a ceiling.

Countersink To drive a fastener below the surface of a board in order to give the surface a more finished appearance. Also, the name given to the bit used to cut a recess in a board in order to make it possible to sink a screwhead below the board's surface.

Cove A general term referring to a concave semicircular profile on a molding.

Crosscut A cut across the grain of a piece of lumber. A general-purpose crosscut saw has a blade designed for this purpose with about eight teeth per inch.

Dado A wide flat-bottomed groove cut at a right angle to the grain of a piece of wood. Also, the lower area of a wall (below a chair rail) that is wallpapered.

Dead-ending The treatment of a piece of molding at its end; usually a chamfer or a return.

Dentil molding A molding with a pattern that includes alternating blocks and spaces.

Door casing The trim applied to a wall around the edge of a door frame.

Drywall A sheet material made of gypsum and paper used to cover the interior walls of most homes.

Egg-and-dart molding A molding pattern that includes egg-shaped relief carvings.

File A long thin metal tool with a rough surface used to shape material. Often, the term *file* is reserved for fine-surfaced tools used on metal, and the term *rasp* is reserved for coarse-surfaced tools used on wood.

Finger joint A joint used to make long lengths of material from shorter lengths. The ends of the short lengths are cut in a fingerlike interlocking pattern and glued together. Less expensive moldings are often made by finger joining short pieces of lumber together.

Hardwood Generally, the wood of large deciduous trees such as maple, oak, and poplar.

Inside corner A corner in which the faces of the walls bend in toward each other at an angle less than 180 degrees.

Jamb The frame around a window or door.

Joint compound A soupy material made primarily of crushed limestone and liquid vinyl used to repair holes and fill joints between panels of gypsum drywall.

Kerf The material a saw blade removes in a single cut, usually about ⅛ of an inch, or the thickness of the blade.

Latex-based Paints that can be thinned and cleaned up with water.

Level Term used to define a surface or line that is perfectly horizontal. Also, the name given to a variety of instruments used to determine whether a surface or line is perfectly horizontal.

Masking Covering a surface when painting near it, usually with masking tape.

Medallion A decorative, usually round relief, carving applied to a wall or ceiling.

Miter An angle cut into the face or thickness of a piece of lumber or other material to form a miter joint.

Miter box A wood, plastic, or metal jig with a saw, designed to manually cut wood at various angles.

Molding Decorative strips of wood or plastic used in various kinds of trimwork.

Monochromatic scheme A paint scheme in which the trim, walls, and ceilings in a room are all painted the same color but with different values.

Nail set A blunt-pointed metal tool used to sink nailheads below the surface of wood. The pointed end is held on the nailhead as the other end is struck with a hammer.

Outside corner A corner in which the faces of the walls project out and away from each other in an angle greater than 180 degrees.

Pilaster A vertical relief molding attached to a wall, usually made to resemble the surface of a pillar.

Pillar A column stretching from the floor or other support base to the ceiling or header above a passageway.

Plate joiner A power tool that cuts slots in the edges of two boards so that they can be joined by inserting and gluing a wooden wafer in the slots; also called a biscuit joiner.

Plumb An expression describing a perfectly vertical surface or line. A plumb surface will meet a level surface at 90 degrees to form a right angle.

Power miter saw A circular saw mounted on a pivoting base with angle measurements that is used to cut accurate angle cuts in lumber and other materials.

Predrill To drill a hole in a piece of lumber before nailing or screwing it to a surface to make driving the fastener easier and to prevent the lumber from splitting.

Rabbet A groove cut across the edge of the face of a piece of lumber, generally so that another piece of lumber can be inserted in the groove in order to join the two pieces at a right angle.

Ragging A decorative paint technique that involves adding or removing layers of paint using a rag.

Rail Horizontal trimwork installed on a wall between the cornice and base trim. It may stand alone, as a chair rail, or be part of a larger framework.

Rasp A long, thin metal tool with a rough-toothed surface used to shape wood.

Return A small piece of molding attached to the end of a long run of molding to carry the profile from the front of the molding back to the wall.

Rip A cut made in the direction of the grain on a piece of lumber. A rip saw with a blade designed for this type of cutting has about six teeth per inch.

Roundover bit A router bit used to cut a semicircular profile along the edge of a board.

Router A power tool with a rotating shaft that accepts a variety of specially shaped bits. Designed for many purposes, such as cutting contours on the edges of molding or grooves through the face of a piece of lumber.

Sandpaper Sandy grit on a paper backing used to smooth wood and other materials. Numbers printed on the backing refer to grit size. Higher numbers indicate finer grits, while lower numbers indicate coarser grits that remove more material.

Scarf joint The connection between two pieces of trim joined by overlapping opposing miters in order to disguise the joint.

Sliding T-bevel An adjustable tool, often called a bevel square or bevel gauge, used to capture and transfer angles.

Softwood Generally, the wood of coniferous, needle-bearing trees such as pine, fir, or spruce.

Sponging Adding or removing layers of paint for decorative effect using a sponge.

Stile The outer vertical members forming the framework of a wainscot wall system.

Stipple Tiny ridges in a paint surface left by the nap of a roller.

Stippling A decorative paint technique that involves spraying bits of paint on to a wall with a stiff bristle brush.

Toenailing Attaching the end of a board to the face of another by nailing at a steep angle through the face of the first board into the second.

Wainscoting Any trim structure installed in the area between a baseboard and a chair rail.

Window casing Trim that surrounds the edges of a window frame.

Window stool The horizontal surface installed below the sash of a window, often called a windowsill.

Wood filler A puttylike material used to fill nailholes and other imperfections in the surface of wood.

Metric Equivalents

Length

1 inch	25.4 mm
1 foot	0.3048 m
1 yard	0.9144 m
1 mile	1.61 km

Area

1 square inch	645 mm^2
1 square foot	0.0929 m^2
1 square yard	0.8361 m^2
1 acre	4046.86 m^2
1 square mile	2.59 km^2

Volume

1 cubic inch	16.3870 cm^3
1 cubic foot	0.03 m^3
1 cubic yard	0.77 m^3

Common Lumber Equivalents

Sizes: Metric cross sections are so close to their U.S. sizes, as noted below, that for most purposes they may be considered equivalents.

Dimensional lumber	1 × 2	19 × 38 mm
	1 × 4	19 × 89 mm
	2 × 2	38 × 38 mm
	2 × 4	38 × 89 mm
	2 × 6	38 × 140 mm
	2 × 8	38 × 184 mm
	2 × 10	38 × 235 mm
	2 × 12	38 × 286 mm
Sheet sizes	4 × 8 ft.	1200 × 2400 mm
	4 × 10 ft.	1200 × 3000 mm
Sheet thicknesses	¼ in.	6 mm
	⅜ in.	9 mm
	½ in.	12 mm
	¾ in.	19 mm
Stud/joist spacing	16 in. o.c.	400 mm o.c.
	24 in. o.c.	600 mm o.c.

Capacity

1 fluid ounce	29.57 mL
1 pint	473.18 mL
1 quart	1.14 L
1 gallon	3.79 L

Weight

1 ounce	28.35g
1 pound	0.45kg

Temperature

Fahrenheit = Celsius × 1.8 + 32

Celsius = Fahrenheit − 32 × 5⁄9

Nail Size & Length

Penny Size	Nail Length
2d	1"
3d	1¼"
4d	1½"
5d	1¾"
6d	2"
7d	2¼"
8d	2½"
9d	2¾"
10d	3"
12d	3¼"
16d	3½"

INDEX